Algorithmic Complexity

Theory and Practice

A Comprehensive Guide to Understanding and Analyzing Algorithm Efficiency

Moaiz Ben Dhaou
moaiz@bendhaou.net

Chokri Ben Dhaou
chokri@bendhaou.net

Algorithmic Complexity

Edited by NAWVA
contact@nawva.com

ISBN: 978-2-488616-04-1

to NEYL, LAYANE, ARMEEN, HELENA, and ILYAN

Contents

Preface

Who This Book Is For

This book is designed for anyone seeking a deep understanding of algorithmic complexity from advanced undergraduate students encountering complexity theory for the first time to seasoned software engineers looking to sharpen their analytical skills, and researchers exploring the theoretical foundations of computation.

If you've ever wondered why one sorting algorithm performs better than another on large datasets, or why certain computational problems seem inherently difficult despite decades of research, this book will provide you with the tools and insights to understand these phenomena. We assume you have some familiarity with basic algorithms and data structures, but we build the complexity-theoretic foundation from the ground up.

The book serves multiple audiences:

Students will find comprehensive coverage of complexity theory fundamentals, with numerous examples and exercises that reinforce key concepts. The progression from basic asymptotic analysis to advanced topics like NP-completeness follows a carefully crafted learning path.

Software Engineers will appreciate the practical perspective woven throughout the theoretical material. We consistently address the gap between theoretical complexity and real-world performance, helping you make informed decisions about algorithm selection and optimization.

Researchers will find rigorous treatment of advanced topics, extensive references to current literature, and discussions of open problems that continue to challenge the field.

Prerequisites and Mathematical Background

To get the most from this book, you should have:

- **Mathematical Maturity**: Comfort with mathematical proofs, particularly induction and contradiction

- **Discrete Mathematics**: Knowledge of sets, functions, relations, and basic combinatorics
- **Basic Algorithms**: Familiarity with fundamental algorithms like sorting, searching, and graph traversal
- **Programming Experience**: While we use pseudocode, programming background helps with implementation discussions

We provide mathematical preliminaries in Chapter 2, but these serve more as review than introduction. If you're uncertain about your mathematical background, spend extra time with Chapter 2's exercises before proceeding.

How to Use This Book

This book is structured to support different reading approaches:

Sequential Reading: The chapters build upon each other, particularly in Parts I-III. This approach provides the most complete understanding.

Topic-Focused Reading: Experienced readers can jump to specific topics using the extensive cross-references. Each chapter begins with prerequisite indicators.

Course Usage: The book supports a two-semester sequence: an introductory course covering Parts I-II and selected topics from Parts III-IV, followed by an advanced course covering the remainder.

Exercise Philosophy: Each chapter contains three types of exercises:

- **Practice Problems**: Reinforce basic concepts and techniques
- **Extension Problems**: Explore variations and applications of main ideas
- **Research Problems**: Connect to current open questions (marked with $\star$)

Part I

Foundations

Chapter 1

Introduction to Algorithmic Complexity

Learning Objectives

After reading this chapter, you will be able to:

- Explain what algorithmic complexity measures and why it matters
- Distinguish between different types of complexity analysis
- Understand the historical development of complexity theory
- Identify the key questions that drive complexity analysis
- Appreciate the role of complexity theory in ccmputer science

1.1 What Is Algorithmic Complexity?

Algorithmic complexity is the study of the computational resources required to solve problems using algorithms. At its core, it seeks to answer fundamental questions about computation: How much time does an algorithm need to solve a problem? How much memory does it require? How do these requirements scale as the problem size grows?

Consider a simple example that illustrates why these questions matter. Suppose you're tasked with finding a specific name in a phone book containing one million entries. You have several approaches:

Linear Search: Start from the first entry and check each name sequentially until you find the target. In the worst case, you might examine all one million entries.

Binary Search: Since the phone book is alphabetically sorted, you can use a divide-and-conquer approach. Start in the middle, determine whether your target comes before or after the middle entry, then repeat the process on the appropriate half. This requires examining at most about 20 entries for a million-entry phone book.

Both algorithms solve the same problem, but their resource requirements differ dramatically. The linear search might require examining 1,000,000 entries, while binary search needs at most $\log_2(1,000,000) \approx 20$ entries. This difference becomes even more pronounced as the problem size growsfor a billion entries, linear search might examine 1,000,000,000 entries while binary search still needs only about 30.

This example captures the essence of algorithmic complexity: understanding how algorithm performance scales with problem size, and using this understanding to make informed choices about algorithm design and selection.

Definition 1.1.1 (Algorithmic Complexity)**.** Algorithmic complexity is the study of the amount of computational resources (primarily time and space) required by algorithms as a function of the input size.

The field encompasses several interconnected areas:

Time Complexity: How does the running time of an algorithm grow with input size?

Space Complexity: How does the memory requirement grow with input size?

Computational Complexity: What problems can be solved efficiently, and what problems appear to require exponential resources?

Approximation Complexity: When exact solutions are too expensive, how well can we approximate the optimal solution?

1.2 Why Complexity Analysis Matters

Understanding algorithmic complexity is crucial for several reasons, ranging from practical software development concerns to fundamental questions about the nature of computation itself.

1.2.1 Practical Importance

In software development, complexity analysis guides critical decisions:

Algorithm Selection: When multiple algorithms solve the same problem, complexity analysis helps identify the most suitable choice for your specific context. For instance, while quicksort has $\mathcal{O}(n^2)$ worst-case behavior, its $\mathcal{O}(n \log n)$ average-case performance and good cache behavior make it preferable to heapsort for many applications.

Scalability Planning: Understanding how algorithms scale helps predict performance as data grows. An $\mathcal{O}(n^2)$ algorithm might work fine for 1,000 elements but become unusable for 1,000,000 elements.

Resource Allocation: Complexity analysis informs decisions about hardware requirements, memory allocation, and system architecture.

Performance Optimization: Identifying algorithmic bottlenecks often yields greater improvements than low-level optimizations.

1.2.2 Theoretical Significance

Beyond practical applications, complexity theory addresses fundamental questions about computation:

Computational Limits: What problems can be solved efficiently? The famous P vs NP question asks whether every problem whose solution can be quickly verified can also be quickly solved.

Problem Classification: Complexity theory provides frameworks for classifying problems by their inherent difficulty, helping us understand which problems are fundamentally hard and which merely lack efficient algorithms.

Resource Tradeoffs: How do different computational resources relate to each other? Can we always trade time for space or vice versa?

1.2.3 Economic Impact

The economic implications of algorithmic complexity are profound:

Industry Competitiveness: Companies like Google built competitive advantages on superior algorithms for search, recommendation systems, and data processing.

Resource Costs: In cloud computing, algorithmic efficiency directly translates to cost savings. An algorithm that runs twice as fast can halve computational costs.

Innovation Enablement: Efficient algorithms enable new applications and services that would be impossible with slower approaches.

1.2.4 Examples Across Domains

Web Search: Modern search engines process billions of queries daily. The difference between an $\mathcal{O}(n)$ and $\mathcal{O}(\log n)$ search algorithm determines whether response times are measured in seconds or milliseconds.

Cryptography: The security of modern cryptographic systems relies on problems that are believed to require exponential time to solve, while legitimate users can perform encryption and decryption efficiently.

Machine Learning: Training large neural networks requires processing massive datasets. Algorithmic improvements in optimization can reduce training time from months to days.

Bioinformatics: Analyzing DNA sequences involves string matching and alignment problems where algorithmic efficiency determines whether analysis takes minutes or years.

1.3 Historical Perspective and Key Contributors

The development of complexity theory represents one of computer science's most significant intellectual achievements, evolving from practical concerns about computation efficiency to deep theoretical insights about the nature of computation itself.

1.3.1 Early Foundations (1930s-1950s)

The roots of complexity theory trace back to the foundational work on computability in the 1930s:

Alan Turing (1936): Introduced Turing machines as a model of computation and proved the existence of undecidable problems. While focused on computability rather than complexity, Turing's work established the mathematical framework for analyzing computation.

John von Neumann (1940s): Developed early models of computer architecture and began considering the efficiency of computations, particularly in the context of numerical methods.

Claude Shannon (1940s): His work on information theory provided mathematical tools that would later prove crucial in complexity analysis, particularly in understanding the relationship between information and computational resources.

1.3.2 Emergence of Algorithm Analysis (1960s)

As computers became more prevalent, the need for systematic algorithm analysis became apparent:

Donald Knuth (1960s-present): Often called the father of algorithm analysis, Knuth's multi-volume work "The Art of Computer Programming" established rigorous methods for analyzing algorithm performance. His detailed analysis of sorting algorithms, for example, revealed subtle performance differences that guided practical implementations.

Jack Edmonds (1965): Introduced the crucial distinction between polynomial and exponential time algorithms in his paper "Paths, Trees, and Flowers." Edmonds argued that polynomial-time algorithms represent "efficient" computationa perspective that became central to complexity theory.

Juris Hartmanis and Richard Stearns (1965): Established formal time and space complexity measures, proving the first hierarchy theorems showing that more time or space allows for solving strictly more problems.

1.3.3 Birth of NP-Completeness Theory (1970s)

The 1970s witnessed the development of one of computer science's most important theoretical frameworks:

Stephen Cook (1971): Proved that the Boolean satisfiability problem (SAT) is NP-complete in his landmark paper "The Complexity of Theorem-Proving Procedures." This work established the theoretical foundation for understanding computational intractability.

Richard Karp (1972): Extended Cook's work by showing that 21 important problems from various domains are NP-complete. Karp's paper "Reducibility Among Combinatorial Problems" demonstrated the widespread nature of computational intractability.

Leonid Levin (1973): Independently developed similar results to Cook's work, leading to the Cook-Levin theorem. Levin's contributions extended beyond NP-completeness to average-case complexity and other areas.

1.3.4 Expansion and Refinement (1980s-1990s)

The field matured with increasingly sophisticated analysis techniques:

Michael Garey and David Johnson (1979): Their book "Computers and Intractability: A Guide to the Theory of NP-Completeness" made complexity theory accessible to practitioners and established standard techniques for proving NP-completeness.

Leslie Valiant (1979): Introduced the complexity class #P, which captures counting problems, and later developed PAC learning theory, bridging complexity theory and machine learning.

Shafi Goldwasser, Silvio Micali, and Charles Rackoff (1980s): Developed the theory of interactive proofs, showing that interaction can dramatically increase the power of verification.

1.3.5 Modern Developments (2000s-Present)

Contemporary complexity theory continues to evolve with new models and techniques:

Computational Complexity and Quantum Computing: Researchers like Peter Shor and Lov Grover developed quantum algorithms that challenged classical complexity assumptions, leading to new complexity classes like BQP.

Approximation Algorithms: Researchers developed sophisticated frameworks for understanding when problems admit good approximations and when they don't.

Fine-Grained Complexity: Recent work focuses on understanding complexity within polynomial time, asking whether $\mathcal{O}(n^2)$ problems can be solved in $\mathcal{O}(n^{1.99})$ time.

1.3.6 Key Themes in Historical Development

Several themes emerge from this historical development:

From Practical to Theoretical: The field began with practical concerns about algorithm efficiency but evolved into deep theoretical insights about computation itself.

Interdisciplinary Connections: Complexity theory draws from and contributes to mathematics, physics, economics, and other fields.

Persistent Questions: Some fundamental questions, particularly P vs NP, have resisted solution for decades, driving continued research and refinement of techniques.

1.4 Overview of Complexity Measures

Algorithmic complexity encompasses several different measures, each capturing different aspects of computational resource usage. Understanding these various measures and their relationships provides essential groundwork for deeper complexity analysis.

1.4.1 Time Complexity

Time complexity measures how the number of elementary operations grows with input size.

Definition 1.4.1 (Time Complexity). For an algorithm A and input size n, the time complexity $T(n)$ represents the maximum number of elementary operations A performs on any input of size n.

Elementary Operations: These include basic arithmetic operations, comparisons, assignments, and array accesses. The specific choice of elementary operations doesn't typically affect asymptotic analysis, though it matters for precise timing analysis.

Example 1.4.1 (Finding Maximum Element). Consider finding the maximum element in an array:

```
function findMax(array A of size n):
    max = A[0]                    # 1 operation
    for i = 1 to n-1:             # loop executes n-1 times
        if A[i] > max:            # 1 comparison per iteration
            max = A[i]            # 1 assignment (worst case)
    return max                    # 1 operation

Total operations: 1 + (n-1) * (1 + 1) + 1 = 2n + 1
Time complexity: T(n) = 2n + 1 = O(n)
```

1.4.2 Space Complexity

Space complexity measures memory usage as a function of input size.

Types of Space:

- **Input Space**: Memory required to store the input (usually not counted in space complexity)
- **Auxiliary Space**: Additional memory used by the algorithm
- **Total Space**: Input space + auxiliary space

Example 1.4.2 (Binary Search Space Complexity). Binary search on a sorted array:

```
function binarySearch(sorted array A, target):
    left = 0                      # 1 unit
    right = length(A) - 1         # 1 unit
    while left <= right:
        mid = (left + right) / 2  # 1 unit
        if A[mid] = target:
            return mid
        else if A[mid] < target:
            left = mid + 1
        else:
            right = mid - 1
    return -1

Auxiliary space: 3 units (left, right, mid)
Space complexity: S(n) = O(1)
```

1.4.3 Best, Worst, and Average Case Analysis

Different inputs of the same size can lead to different performance, necessitating multiple complexity measures:

Worst-Case Complexity: Maximum resources required over all possible inputs of size n. This provides performance guaranteesthe algorithm will never perform worse than the worst-case bound.

Best-Case Complexity: Minimum resources required over all possible inputs of size n. While less commonly used, best-case analysis helps understand algorithm behavior under favorable conditions.

Average-Case Complexity: Expected resources required over all possible inputs of size n, assuming some probability distribution over inputs.

Example 1.4.3 (Insertion Sort Complexity)**.** Insertion Sort on an array:

```
function insertionSort(array A):
    for i = 1 to length(A) - 1:
        key = A[i]
        j = i - 1
        while j >= 0 and A[j] > key:
            A[j + 1] = A[j]
            j = j - 1
        A[j + 1] = key
```

- **Best Case**: Array already sorted; inner while loop never executes. Time: $\mathcal{O}(n)$
- **Worst Case**: Array sorted in reverse order; inner loop executes maximally. Time: $\mathcal{O}(n^2)$
- **Average Case**: Random permutation; inner loop executes about half-maximally. Time: $\mathcal{O}(n^2)$

1.4.4 Amortized Complexity

Some algorithms have operations with varying costs, but the expensive operations are rare enough that the average cost per operation remains low.

Definition 1.4.2 (Amortized Complexity)**.** Amortized complexity analyzes the average time per operation over a sequence of operations, even when individual operations may be expensive.

Example: Dynamic array (like C++ vector or Python list) that doubles in size when full:

- Most insertions: $\mathcal{O}(1)$ time
- Occasional resize: $\mathcal{O}(n)$ time to copy all elements
- Amortized time per insertion: $\mathcal{O}(1)$

1.4.5 Parameterized Complexity

Traditional complexity analysis uses input size as the only parameter, but some problems have natural parameters that better capture difficulty.

Definition 1.4.3 (Parameterized Complexity)**.** Parameterized complexity analyzes running time as a function of both input size n and some parameter k, seeking algorithms with running time $f(k) \times n^c$ where f is arbitrary and c is constant.

Example: The vertex cover problem asks whether a graph has a vertex cover of size k. A brute-force approach trying all possible k-subsets takes $\mathcal{O}(n^k)$ time, but a more sophisticated algorithm achieves $\mathcal{O}(2^k \times n)$ timeexponential in k but polynomial in n.

1.4.6 Parallel Complexity

With multicore processors and distributed systems, parallel complexity measures become important:

- **Work**: Total number of operations performed by all processors
- **Depth (Span)**: Length of the longest sequential chain of dependencies
- **Parallelism**: Ratio of work to depth, indicating potential speedup from parallelization

1.4.7 Communication Complexity

In distributed settings, communication costs often dominate computation costs:

Definition 1.4.4 (Communication Complexity)**.** Communication complexity measures the amount of information that must be exchanged between parties to solve a problem.

Example: Two parties each hold half of a database and want to compute some joint function. How much information must they exchange?

1.5 The Role of Complexity in Computer Science

Complexity theory occupies a central position in computer science, influencing virtually every area of the field and providing both theoretical foundations and practical guidance.

1.5.1 Theoretical Computer Science

Complexity theory provides the mathematical framework for understanding computation itself:

Computational Models: Different models of computation (Turing machines, RAM model, circuit model) provide different perspectives on complexity, each capturing certain aspects of real computation.

Hierarchy Theorems: These fundamental results show that more computational resources (time, space) strictly increase computational power, providing the theoretical basis for complexity classes.

Lower Bounds: Complexity theory develops techniques for proving that certain problems require substantial resources, helping identify fundamental computational limits.

1.5.2 Algorithm Design and Analysis

Complexity analysis guides algorithm development at every stage:

Design Principles: Understanding complexity helps identify promising algorithmic approaches. For instance, divide-and-conquer often yields $\mathcal{O}(n \log n)$ algorithms, while greedy approaches might achieve linear time.

Algorithm Comparison: When multiple algorithms solve the same problem, complexity analysis provides objective criteria for comparison.

Optimization Focus: Complexity analysis identifies bottlenecks, directing optimization efforts where they'll have the greatest impact.

Example: The development of fast matrix multiplication algorithms illustrates this interplay. The straightforward $\mathcal{O}(n^3)$ algorithm was improved through sophisticated techniques to $\mathcal{O}(n^{2.376})$, with complexity theory both motivating the search for better algorithms and providing tools to analyze new approaches.

1.5.3 Software Engineering

Complexity considerations influence software design decisions:

Data Structure Selection: Choosing between arrays, linked lists, hash tables, or trees depends on the complexity characteristics of required operations.

System Architecture: Understanding algorithmic complexity helps architects design systems that scale efficiently.

Performance Prediction: Complexity analysis enables performance modeling before implementation, helping identify potential scaling issues.

Code Review and Optimization: Complexity analysis provides objective criteria for evaluating code efficiency and guiding optimization efforts.

1.5.4 Database Systems

Database systems heavily rely on complexity theory:

Query Optimization: Database query optimizers use complexity analysis to choose among alternative query execution plans.

Index Design: Understanding search complexity motivates different indexing strategies (B-trees, hash indexes, etc.).

Join Algorithms: The choice among nested-loop joins, hash joins, and sort-merge joins depends on complexity analysis of different approaches.

1.5.5 Machine Learning and AI

Complexity theory increasingly influences machine learning:

Learning Theory: PAC learning theory uses complexity-theoretic concepts to understand when learning is possible and how much data is required.

Optimization: Understanding the complexity of optimization landscapes guides the development of training algorithms for neural networks.

Computational Limits: Complexity theory helps identify fundamental limits on learning and inference.

1.5.6 Cryptography

Modern cryptography fundamentally depends on complexity theory:

One-Way Functions: Cryptographic security assumes the existence of functions that are easy to compute but hard to invert.

Complexity-Based Security: The security of RSA, elliptic curve cryptography, and other systems depends on the assumed difficulty of certain mathematical problems.

Provable Security: Complexity theory provides frameworks for proving cryptographic security under specific assumptions.

1.5.7 Computational Biology

Biological applications increasingly rely on sophisticated algorithms:

Sequence Analysis: Algorithms for DNA/protein sequence alignment, phylogenetic reconstruction, and gene finding must handle massive datasets efficiently.

Structure Prediction: Protein folding prediction involves complex optimization problems where algorithmic efficiency determines feasibility.

Systems Biology: Modeling biological networks requires algorithms that can handle large-scale systems efficiently.

1.5.8 Economics and Game Theory

Complexity theory contributes to understanding economic computation:

Algorithmic Game Theory: Studies the complexity of computing equilibria in games and designing mechanisms with good computational properties.

Market Design: Understanding the complexity of matching problems influences the design of markets for kidneys, school choice, and other applications.

Auction Theory: The complexity of optimal bidding strategies affects auction design.

1.5.9 Emerging Areas

New areas continue to develop at the intersection of complexity theory and other fields:

Quantum Complexity: Understanding the power of quantum computation and its relationship to classical complexity classes.

Social Networks: Analyzing the complexity of information propagation, influence maximization, and community detection in large networks.

Big Data: Developing algorithms that can handle datasets too large for traditional approaches, leading to streaming algorithms and other specialized techniques.

1.5.10 Meta-Theoretical Impact

Complexity theory also influences how we think about computer science itself:

Problem Classification: Complexity classes provide a taxonomy for computational problems, helping organize our understanding of what can be computed efficiently.

Fundamental Questions: Questions like P vs NP drive research directions and highlight deep connections between different areas of mathematics and computer science.

Methodology: Complexity-theoretic thinkingfocusing on scaling behavior, worst-case guarantees, and resource tradeoffsinfluences how computer scientists approach problems across all areas of the field.

The pervasive influence of complexity theory demonstrates its fundamental importance in computer science. Whether developing new algorithms, designing software systems, or exploring theoretical questions, complexity analysis provides essential tools for understanding computational phenomena. As computer science continues to evolve, complexity theory adapts and grows, providing both stability through fundamental principles and flexibility through new models and techniques.

Chapter Summary

This introductory chapter has laid the groundwork for our journey through algorithmic complexity theory. We've seen that complexity analysis serves multiple roles: providing practical guidance for algorithm selection and system design, offering theoretical insights into the nature of computation, and establishing mathematical foundations for understanding computational limits.

Key takeaways from this chapter:

1. **Complexity analysis** measures how computational resource requirements scale with problem size, providing both practical guidance and theoretical insights.

2. **Multiple measures** capture different aspects of computational cost: time, space, average-case, worst-case, amortized, and others.

3. **Historical development** shows the evolution from practical concerns about algorithm efficiency to deep theoretical questions about computation itself.

4. **Broad impact** extends across all areas of computer science, from software engineering to theoretical computer science to emerging interdisciplinary fields.

As we proceed through this book, we'll develop the mathematical tools needed for rigorous complexity analysis, explore the theoretical frameworks that classify problems by their inherent difficulty, and examine how complexity considerations influence algorithm design and system implementation across diverse application domains.

The journey ahead will take us from basic asymptotic notation to advanced topics like quantum complexity and approximation algorithms. Each step builds upon the foundations laid in this introduction, developing both theoretical understanding and practical skills for analyzing and designing efficient algorithms.

Exercises

Practice Problems

1. For each of the following algorithms, identify what problem it solves and analyze its time complexity:

   (a) Linear search through an unsorted array

   (b) Binary search through a sorted array
   (c) Bubble sort
   (d) Finding the sum of elements in an array

2. Explain the difference between worst-case, average-case, and best-case complexity using insertion sort as an example.

3. Give three examples of problems from different domains (not mentioned in this chapter) where algorithmic complexity analysis would be crucial.

Extension Problems

4. Consider the problem of multiplying two $n \times n$ matrices using the standard algorithm. Analyze both time and space complexity.

5. Research and briefly describe one significant contribution to complexity theory not mentioned in the historical section.

6. Explain how the concept of polynomial time captures our intuitive notion of "efficient" computation.

Research Problems $\star$

$\star$ 7. Investigate the relationship between P and NP by researching current perspectives on whether P = NP. What would be the implications if P = NP? If P $\neq$ NP?

$\star$ 8. Explore how complexity theory applies to quantum computing. What complexity classes are relevant to quantum algorithms?

$\star$ 9. Research "fine-grained complexity theory" and explain how it refines our understanding of problems within P.

Chapter 2

Mathematical Preliminaries

Before diving deep into algorithmic complexity analysis, we must establish a solid mathematical foundation. This chapter introduces the essential mathematical concepts, notation, and techniques that will be used throughout this book. While some readers may be familiar with these topics, we present them here with a specific focus on their application to complexity analysis.

2.1 Essential Mathematical Concepts

2.1.1 Sets and Set Operations

In algorithmic analysis, we frequently work with sets to describe inputs, outputs, and problem spaces. A set is a collection of distinct objects, called elements or members.

Definition 2.1.1 (Set Membership). For a set S and an element x, we write $x \in S$ if x is a member of S, and $x \notin S$ otherwise.

Common Set Notations:

- $\emptyset$ or $\{\}$ denotes the empty set
- $\mathbb{N} = \{0, 1, 2, 3, \ldots\}$ represents natural numbers
- $\mathbb{Z} = \{\ldots, -2, -1, 0, 1, 2, \ldots\}$ represents integers
- $\mathbb{Q}$ represents rational numbers
- $\mathbb{R}$ represents real numbers
- $\mathbb{R}^+$ represents positive real numbers

Set Operations:

- Union: $A \cup B = \{x : x \in A \text{ or } x \in B\}$
- Intersection: $A \cap B = \{x : x \in A \text{ and } x \in B\}$
- Difference: $A \setminus B = \{x : x \in A \text{ and } x \notin B\}$
- Cartesian Product: $A \times B = \{(a, b) : a \in A \text{ and } b \in B\}$

The cardinality of a set S, denoted $|S|$, represents the number of elements in S. For infinite sets, we distinguish between countably infinite (like $\mathbb{N}$) and uncountably infinite (like $\mathbb{R}$) sets.

2.1.2 Logic and Proof Techniques

Logical Operators:

- Conjunction (AND): $p \wedge q$
- Disjunction (OR): $p \vee q$
- Negation (NOT): $\neg p$
- Implication: $p \to q$ (if p then q)
- Biconditional: $p \leftrightarrow q$ (p if and only if q)

Common Proof Techniques:

1. **Direct Proof:** To prove $p \to q$, assume p is true and show q must follow.
2. **Proof by Contradiction:** To prove statement p, assume $\neg p$ and derive a contradiction.
3. **Proof by Induction:** Particularly useful for analyzing recursive algorithms.
   - Base case: Prove $P(n_0)$ for some starting value n_0
   - Inductive step: Prove that $P(k) \to P(k+1)$ for all $k \geq n_0$

Example 2.1.1 (Induction for Algorithm Analysis)**.** Prove that the sum of the first n positive integers equals $\frac{n(n+1)}{2}$.

Proof. **Base case** ($n = 1$): $1 = \frac{1(1+1)}{2} = 1$ ✓

Inductive step: Assume $\sum_{i=1}^{k} i = \frac{k(k+1)}{2}$

Then:

$$\sum_{i=1}^{k+1} i = \left(\sum_{i=1}^{k} i\right) + (k+1) \tag{2.1}$$

$$= \frac{k(k+1)}{2} + (k+1) \tag{2.2}$$

$$= (k+1)\left(\frac{k}{2} + 1\right) \tag{2.3}$$

$$= \frac{(k+1)(k+2)}{2} \checkmark \tag{2.4}$$

2.1.3 Floors and Ceilings

Definition 2.1.2. For any real number x:

- Floor: $\lfloor x \rfloor$ = largest integer $\leq x$
- Ceiling: $\lceil x \rceil$ = smallest integer $\geq x$

Properties:

- $\lfloor x \rfloor \leq x < \lfloor x \rfloor + 1$
- $\lceil x \rceil - 1 < x \leq \lceil x \rceil$
- $\lfloor x \rfloor = \lceil x \rceil$ if and only if x is an integer
- $\lceil n/2 \rceil + \lfloor n/2 \rfloor = n$ for any integer n

These functions frequently appear in algorithm analysis, particularly when dealing with array indices, loop iterations, and divide-and-conquer algorithms.

2.1.4 Modular Arithmetic

Definition 2.1.3. For integers a, b, and $n > 0$, we say $a \equiv b \pmod{n}$ if n divides $(a - b)$.

Properties:

- $a \bmod n \in \{0, 1, \ldots, n-1\}$
- $(a + b) \bmod n = ((a \bmod n) + (b \bmod n)) \bmod n$
- $(a \times b) \bmod n = ((a \bmod n) \times (b \bmod n)) \bmod n$

Modular arithmetic is essential in hash function analysis, cryptographic algorithms, and cyclic data structures.

2.2 Functions and Their Growth Rates

Understanding how functions grow is fundamental to complexity analysis. We categorize functions by their asymptotic behavior as input size increases.

2.2.1 Function Classification

Definition 2.2.1 (Monotonicity).

- A function f is monotonically increasing if $x < y$ implies $f(x) \leq f(y)$
- A function f is strictly increasing if $x < y$ implies $f(x) < f(y)$
- Similar definitions apply for decreasing functions

Definition 2.2.2 (Polynomial Functions). A polynomial of degree d has the form:

$$f(n) = a_d n^d + a_{d-1} n^{d-1} + \cdots + a_1 n + a_0$$

where $a_d \neq 0$. The growth rate is dominated by the highest-degree term.

2.2.2 Common Growth Rates

Listed from slowest to fastest growth:

1. **Constant:** $\mathcal{O}(1)$
   - Example: Array access by index
   - $f(n) = c$ for some constant c
2. **Logarithmic:** $\mathcal{O}(\log n)$
   - Example: Binary search
   - Growth is extremely slow
3. **Linear:** $\mathcal{O}(n)$
   - Example: Linear search
   - $f(n) = an + b$
4. **Linearithmic:** $\mathcal{O}(n \log n)$
   - Example: Efficient sorting algorithms
   - Common in divide-and-conquer algorithms
5. **Quadratic:** $\mathcal{O}(n^2)$

- Example: Simple sorting algorithms
- $f(n) = an^2 + bn + c$

6. **Cubic:** $\mathcal{O}(n^3)$
   - Example: Naive matrix multiplication
   - Generally the practical limit for large inputs
7. **Exponential:** $\mathcal{O}(2^n)$
   - Example: Subset generation
   - Quickly becomes intractable
8. **Factorial:** $\mathcal{O}(n!)$
   - Example: Permutation generation
   - Grows faster than exponential

Theorem 2.2.1 (Growth Rate Hierarchy). *For sufficiently large n and constants $a, b > 1$:*

$$1 < \log n < n^\epsilon < n < n \log n < n^2 < n^3 < 2^n < n! < n^n$$

where ϵ is any positive constant less than 1.

2.2.3 Limits and Continuity

Definition 2.2.3 (Limit). We say $\lim_{n\to\infty} f(n) = L$ if for every $\epsilon > 0$, there exists N such that for all $n > N$, $|f(n) - L| < \epsilon$.

L'Hôpital's Rule: Often useful for comparing growth rates:
If $\lim_{n\to\infty} f(n) = \lim_{n\to\infty} g(n) = \infty$, then:

$$\lim_{n\to\infty} \frac{f(n)}{g(n)} = \lim_{n\to\infty} \frac{f'(n)}{g'(n)}$$

Example 2.2.1. Show that $\log n$ grows slower than $\sqrt{n}$.

$$\lim_{n\to\infty} \frac{\log n}{\sqrt{n}} = \lim_{n\to\infty} \frac{1/n}{1/(2\sqrt{n})} = \lim_{n\to\infty} \frac{2}{\sqrt{n}} = 0$$

Therefore, $\log n = o(\sqrt{n})$.

2.3 Logarithms and Exponentials

Logarithms appear constantly in algorithm analysis, particularly in divide-and-conquer algorithms and tree-based data structures.

2.3.1 Logarithm Properties

Definition 2.3.1. For $b > 0$, $b \neq 1$, and $x > 0$:

$$y = \log_b(x) \text{ if and only if } b^y = x$$

Fundamental Properties:

1. $\log_b(xy) = \log_b(x) + \log_b(y)$
2. $\log_b(x/y) = \log_b(x) - \log_b(y)$
3. $\log_b(x^r) = r \cdot \log_b(x)$
4. $\log_b(x) = \frac{\log_c(x)}{\log_c(b)}$ (change of base)
5. $b^{\log_b(x)} = x$
6. $\log_b(b^x) = x$

Special Values:

- $\log_b(1) = 0$
- $\log_b(b) = 1$
- $\log_b(b^k) = k$

2.3.2 Common Logarithm Bases in Computer Science

1. **Binary Logarithm** ($\log_2$)**:**
   - Most common in algorithm analysis
   - Represents the number of times we can divide n by 2 until reaching 1
   - Height of a balanced binary tree with n nodes $\approx \log_2(n)$
2. **Natural Logarithm** (ln **or** $\log_e$)**:**
   - Appears in mathematical analysis and probability
   - Useful for calculus-based derivations
3. **Common Logarithm** ($\log_{10}$)**:**
   - Less common in complexity analysis
   - Sometimes used for decimal digit counting

Note: In complexity analysis, when the base is omitted, we typically mean $\log_2$. However, for asymptotic analysis, the base doesn't matter since logarithms of different bases differ only by a constant factor.

2.3.3 Exponential Functions

Definition 2.3.2. An exponential function has the form $f(x) = b^x$ where $b > 0$, $b \neq 1$.

Properties:

1. $b^{x+y} = b^x \cdot b^y$
2. $b^{x-y} = b^x / b^y$
3. $(b^x)^y = b^{xy}$
4. $b^0 = 1$
5. $b^{-x} = 1/b^x$

Important Series:

- Geometric series: $\sum_{i=0}^{n-1} r^i = \frac{1-r^n}{1-r}$ for $r \neq 1$
- For $|r| < 1$: $\sum_{i=0}^{\infty} r^i = \frac{1}{1-r}$

2.3.4 Applications in Algorithm Analysis

Example 2.3.1 (Binary Search Complexity)**.** In binary search, we repeatedly halve the search space. Starting with n elements:

- After 1 comparison: $n/2$ elements remain
- After 2 comparisons: $n/4$ elements remain
- After k comparisons: $n/2^k$ elements remain

We stop when $n/2^k \leq 1$, which gives $k \geq \log_2(n)$. Therefore, binary search requires $\mathcal{O}(\log n)$ comparisons.

Example 2.3.2 (Merge Sort Recurrence)**.** The recurrence $T(n) = 2T(n/2) + n$ represents merge sort's time complexity.

- At depth 0: 1 problem of size n, work $= n$
- At depth 1: 2 problems of size $n/2$, work $= 2(n/2) = n$
- At depth i: 2^i problems of size $n/2^i$, work $= 2^i(n/2^i) = n$

The depth is $\log_2(n)$, giving total work: $n \cdot \log_2(n) = \mathcal{O}(() \, n \log n)$.

2.4 Summations and Recurrence Relations

2.4.1 Common Summations

Summations frequently arise when analyzing loops and recursive algorithms.

Arithmetic Series:

$$\sum_{i=1}^{n} i = \frac{n(n+1)}{2} = \Theta\left(()\, n^2\right)$$

Geometric Series:

$$\sum_{i=0}^{n-1} r^i = \frac{1-r^n}{1-r} \text{ for } r \neq 1$$

Harmonic Series:

$$H_n = \sum_{i=1}^{n} \frac{1}{i} = \ln(n) + \gamma + \mathcal{O}\left(()\, 1/n\right)$$

where $\gamma \approx 0.5772$ is the Euler-Mascheroni constant.

Power Sums:

- $\sum_{i=1}^{n} i^2 = \frac{n(n+1)(2n+1)}{6} = \Theta\left(()\, n^3\right)$
- $\sum_{i=1}^{n} i^3 = \left[\frac{n(n+1)}{2}\right]^2 = \Theta\left(()\, n^4\right)$
- In general: $\sum_{i=1}^{n} i^k = \Theta\left(()\, n^{k+1}\right)$

2.4.2 Summation Techniques

1. Splitting Summations:

$$\sum_{i=1}^{n} (a_i + b_i) = \sum_{i=1}^{n} a_i + \sum_{i=1}^{n} b_i$$

2. Change of Variables:

$$\sum_{i=0}^{n-1} f(i) = \sum_{j=1}^{n} f(j-1)$$

3. Bounding Summations: For monotonic functions:

- If f is increasing: $\int_1^n f(x)dx \leq \sum_{i=1}^{n} f(i) \leq \int_1^{n+1} f(x)dx$
- If f is decreasing: $\int_1^{n+1} f(x)dx \leq \sum_{i=1}^{n} f(i) \leq \int_1^{n} f(x)dx$

2.4.3 Recurrence Relations

Definition 2.4.1. A recurrence relation defines a sequence where each term is a function of preceding terms.

Common Forms:

1. **Linear Homogeneous:**

$$T(n) = a_1T(n-1) + a_2T(n-2) + \cdots + a_kT(n-k)$$

2. **Divide-and-Conquer:**

$$T(n) = aT(n/b) + f(n)$$

where $a \geq 1$ is the number of subproblems, $b > 1$ is the size reduction factor, and $f(n)$ is the work done outside recursion.

3. **Linear Non-homogeneous:**

$$T(n) = T(n-1) + f(n)$$

Solution Methods Preview:

1. **Substitution Method:** Guess the solution and prove by induction
2. **Recursion Tree Method:** Visualize the recursion as a tree
3. **Master Theorem:** Direct formula for divide-and-conquer recurrences
4. **Characteristic Equation:** For linear homogeneous recurrences

Example 2.4.1 (Fibonacci Recurrence). $F(n) = F(n-1) + F(n-2)$ with $F(0) = 0$, $F(1) = 1$

The characteristic equation $r^2 = r + 1$ has roots:

$$r_1 = \frac{1+\sqrt{5}}{2} \text{ (golden ratio } \varphi) \tag{2.5}$$

$$r_2 = \frac{1-\sqrt{5}}{2} \tag{2.6}$$

General solution: $F(n) = A\varphi^n + B\left(\frac{1-\sqrt{5}}{2}\right)^n$

Using initial conditions: $F(n) = \frac{\varphi^n - \psi^n}{\sqrt{5}}$ where $\psi = \frac{1-\sqrt{5}}{2}$

This shows $F(n) = \Theta(() \varphi^n) \approx \Theta(() 1.618^n)$, demonstrating exponential growth.

2.5 Probability Theory Basics

Probabilistic analysis is crucial for understanding average-case complexity and randomized algorithms.

2.5.1 Probability Spaces and Events

Definition 2.5.1 (Probability Space)**.** A probability space consists of:

- Sample space Ω: set of all possible outcomes
- Event space $\mathcal{F}$: set of events (subsets of Ω)
- Probability function $\mathbb{P} : \mathcal{F} \to [0, 1]$

Axioms of Probability:

1. $\mathbb{P}(E) \geq 0$ for any event E
2. $\mathbb{P}(\Omega) = 1$
3. For disjoint events $E_1, E_2, \ldots$: $\mathbb{P}\left(\bigcup_i E_i\right) = \sum_i \mathbb{P}(E_i)$

Basic Properties:

- $\mathbb{P}(\emptyset) = 0$
- $\mathbb{P}(\bar{E}) = 1 - \mathbb{P}(E)$ where $\bar{E}$ is the complement of E
- $\mathbb{P}(A \cup B) = \mathbb{P}(A) + \mathbb{P}(B) - \mathbb{P}(A \cap B)$
- If $A \subseteq B$, then $\mathbb{P}(A) \leq \mathbb{P}(B)$

2.5.2 Random Variables and Expectation

Definition 2.5.2 (Random Variable)**.** A random variable X is a function $X : \Omega \to \mathbb{R}$ that assigns a real number to each outcome.

Discrete Random Variables:

- Probability Mass Function (PMF): $\mathbb{P}(X = x)$
- Expectation: $\mathbb{E}[X] = \sum_x x \cdot \mathbb{P}(X = x)$
- Variance: $\text{Var}(X) = \mathbb{E}[(X - \mathbb{E}[X])^2] = \mathbb{E}[X^2] - (\mathbb{E}[X])^2$
- Standard Deviation: $\sigma = \sqrt{\text{Var}(X)}$

Continuous Random Variables:

- Probability Density Function (PDF): $f(x)$
- Cumulative Distribution Function (CDF): $F(x) = \mathbb{P}(X \leq x)$
- Expectation: $\mathbb{E}[X] = \int_{-\infty}^{\infty} x \cdot f(x)dx$

2.5.3 Important Probability Distributions

1. Bernoulli Distribution:

- Single trial with success probability p
- $\mathbb{P}(X = 1) = p$, $\mathbb{P}(X = 0) = 1 - p$
- $\mathbb{E}[X] = p$, $\text{Var}(X) = p(1 - p)$

2. Binomial Distribution:

- Number of successes in n independent Bernoulli trials
- $\mathbb{P}(X = k) = \binom{n}{k}p^k(1 - p)^{n-k}$
- $\mathbb{E}[X] = np$, $\text{Var}(X) = np(1 - p)$

3. Geometric Distribution:

- Number of trials until first success
- $\mathbb{P}(X = k) = (1 - p)^{k-1}p$
- $\mathbb{E}[X] = 1/p$, $\text{Var}(X) = (1 - p)/p^2$

4. Uniform Distribution:

- Discrete: $\mathbb{P}(X = k) = 1/n$ for $k \in \{1, 2, \ldots, n\}$
- Continuous: $f(x) = 1/(b - a)$ for $x \in [a, b]$

2.5.4 Conditional Probability and Independence

Definition 2.5.3 (Conditional Probability)**.** $\mathbb{P}(A|B) = \frac{\mathbb{P}(A \cap B)}{\mathbb{P}(B)}$ for $\mathbb{P}(B) > 0$

Bayes' Theorem:

$$\mathbb{P}(A|B) = \frac{\mathbb{P}(B|A) \cdot \mathbb{P}(A)}{\mathbb{P}(B)}$$

Definition 2.5.4 (Independence)**.** Events A and B are independent if $\mathbb{P}(A \cap B) = \mathbb{P}(A) \cdot \mathbb{P}(B)$

Linearity of Expectation:

$$\mathbb{E}[X + Y] = \mathbb{E}[X] + \mathbb{E}[Y]$$

(always true, even if X and Y are dependent)

For independent random variables:

- $\mathbb{E}[XY] = \mathbb{E}[X] \cdot \mathbb{E}[Y]$
- $\text{Var}(X + Y) = \text{Var}(X) + \text{Var}(Y)$

2.5.5 Applications in Algorithm Analysis

Example 2.5.1 (Expected Comparisons in Quicksort)**.** Let X_{ij} be an indicator variable for whether elements i and j are compared.

- $\mathbb{P}(X_{ij} = 1) = \frac{2}{j-i+1}$ (probability that i or j is chosen as pivot first)
- Total comparisons: $X = \sum_{i=1}^{n-1} \sum_{j=i+1}^{n} X_{ij}$
- $\mathbb{E}[X] = \sum_{i=1}^{n-1} \sum_{j=i+1}^{n} \frac{2}{j-i+1} = \mathcal{O}(()\, n \log n)$

Example 2.5.2 (Hash Table Collisions)**.** With n keys and m slots using uniform hashing:

- Probability of specific collision: $1/m$
- Expected collisions for one key: $(n - 1)/m$
- Load factor $\alpha = n/m$ determines average-case performance

2.6 Graph Theory Fundamentals

Graphs are fundamental data structures in computer science, and many algorithms operate on graph representations.

2.6.1 Basic Definitions

Definition 2.6.1 (Graph)**.** A graph $G = (V, E)$ consists of:

- V: set of vertices (or nodes)
- E: set of edges connecting vertices

Types of Graphs:

1. **Undirected Graph:** Edges have no direction

- Edge $\{u, v\}$ connects u and v bidirectionally

2. **Directed Graph (Digraph):** Edges have direction
   - Edge (u, v) goes from u to v
3. **Weighted Graph:** Each edge has an associated weight
   - $w : E \to \mathbb{R}$ assigns weights to edges
4. **Simple Graph:** No self-loops or multiple edges between vertices

Graph Terminology:

- **Adjacent vertices:** Connected by an edge
- **Degree:** Number of edges incident to a vertex
  - In-degree: incoming edges (directed graphs)
  - Out-degree: outgoing edges (directed graphs)
- **Path:** Sequence of vertices $v_1, v_2, \ldots, v_k$ where each consecutive pair is connected
- **Cycle:** Path where first and last vertices are the same
- **Connected:** There exists a path between every pair of vertices
- **Component:** Maximal connected subgraph

2.6.2 Graph Representations

1. Adjacency Matrix:

- $n \times n$ matrix A where $A[i][j] = 1$ if edge exists, 0 otherwise
- Space: $\mathcal{O}(n^2)$
- Edge query: $\mathcal{O}(1)$
- Neighbor iteration: $\mathcal{O}(n)$

2. Adjacency List:

- Array of lists, each containing a vertex's neighbors
- Space: $\mathcal{O}(n + m)$ where $m = |E|$
- Edge query: $\mathcal{O}(\text{degree}(v))$

- Neighbor iteration: $\mathcal{O}(\text{degree}(v))$

3. Edge List:

- List of all edges as pairs (or triples for weighted graphs)
- Space: $\mathcal{O}(m)$
- Edge query: $\mathcal{O}(m)$
- Useful for algorithms that process edges sequentially

2.6.3 Special Graph Classes

Trees:

- Connected acyclic graph
- n vertices, $n-1$ edges
- Unique path between any two vertices
- Adding any edge creates exactly one cycle

Bipartite Graphs:

- Vertices partitioned into two sets U and V
- All edges connect a vertex in U to a vertex in V
- Characterization: Contains no odd-length cycles

Complete Graphs:

- Every pair of vertices is connected
- Denoted K_n for n vertices
- Number of edges: $\frac{n(n-1)}{2}$

Planar Graphs:

- Can be drawn in the plane without edge crossings
- Euler's formula: $V - E + F = 2$ (V vertices, E edges, F faces)
- Maximum edges: $3V - 6$ for $V \geq 3$

2.6.4 Graph Properties and Theorems

Theorem 2.6.1 (Handshaking Lemma). *In any undirected graph:* $\sum_{v \in V} degree(v) = 2|E|$

Theorem 2.6.2 (Tree Characterizations). *The following are equivalent for a graph G with n vertices:*

1. *G is a tree*
2. *G is connected and has $n-1$ edges*
3. *G is acyclic and has $n-1$ edges*
4. *G is connected and removing any edge disconnects it*
5. *G is acyclic and adding any edge creates exactly one cycle*

Theorem 2.6.3 (Graph Coloring).

- *Chromatic number $\chi(G)$: Minimum colors needed to color vertices so no adjacent vertices share a color*
- *For bipartite graphs: $\chi(G) = 2$*
- *For complete graphs: $\chi(K_n) = n$*
- *For planar graphs: $\chi(G) \leq 4$ (Four Color Theorem)*

2.6.5 Graph Algorithms Preview

Common graph problems and their complexities:

1. **Traversal (BFS/DFS):** $\mathcal{O}(V+E)$
2. **Shortest Path:**
   - Unweighted: BFS, $\mathcal{O}(V+E)$
   - Non-negative weights: Dijkstra, $\mathcal{O}((V+E)\log V)$
   - General: Bellman-Ford, $\mathcal{O}(VE)$
3. **Minimum Spanning Tree:**
   - Kruskal: $\mathcal{O}(E\log E)$
   - Prim: $\mathcal{O}((V+E)\log V)$
4. **Topological Sort:** $\mathcal{O}(V+E)$
5. **Strongly Connected Components:** $\mathcal{O}(V+E)$

2.6.6 Applications in Complexity Analysis

Example 2.6.1 (Social Network Analysis). In a social network with n users and m friendships:

- Average degree: $2m/n$
- Clustering coefficient measures local density
- Small-world property: diameter is $\mathcal{O}(\log n)$

Example 2.6.2 (Web Graph). The web can be modeled as a directed graph:

- Vertices: web pages
- Edges: hyperlinks
- PageRank algorithm complexity: $\mathcal{O}(k(V+E))$ for k iterations

Chapter Summary

This chapter has established the mathematical foundation necessary for algorithmic complexity analysis:

1. **Set theory and logic** provide the language for precise algorithm specification
2. **Functions and growth rates** form the basis for comparing algorithm efficiency
3. **Logarithms and exponentials** appear throughout divide-and-conquer and tree-based algorithms
4. **Summations and recurrences** are essential for analyzing loops and recursion
5. **Probability theory** enables average-case and randomized algorithm analysis
6. **Graph theory** provides the framework for network and relationship-based problems

These mathematical tools will be applied throughout the remainder of this book. Readers should be comfortable with these concepts before proceeding, as they form the theoretical underpinning of all complexity analysis.

Exercises

Conceptual Questions

2.1. Prove that for any positive integer n: $\lfloor n/2 \rfloor + \lceil n/2 \rceil = n$

2.2. Show that $\log(n!) = \Theta\left(()\, n \log n\right)$ using Stirling's approximation.

2.3. Prove that if $f(n) = \mathcal{O}\left(()\, g(n)\right)$ and $g(n) = \mathcal{O}\left(()\, h(n)\right)$, then $f(n) = \mathcal{O}\left(()\, h(n)\right)$.

2.4. Find a closed form for the recurrence: $T(n) = T(n-1) + n$ with $T(1) = 1$.

2.5. In a hash table with n keys and m slots, what is the probability that at least two keys hash to the same slot? (Birthday paradox)

Computational Problems

2.6. Rank the following functions by growth rate:

$$n^{1.5}, \quad 2^{\log n}, \quad n \log\log n, \quad n!, \quad (\log n)!, \quad 2^{2^n}$$

2.7. Solve the recurrence $T(n) = 3T(n/2) + n$ using the recursion tree method.

2.8. Calculate $\mathbb{E}[X^2]$ where X is the number of comparisons in a successful linear search of n elements.

2.9. Prove that a tree with n vertices has exactly $n-1$ edges using induction.

2.10. Show that the sum of all node depths in a complete binary tree with n nodes is $\Theta\left(n \log n\right)$.

Advanced Problems

2.11. Prove that the harmonic series $H_n = \Theta\left(()\, \log n\right)$ by bounding it with integrals.

2.12. Analyze the expected number of cycles of length k in a random graph $G(n, p)$.

2.13. Show that any comparison-based sorting algorithm requires $\Omega\left(n \log n\right)$ comparisons in the worst case.

2.14. Derive the probability generating function for the binomial distribution and use it to find the mean and variance.

2.15. Prove Cayley's formula: The number of labeled trees on n vertices is n^{n-2}.

Further Reading

- *Concrete Mathematics* by Graham, Knuth, and Patashnik - Comprehensive mathematical techniques for computer science
- *Introduction to Probability* by Bertsekas and Tsitsiklis - Thorough probability theory treatment
- *Graph Theory* by Diestel - Advanced graph theory concepts
- *Generating Functions* by Wilf - Powerful techniques for summations and recurrences
- *The Art of Computer Programming, Vol. 1* by Knuth - Mathematical foundations and analysis

Chapter 3

Asymptotic Notation

3.1 The Need for Asymptotic Analysis

3.1.1 Introduction

When analyzing algorithms, we face a fundamental challenge: how do we compare the efficiency of different algorithms in a way that is both meaningful and machine-independent? Consider two sorting algorithms: one that takes $100n^2 + 50n + 1000$ microseconds and another that takes $2n^3 + 10n$ microseconds to sort n elements. Which is better?

The answer depends on the input size. For small values of n, the cubic algorithm might be faster due to its smaller constants. However, as n grows large, the quadratic algorithm will eventually outperform the cubic one, regardless of the constants involved. This observation leads us to *asymptotic analysis*the study of algorithm behavior as input size approaches infinity.

3.1.2 Why Exact Analysis Falls Short

Exact runtime analysis, while theoretically possible, presents several practical challenges:

1. **Machine Dependency**: The exact number of operations depends on the specific computer architecture, processor speed, and instruction set.

2. **Implementation Details**: Minor coding choices (loop structure, variable initialization) can affect the exact count but not the fundamental efficiency.

3. **Compiler Optimizations**: Modern compilers perform numerous optimizations that can dramatically change the actual number of executed instructions.

4. **Input Variability**: Different inputs of the same size may require different numbers of operations.

3.1.3 The Asymptotic Approach

Asymptotic analysis abstracts away these details by focusing on the growth rate of functions as input size increases. This approach provides several benefits:

- **Simplicity**: We can ignore lower-order terms and constant factors that become insignificant for large inputs.
- **Portability**: Analysis remains valid across different machines and implementations.
- **Clarity**: The fundamental efficiency characteristics become apparent.
- **Predictability**: We can predict performance on large inputs even from small-scale experiments.

3.1.4 Mathematical Foundation

Asymptotic notation is rooted in the mathematical concept of limits. When we say $f(n)$ grows asymptotically like $g(n)$, we're essentially examining:

$$\lim_{n \to \infty} \frac{f(n)}{g(n)}$$

This limit, when it exists and is finite and non-zero, tells us that f and g have the same growth rate. Asymptotic notation provides a precise language for expressing these relationships.

3.2 Big O Notation ($\mathcal{O}$)

3.2.1 Definition

Big O notation provides an asymptotic upper bound on a function's growth rate.

Definition 3.2.1 (Big O)**.** We say $f(n) = \mathcal{O}(g(n))$ if there exist positive constants c and n_0 such that:

$$0 \leq f(n) \leq c \cdot g(n) \quad \text{for all } n \geq n_0$$

This means that $f(n)$ grows no faster than $g(n)$ up to a constant factor, for sufficiently large n.

3.2.2 Intuitive Understanding

Think of $\mathcal{O}(g(n))$ as defining a set of functions that grow no faster than $g(n)$. When we write $f(n) = \mathcal{O}(g(n))$, we're asserting that f belongs to this set. Some computer scientists prefer the notation $f(n) \in \mathcal{O}(g(n))$ to emphasize this set membership.

3.2.3 Examples and Applications

Example 3.2.1. Prove that $3n^2 + 5n + 2 = \mathcal{O}(n^2)$.

Proof. We need to find constants c and n_0 such that:

$$3n^2 + 5n + 2 \leq c \cdot n^2 \quad \text{for all } n \geq n_0$$

For $n \geq 1$, we have:

$$5n \leq 5n^2 \tag{3.1}$$

$$2 \leq 2n^2 \tag{3.2}$$

Therefore:

$$3n^2 + 5n + 2 \leq 3n^2 + 5n^2 + 2n^2 = 10n^2$$

So we can choose $c = 10$ and $n_0 = 1$.

Example 3.2.2. Is $2^n = \mathcal{O}(n^2)$?

Analysis: For this to be true, we would need:

$$2^n \leq c \cdot n^2 \quad \text{for some constant } c \text{ and all } n \geq n_0$$

However, $\lim_{n\to\infty} \frac{2^n}{n^2} = \infty$, so no such constant exists. Therefore, $2^n \neq \mathcal{O}(n^2)$.

3.2.4 Properties of Big O

1. **Transitivity**: If $f(n) = \mathcal{O}(g(n))$ and $g(n) = \mathcal{O}(h(n))$, then $f(n) = \mathcal{O}(h(n))$
2. **Sum Rule**: $\mathcal{O}(f(n)) + \mathcal{O}(g(n)) = \mathcal{O}(\max(f(n), g(n)))$
3. **Product Rule**: $\mathcal{O}(f(n)) \cdot \mathcal{O}(g(n)) = \mathcal{O}(f(n) \cdot g(n))$
4. **Constant Multiplication**: For any constant $k > 0$, $\mathcal{O}(k \cdot f(n)) = \mathcal{O}(f(n))$

3.2.5 Common Big O Classes

In order of increasing growth rate:

- $\mathcal{O}(1)$ — Constant time
- $\mathcal{O}(\log n)$ — Logarithmic time
- $\mathcal{O}(n)$ — Linear time
- $\mathcal{O}(n \log n)$ — Linearithmic time
- $\mathcal{O}(n^2)$ — Quadratic time
- $\mathcal{O}(n^3)$ — Cubic time
- $\mathcal{O}(2^n)$ — Exponential time
- $\mathcal{O}(n!)$ — Factorial time

3.3 Omega Notation (Ω)

3.3.1 Definition

While Big O provides an upper bound, Omega notation provides an asymptotic lower bound.

Definition 3.3.1 (Big Omega)**.** We say $f(n) = \Omega(g(n))$ if there exist positive constants c and n_0 such that:

$$0 \leq c \cdot g(n) \leq f(n) \quad \text{for all } n \geq n_0$$

3.3.2 Relationship with Big O

An important relationship exists between $\mathcal{O}$ and Ω:

Theorem 3.3.1. *$f(n) = \Omega(g(n))$ if and only if $g(n) = \mathcal{O}(f(n))$*

This duality means that proving lower bounds is essentially the mirror image of proving upper bounds.

3.3.3 Applications in Algorithm Analysis

Omega notation is particularly useful for:

1. **Best-case analysis**: When we want to show that an algorithm must take at least a certain amount of time.

2. **Lower bounds for problems**: Proving that any algorithm solving a problem must have at least a certain complexity.

Example 3.3.1 (Comparison-based sorting lower bound). Any comparison-based sorting algorithm must make $\Omega(n \log n)$ comparisons in the worst case. This is a fundamental lower bound that tells us algorithms like mergesort and heapsort are asymptotically optimal.

3.3.4 Examples

Example 3.3.2. Prove that $n^2 - 3n = \Omega(n^2)$.

Proof. We need to show that $c \cdot n^2 \leq n^2 - 3n$ for some $c > 0$ and all $n \geq n_0$.

For $n \geq 6$:

$$n^2 - 3n = n^2\left(1 - \frac{3}{n}\right) \geq n^2\left(1 - \frac{3}{6}\right) = \frac{n^2}{2}$$

Therefore, we can choose $c = \frac{1}{2}$ and $n_0 = 6$.

3.4 Theta Notation (Θ)

3.4.1 Definition

Theta notation provides a tight asymptotic bound, combining both upper and lower bounds.

Definition 3.4.1 (Big Theta). We say $f(n) = \Theta(g(n))$ if there exist positive constants c_1, c_2, and n_0 such that:

$$0 \leq c_1 \cdot g(n) \leq f(n) \leq c_2 \cdot g(n) \quad \text{for all } n \geq n_0$$

Equivalently: $f(n) = \Theta(g(n))$ if and only if $f(n) = \mathcal{O}(g(n))$ and $f(n) = \Omega(g(n))$.

3.4.2 Significance

Theta notation is the most precise of the three notations when applicable. It tells us that a function grows at exactly the same rate as another function, up to constant factors.

3.4.3 Examples and Non-examples

Example 3.4.1. Prove that $6n^3 + 2n^2 - 5n + 11 = \Theta(n^3)$.

Proof. We need to show both $\mathcal{O}(n^3)$ and $\Omega(n^3)$.

For the upper bound (when $n \geq 1$):

$$6n^3 + 2n^2 - 5n + 11 \leq 6n^3 + 2n^3 + 11n^3 = 19n^3$$

For the lower bound (when $n \geq 11$):

$$6n^3 + 2n^2 - 5n + 11 \geq 6n^3 - 5n^3 = n^3$$

Therefore, $n^3 \leq 6n^3 + 2n^2 - 5n + 11 \leq 19n^3$ for $n \geq 11$.

Example 3.4.2. Why $2n \neq \Theta(n^2)$?

While $2n = \mathcal{O}(n^2)$ (upper bound exists), we cannot establish $2n = \Omega(n^2)$ because $2n$ grows much slower than n^2. Therefore, no tight bound exists.

3.4.4 Use in Average-Case Analysis

Theta notation is particularly valuable when describing average-case complexity, where we often know the exact growth rate. For instance, quicksort has average-case complexity $\Theta(n \log n)$, meaning it takes exactly $n \log n$ time up to constant factors.

3.5 Little o and Little Omega

3.5.1 Little o Notation

Little o provides a strict upper bound, indicating that one function grows strictly slower than another.

Definition 3.5.1 (Little o). $f(n) = o(g(n))$ if for every constant $c > 0$, there exists n_0 such that:

$$0 \leq f(n) < c \cdot g(n) \quad \text{for all } n \geq n_0$$

Equivalently: $\lim_{n\to\infty} \frac{f(n)}{g(n)} = 0$

3.5.2 Little Omega Notation

Little omega provides a strict lower bound.

Definition 3.5.2 (Little Omega). $f(n) = \omega(g(n))$ if for every constant $c > 0$, there exists n_0 such that:

$$0 \leq c \cdot g(n) < f(n) \quad \text{for all } n \geq n_0$$

Equivalently: $\lim_{n\to\infty} \frac{f(n)}{g(n)} = \infty$

3.5.3 Relationships and Distinctions

The relationship between big and little notations:

- $f(n) = o(g(n))$ implies $f(n) = \mathcal{O}(g(n))$, but not conversely
- $f(n) = \omega(g(n))$ implies $f(n) = \Omega(g(n))$, but not conversely
- $f(n) = o(g(n))$ means $f(n) \neq \Theta(g(n))$

3.5.4 Examples

Example 3.5.1 (Relationships between polynomial degrees).

- $n = o(n^2)$ because $\lim_{n\to\infty} \frac{n}{n^2} = 0$
- $n^2 \neq o(n^2)$ because $\lim_{n\to\infty} \frac{n^2}{n^2} = 1$
- $n^2 = o(n^{2+\epsilon})$ for any $\epsilon > 0$

Example 3.5.2 (Logarithmic vs. polynomial growth). $\log n = o(n^\epsilon)$ for any $\epsilon > 0$, no matter how small. This captures the intuition that logarithmic functions grow strictly slower than any polynomial function.

3.6 Common Misconceptions and Proper Usage

3.6.1 Misconception 1: Equality vs. Set Membership

Incorrect thinking: "$f(n) = \mathcal{O}(g(n))$ means $f(n)$ equals something"

Correct understanding: $\mathcal{O}(g(n))$ represents a set of functions. The notation $f(n) = \mathcal{O}(g(n))$ is a convenient abuse of notation meaning $f(n) \in \mathcal{O}(g(n))$.

3.6.2 Misconception 2: Unique Representation

Incorrect thinking: "Each function has a unique Big O representation"

Correct understanding: A function belongs to infinitely many Big O classes. If $f(n) = \mathcal{O}(n^2)$, then $f(n) = \mathcal{O}(n^3)$, $\mathcal{O}(n^4)$, etc. We typically use the tightest bound that's easy to express.

3.6.3 Misconception 3: Big O Always Means Worst Case

Incorrect thinking: "Big O notation always describes worst-case behavior"

Correct understanding: Big O is a mathematical tool that can be applied to best-case, average-case, or worst-case analysis. The confusion arises because we often use Big O to express worst-case bounds.

3.6.4 Misconception 4: Constants Never Matter

Incorrect thinking: "Since we ignore constants, $10^{100}n$ is better than n^2"

Correct understanding: Asymptotic notation is meaningful for sufficiently large n. For practical input sizes, constants can be crucial. An algorithm with complexity $10^{100}n$ would be useless for any realistic input.

3.6.5 Best Practices

1. **Use the tightest bound possible**: If $f(n) = \Theta(n^2)$, say so rather than just $\mathcal{O}(n^2)$.
2. **Simplify expressions**: Write $\mathcal{O}(n)$ instead of $\mathcal{O}(2n + 5)$.
3. **Be precise about what you're measuring**: Specify whether you're analyzing time complexity, space complexity, number of comparisons, etc.
4. **Consider the context**: For small inputs or real-time systems, constant factors and lower-order terms matter.

3.6.6 Common Notation Abuses

While technically incorrect, certain notational conveniences are widely accepted:

1. **Equations with Big O**: Writing $T(n) = 2n^2 + \mathcal{O}(n)$ to mean $T(n) = 2n^2 + f(n)$ where $f(n) = \mathcal{O}(n)$.
2. **Arithmetic with Big O**: Expressions like $\mathcal{O}(n) + \mathcal{O}(n^2) = \mathcal{O}(n^2)$.
3. **Conditional Big O**: $\mathcal{O}(n)$ if condition A, $\mathcal{O}(n^2)$ otherwise.

3.7 Comparing Growth Rates

3.7.1 Fundamental Growth Rate Hierarchy

Understanding the relative growth rates of common functions is essential for algorithm analysis. Here's the fundamental hierarchy from slowest to fastest growing:

$$\mathcal{O}(1) \ll \mathcal{O}(\log\log n) \ll \mathcal{O}(\log n) \ll \mathcal{O}(\sqrt{n}) \ll \mathcal{O}(n) \ll \mathcal{O}(n\log n) \ll \mathcal{O}(n^2) \tag{3.3}$$

$$\ll \mathcal{O}(n^3) \ll \mathcal{O}(2^n) \ll \mathcal{O}(n!) \ll \mathcal{O}(n^n) \tag{3.4}$$

Where $f \ll g$ means $f = o(g)$.

3.7.2 Logarithmic Functions

All logarithmic functions have the same growth rate regardless of base:

Theorem 3.7.1. $\log_a n = \Theta(\log_b n)$ *for any constants* $a, b > 1$

This is because $\log_a n = \frac{\log_b n}{\log_b a}$, and $\log_b a$ is just a constant.

3.7.3 Polynomial vs. Exponential

A fundamental divide exists between polynomial and exponential growth:

Theorem 3.7.2. $n^k = o(c^n)$ *for any constant* $k > 0$ *and* $c > 1$

This means that any polynomial function grows strictly slower than any exponential function.

3.7.4 Techniques for Comparison

Method 1: Limit Test

To compare $f(n)$ and $g(n)$, compute $\lim_{n\to\infty} \frac{f(n)}{g(n)}$:

- If limit $= 0$: $f(n) = o(g(n))$
- If limit $=$ constant $c > 0$: $f(n) = \Theta(g(n))$
- If limit $= \infty$: $f(n) = \omega(g(n))$

Method 2: Logarithmic Comparison

For products and powers, taking logarithms can simplify comparison:

- Compare $n^{\log n}$ with 2^n
- $\log(n^{\log n}) = (\log n)^2$
- $\log(2^n) = n \log 2$
- Since $(\log n)^2 = o(n)$, we have $n^{\log n} = o(2^n)$

Method 3: L'Hôpital's Rule

When limits yield indeterminate forms, L'Hôpital's rule can help:

$$\lim_{n\to\infty} \frac{f(n)}{g(n)} = \lim_{n\to\infty} \frac{f'(n)}{g'(n)}$$

3.7.5 Special Cases and Subtleties

Iterated Logarithm: $\log^* n$ (log star) is the number of times logarithm must be applied before the result is ≤ 1. It grows extremely slowly: $\log^*(2^{65536}) = 5$.

Ackermann Function Inverse: $\alpha(n)$ grows even slower than $\log^* n$ and appears in the analysis of union-find data structures.

Factorial Approximation: Using Stirling's approximation:

$$n! \approx \sqrt{2\pi n} \cdot \left(\frac{n}{e}\right)^n$$

We can show that $\log(n!) = \Theta(n \log n)$.

3.7.6 Practical Examples

Example 3.7.1 (Comparing complex expressions)**.** Order these functions by growth rate: $n^{1.5}$, $n \log^2 n$, $n^{1+1/\log n}$, $2^{\sqrt{n}}$

Solution:

1. $n \log^2 n = o(n^{1.5})$ since $\log^2 n = o(n^{0.5})$
2. $n^{1+1/\log n} = n \cdot n^{1/\log n} = n \cdot 2$, so this is $\Theta(n)$
3. $2^{\sqrt{n}} = o(2^n)$ but $2^{\sqrt{n}} = \omega(n^k)$ for any constant k

Therefore: $n^{1+1/\log n} < n \log^2 n < n^{1.5} < 2^{\sqrt{n}}$

Summary

Asymptotic notation provides the mathematical foundation for algorithm analysis. By abstracting away machine-dependent constants and focusing on growth rates, we can:

- Compare algorithms objectively
- Predict performance on large inputs
- Identify fundamental efficiency limits
- Communicate complexity concisely

The five notations$\mathcal{O}$, Ω, Θ, o, and ωeach serve specific purposes:

- **Big O**: Upper bounds (at most)

- **Omega**: Lower bounds (at least)
- **Theta**: Tight bounds (exactly)
- **Little o**: Strict upper bounds (strictly less than)
- **Little omega**: Strict lower bounds (strictly greater than)

Mastery of these notations is essential for understanding algorithm efficiency, proving complexity bounds, and designing efficient algorithms. As we progress through this book, these notations will be our primary language for expressing and comparing algorithmic complexity.

Exercises

Conceptual Understanding

1. Explain why $f(n) = \mathcal{O}(g(n))$ does not imply $g(n) = \mathcal{O}(f(n))$. Provide a counterexample.
2. If $f(n) = \Theta(g(n))$, what can you say about $g(n)$ in terms of $f(n)$?
3. Prove or disprove: If $f(n) = \mathcal{O}(g(n))$ and $g(n) = \mathcal{O}(f(n))$, then $f(n) = \Theta(g(n))$.

Proving Bounds

1. Prove that $n^3 + 100n^2 + 10n + 5 = \Theta(n^3)$.
2. Show that $\log(n!) = \Theta(n \log n)$.
3. Prove that $\sum_{i=1}^{n} i^2 = \Theta(n^3)$.

Growth Rate Comparison

1. Order these functions by growth rate: 2^{2n}, 2^n, $n^{\log n}$, $(\log n)^n$, $n!$, $\sqrt{n!}$, $n^{\sqrt{n}}$
2. For which values of a and b is $n^a = o(n \log^b n)$?

Advanced Problems

1. Define $f(n) = n$ if n is odd, and $f(n) = n^2$ if n is even. What is the tightest asymptotic bound for $f(n)$?
2. Prove that for any positive integer k, $(\log n)^k = o(n^\epsilon)$ for any $\epsilon > 0$.

Practical Applications

1. An algorithm has time complexity $T(n) = 100n \log n + 10000n$. For what values of n is this better than an algorithm with complexity $T'(n) = n^2$?

2. You have two algorithms: one runs in $\Theta(n^{1.5})$ time and $\Theta(1)$ space, another runs in $\Theta(n \log n)$ time and $\Theta(n)$ space. Under what circumstances would you choose each?

Further Reading

- Knuth, D. E. (1976). "Big Omicron and Big Omega and Big Theta"
- Cormen, T. H., et al. (2009). *Introduction to Algorithms* — Chapter 3
- Sedgewick, R. (2011). *Algorithms* — Mathematical foundations section
- Graham, R. L., Knuth, D. E., & Patashnik, O. (1994). *Concrete Mathematics* — Asymptotic methods

Part II

Time and Space Complexity Analysis

Chapter 4

Time Complexity Fundamentals

Time complexity analysis forms the backbone of algorithm efficiency evaluation. This chapter introduces the fundamental concepts and techniques for analyzing how an algorithm's runtime grows with input size. We'll explore different analysis scenarios, examine common patterns, and develop intuition for recognizing complexity in various algorithmic structures.

4.1 Measuring Time Complexity

4.1.1 Introduction to Time Measurement

Time complexity represents the amount of time an algorithm takes to complete as a function of the input size. Rather than measuring actual clock time, which varies across machines and implementations, we count the number of fundamental operations performed.

4.1.2 Fundamental Operations

Definition 4.1.1 (Fundamental Operation). A **fundamental operation** is a basic computational step that takes constant time. Examples include:

- Arithmetic operations ($+, -, \times, /, \mod$)
- Comparison operations ($<, >, =, \neq$)
- Assignment operations
- Array element access by index
- Simple conditional checks

4.1.3 The Cost Model

We adopt a **uniform cost model** where each fundamental operation takes one unit of time. This abstraction allows us to:

1. Compare algorithms independently of hardware
2. Focus on algorithmic efficiency rather than implementation details
3. Predict scalability for large inputs

4.1.4 Counting Operations

Consider this simple algorithm for finding the maximum element in an array:

Algorithm 1 FindMax($A[1 \ldots n]$)

```
1: max ← A[1]                          ▷ 1 assignment
2: for i ← 2 to n do                   ▷ n − 1 iterations
3:     if A[i] > max then              ▷ 1 comparison per iteration
4:         max ← A[i]                  ▷ 0 to n − 1 assignments
5:     end if
6: end for
7: return max                          ▷ 1 return
```

Analysis:

- Line 1: 1 operation
- Line 2: Loop executes $n-1$ times
- Line 3: $n-1$ comparisons
- Line 4: At most $n-1$ assignments
- Line 6: 1 operation

Total operations: $T(n) \leq 1 + (n-1) + (n-1) + 1 = 2n$ operations in the worst case.

4.1.5 Input Size Parameters

The choice of input size parameter depends on the problem:

- **Arrays/Lists:** Number of elements (n)
- **Matrices:** Dimensions ($m \times n$)

- **Graphs:** Number of vertices (V) and edges (E)
- **Strings:** Length of string(s)
- **Numbers:** Number of bits in representation

4.1.6 Growth Rate Focus

As n approaches infinity, constant factors and lower-order terms become insignificant. We focus on the **dominant term** that determines the growth rate:

- $T(n) = 3n^2 + 7n + 10 \to \mathcal{O}(n^2)$
- $T(n) = 2^n + n^3 \to \mathcal{O}(2^n)$
- $T(n) = \log n + \sqrt{n} \to \mathcal{O}(\sqrt{n})$

4.2 Best, Worst, and Average Case Analysis

4.2.1 The Need for Multiple Perspectives

Algorithm performance often varies depending on the specific input, even for inputs of the same size. We analyze three key scenarios:

4.2.2 Worst-Case Analysis

Definition 4.2.1 (Worst-Case Time Complexity). The maximum time taken over all possible inputs of size n.

$$T_{\text{worst}}(n) = \max\{T(I) : |I| = n\}$$

Advantages:

- Provides performance guarantee
- No input will cause worse behavior
- Most commonly used in algorithm analysis

Algorithm 2 LinearSearch($A[1 \dots n]$, key)

Example 4.2.1 (Linear Search).

```
for i ← 1 to n do
    if A[i] = key then
        return i
    end if
end for
return −1
```

Worst case: Key is not present or at the last position $\to \mathcal{O}(n)$ comparisons

4.2.3 Best-Case Analysis

Definition 4.2.2 (Best-Case Time Complexity)**.** The minimum time taken over all possible inputs of size n.

$$T_{\text{best}}(n) = \min\{T(I) : |I| = n\}$$

Use Cases:

- Understanding optimal behavior
- Identifying if an algorithm has early termination
- Useful for algorithms that adapt to input characteristics

Example - Linear Search: Best case: Key is at the first position $\to \mathcal{O}(1)$ comparisons

4.2.4 Average-Case Analysis

Definition 4.2.3 (Average-Case Time Complexity)**.** The expected time taken over all possible inputs of size n, assuming a probability distribution.

$$T_{\text{avg}}(n) = \sum_{I:|I|=n} P(I) \times T(I)$$

Challenges:

- Requires assumptions about input distribution
- Often assumes uniform distribution
- Can be mathematically complex

Example 4.2.2 (Linear Search - Successful Search)**.** Assuming key is equally likely to be at any position:

$$T_{\text{avg}}(n) = \frac{1 + 2 + \ldots + n}{n} = \frac{n+1}{2} \to \mathcal{O}(n)$$

4.2.5 Amortized Analysis Preview

Sometimes worst-case analysis is too pessimistic. **Amortized analysis** considers the average performance of a sequence of operations, accounting for the fact that expensive operations cannot occur too frequently. (Detailed coverage in Section 4.6)

4.3 Analyzing Simple Algorithms

4.3.1 Sequential Statements

For sequential statements, we sum the complexities:

$$\text{Statement 1;} \quad //\mathcal{O}(f_1(n)) \tag{4.1}$$
$$\text{Statement 2;} \quad //\mathcal{O}(f_2(n)) \tag{4.2}$$
$$\text{Statement 3;} \quad //\mathcal{O}(f_3(n)) \tag{4.3}$$

Total complexity: $\mathcal{O}(f_1(n)+f_2(n)+f_3(n)) = \mathcal{O}(\max\{f_1(n), f_2(n), f_3(n)\})$

4.3.2 Conditional Statements

For if-else statements, we take the maximum of both branches:

```
if condition then                ▷ O(1) for condition check
    Block A                      ▷ O(f_A(n))
else
    Block B                      ▷ O(f_B(n))
end if
```

Total complexity: $\mathcal{O}(1 + \max\{f_A(n), f_B(n)\})$

4.3.3 Example: Finding Minimum and Maximum

Algorithm 3 FindMinMax($A[1 \ldots n]$)

```
if n = 1 then
    return (A[1], A[1])
end if
min ← A[1]
max ← A[1]
for i ← 2 to n do
    if A[i] < min then
        min ← A[i]
    else if A[i] > max then
        max ← A[i]
    end if
end for
return (min, max)
```

Analysis:

- Lines 1-3: $\mathcal{O}(1)$
- Lines 4-5: $\mathcal{O}(1)$
- Lines 6-12: Loop runs $n-1$ times, each iteration $\mathcal{O}(1)$
- Line 13: $\mathcal{O}(1)$

Total: $\mathcal{O}(1) + \mathcal{O}(n-1) + \mathcal{O}(1) = \mathcal{O}(n)$

4.3.4 Algorithm Comparison Example

Problem: Check if an array has duplicate elements

Algorithm 1: Nested Loop Approach

```
for i ← 1 to n − 1 do
    for j ← i + 1 to n do
        if A[i] = A[j] then
            return true
        end if
    end for
end for
return false
```

Time Complexity: $\mathcal{O}(n^2)$

Algorithm 2: Sorting Approach

```
Sort(A)                                  ▷ O(n log n)
for i ← 1 to n − 1 do                    ▷ O(n)
    if A[i] = A[i + 1] then
        return true
    end if
end for
return false
```

Time Complexity: $\mathcal{O}(n \log n)$

Algorithm 3: Hash Table Approach

```
Create empty hash table H
for i ← 1 to n do
    if H.contains(A[i]) then
        return true
    end if
    H.insert(A[i])
end for
return false
```

Time Complexity: $\mathcal{O}(n)$ average case, $\mathcal{O}(n^2)$ worst case

4.4 Loop Analysis Techniques

4.4.1 Single Loops

For a simple loop:

```
for i ← 1 to n do
    // O(f(n)) operations
end for
```

Total complexity: $\mathcal{O}(n \times f(n))$

4.4.2 Nested Loops

Independent Loops

When loop variables are independent:

```
for i ← 1 to n do
    for j ← 1 to m do
        // O(1) operations
    end for
end for
```

Total complexity: $\mathcal{O}(n \times m)$

Dependent Loops

When inner loop depends on outer loop variable:

```
for i ← 1 to n do
    for j ← 1 to i do
        // O(1) operations
    end for
end for
```

Analysis:

- When $i = 1$: 1 iteration
- When $i = 2$: 2 iterations
- When $i = n$: n iterations
- Total: $1 + 2 + \ldots + n = \frac{n(n+1)}{2} = \mathcal{O}(n^2)$

4.4.3 Logarithmic Loops

Loops where the variable changes multiplicatively:

$i \leftarrow 1$

```
while i < n do
    // O(1) operations
    i ← i × 2
end while
```

Analysis:

- i takes values: $1, 2, 4, 8, \ldots, 2^k$ where $2^k < n$
- Number of iterations: k where $2^k < n \leq 2^{k+1}$
- Therefore: $k = \lfloor \log_2 n \rfloor$
- Complexity: $\mathcal{O}(\log n)$

4.4.4 Complex Loop Patterns

Example 4.4.1 (Triangle Pattern).

```
for i ← 1 to n do
    for j ← i to n do
        for k ← 1 to j do
            // O(1) operation
        end for
    end for
end for
```

Analysis: For fixed i and j, the innermost loop runs j times. Sum over all valid (i, j) pairs:

$$\sum_{i=1}^{n} \sum_{j=i}^{n} j = \sum_{i=1}^{n} [i + (i+1) + \ldots + n]$$

Using summation formulas:

$$= \sum_{i=1}^{n} \left[\frac{n(n+1)}{2} - \frac{(i-1)i}{2} \right] = \mathcal{O}(n^3)$$

4.4.5 Loop Invariants and Termination

Definition 4.4.1 (Loop Invariant). A property that remains true before and after each iteration.

Algorithm 4 BinarySearch($A[1 \ldots n]$, key)

Example 4.4.2 (Binary Search). left $\leftarrow 1$, right $\leftarrow n$

while left $\leq$ right **do**
  mid $\leftarrow \lfloor(\text{left} + \text{right})/2\rfloor$
  if $A[\text{mid}] = \text{key}$ **then**
    return mid
  else if $A[\text{mid}] < \text{key}$ **then**
    left $\leftarrow$ mid $+ 1$
  else
    right $\leftarrow$ mid $- 1$
  end if
end while
return -1

Invariant: If key exists in A, then key $\in A[\text{left} \ldots \text{right}]$
Termination: The range [left, right] halves each iteration

- Iterations: $\mathcal{O}(\log n)$
- Total complexity: $\mathcal{O}(\log n)$

4.5 Recursive Algorithm Analysis

4.5.1 The Recursion Tree Method

Visualize recursive calls as a tree where:

- Each node represents a recursive call
- Node value = work done in that call (excluding recursive calls)
- Total work = sum of all node values

Algorithm 5 MergeSort($A[1 \ldots n]$)

Example 4.5.1 (Merge Sort). **if** $n \leq 1$ **then**
  return A
end if
mid $\leftarrow \lfloor n/2 \rfloor$
$L \leftarrow$ MergeSort($A[1 \ldots \text{mid}]$)
$R \leftarrow$ MergeSort($A[\text{mid} + 1 \ldots n]$)
return Merge(L, R)

Recursion tree:

- Level 0: 1 problem of size n, work = $\mathcal{O}(n)$ for merge
- Level 1: 2 problems of size $n/2$, work = $2 \times \mathcal{O}(n/2) = \mathcal{O}(n)$
- Level 2: 4 problems of size $n/4$, work = $4 \times \mathcal{O}(n/4) = \mathcal{O}(n)$
- $\vdots$
- Level $\log n$: n problems of size 1, work = $n \times \mathcal{O}(1) = \mathcal{O}(n)$

Total: $\mathcal{O}(n)$ work per level $\times$ $\mathcal{O}(\log n)$ levels = $\mathcal{O}(n \log n)$

4.5.2 Recurrence Relations

Recursive algorithms naturally lead to recurrence relations:

General Form:

$$T(n) = aT(n/b) + f(n)$$

Where:

- a = number of recursive calls
- n/b = size of each subproblem
- $f(n)$ = work done outside recursive calls

Common Patterns:

1. **Decrease by Constant:**

$$T(n) = T(n-1) + \mathcal{O}(1) \rightarrow \mathcal{O}(n)$$

   Example: Linear search

2. **Decrease by Factor:**

$$T(n) = T(n/2) + \mathcal{O}(1) \rightarrow \mathcal{O}(\log n)$$

   Example: Binary search

3. **Divide and Conquer:**

$$T(n) = 2T(n/2) + \mathcal{O}(n) \rightarrow \mathcal{O}(n \log n)$$

   Example: Merge sort

4. **Multiple Recursion:**

$$T(n) = 2T(n-1) + \mathcal{O}(1) \rightarrow \mathcal{O}(2^n)$$

   Example: Towers of Hanoi

4.5.3 Substitution Method Example

Theorem 4.5.1. *For the recurrence $T(n) = 2T(n/2) + n$, we have $T(n) = \mathcal{O}(n \log n)$.*

Proof. **Guess:** $T(n) = \mathcal{O}(n \log n)$

Proof by Induction: Assume $T(k) \leq ck \log k$ for all $k < n$. Need to show: $T(n) \leq cn \log n$

$$
\begin{aligned}
T(n) &= 2T(n/2) + n && (4.4)\\
&\leq 2c(n/2)\log(n/2) + n && (4.5)\\
&= cn(\log n - 1) + n && (4.6)\\
&= cn \log n - cn + n && (4.7)\\
&\leq cn \log n \quad (\text{for } c \geq 1) && (4.8)
\end{aligned}
$$

Therefore, $T(n) = \mathcal{O}(n \log n)$.

4.5.4 Tail Recursion and Optimization

Definition 4.5.1 (Tail Recursive). A function where the recursive call is the last operation.

Algorithm 6 FactorialTail(n, acc)

Example 4.5.2 (Factorial - Tail Recursive).

```
if n = 0 then
    return acc
end if
return FactorialTail(n − 1, n × acc)
```

- Can be optimized to iterative form
- Space complexity: $\mathcal{O}(1)$ instead of $\mathcal{O}(n)$
- Time complexity remains $\mathcal{O}(n)$

4.5.5 Common Recursive Patterns

Linear Recursion:

- One recursive call per function
- Example: Factorial, Linear Search

- Typical complexity: $\mathcal{O}(n)$ or $\mathcal{O}(\log n)$

Binary Recursion:

- Two recursive calls per function
- Example: Fibonacci (naive), Tree traversal
- Typical complexity: $\mathcal{O}(2^n)$ or $\mathcal{O}(n)$

Multiple Recursion:

- k recursive calls per function
- Example: n-ary tree traversal
- Typical complexity: $\mathcal{O}(k^n)$ or $\mathcal{O}(n)$

4.6 Amortized Analysis Introduction

4.6.1 Motivation

Some data structures have operations that occasionally take much longer than usual, but these expensive operations are "paid for" by many cheap operations. Amortized analysis provides a more accurate picture than worst-case analysis alone.

4.6.2 Key Concept

Amortized cost = Average cost per operation over a worst-case sequence of operations

Important: This is NOT the same as average-case analysis, which assumes probabilistic input distribution.

4.6.3 Dynamic Array Example

Consider a dynamic array that doubles in size when full:

Operations:

- Append when not full: $\mathcal{O}(1)$
- Append when full: $\mathcal{O}(n)$ to copy all elements to new array

Worst-case analysis: $\mathcal{O}(n)$ per append

Amortized analysis: Starting from size 1, after n insertions:

- Copying costs: $1 + 2 + 4 + 8 + \ldots + n/2 < 2n$
- Total cost for n operations: $\mathcal{O}(n)$
- Amortized cost per operation: $\mathcal{O}(1)$

4.6.4 The Accounting Method

Assign an "amortized cost" to each operation:

- Some operations are "overcharged" (pay more than actual cost)
- Extra payment is stored as "credit"
- Expensive operations use accumulated credit

Dynamic Array with Accounting:

- Charge 3 units for each append
- Actual cost when not full: 1 unit (2 units saved as credit)
- When doubling: Use saved credits to pay for copying
- Result: Amortized $\mathcal{O}(1)$ per operation

4.6.5 The Potential Method

Define a **potential function** Φ that maps data structure states to non-negative real numbers.

Amortized cost = Actual cost + $\Delta\Phi$
Where $\Delta\Phi = \Phi(\text{after}) - \Phi(\text{before})$
Dynamic Array with Potential:

- Let $\Phi = 2 \times \text{num\_elements} - \text{capacity}$
- After doubling: Φ drops to 0
- Each insertion increases Φ by 2
- Amortized cost $= 1 + 2 = \mathcal{O}(1)$

4.6.6 Stack with Multipop Example

Consider a stack supporting:

- Push(x): $\mathcal{O}(1)$
- Pop(): $\mathcal{O}(1)$
- Multipop(k): Pop $\min(k, \text{size})$ elements - $\mathcal{O}(\min(k, n))$

Worst-case for Multipop: $\mathcal{O}(n)$
Amortized Analysis:

- Each element is pushed once: $\mathcal{O}(1)$
- Each element is popped at most once: $\mathcal{O}(1)$
- Total cost for n operations: $\mathcal{O}(n)$
- Amortized cost per operation: $\mathcal{O}(1)$

4.6.7 When to Use Amortized Analysis

Amortized analysis is appropriate when:

1. Operations have varying costs
2. Expensive operations are infrequent
3. There's a pattern to cost distribution
4. We care about total cost over many operations

Common applications:

- Dynamic arrays
- Union-Find data structure
- Splay trees
- Fibonacci heaps
- Hash table resizing

4.6.8 Limitations

- Doesn't help with single-operation guarantees
- Not suitable for real-time systems requiring consistent response times
- Requires analyzing sequences of operations

4.7 Chapter Summary

This chapter established the fundamental framework for analyzing algorithm time complexity:

1. **Measuring Complexity:** We count fundamental operations as a function of input size, focusing on growth rates rather than exact counts.

2. **Case Analysis:** Different inputs of the same size can yield different performance. We analyze best, worst, and average cases to understand algorithm behavior comprehensively.

3. **Simple Algorithms:** Sequential statements add complexities, conditionals take the maximum, and we can compare algorithms by their asymptotic behavior.

4. **Loop Analysis:** Single loops multiply iterations by body complexity. Nested loops require careful counting, especially with dependencies. Logarithmic loops arise from multiplicative changes.

5. **Recursive Analysis:** Recursion trees visualize the work distribution. Recurrence relations capture recursive behavior mathematically. Different recursion patterns lead to vastly different complexities.

6. **Amortized Analysis:** When operations have varying costs, amortized analysis provides a tighter bound by considering sequences of operations rather than individual worst cases.

These techniques form the foundation for analyzing more complex algorithms. The next chapter will explore space complexity, examining how memory usage scales with input size and the fundamental tradeoffs between time and space.

4.8 Exercises

Conceptual Questions

1. Explain why we count operations rather than measuring actual runtime.

2. Give an example where best-case and worst-case complexities differ by more than a constant factor.

3. Why might average-case analysis be misleading in practice?

4. Construct an algorithm where amortized analysis gives a tighter bound than worst-case analysis.

Analysis Problems

5. Analyze the time complexity of the following algorithm:

    for $i \leftarrow 1$ **to** n **do**

```
        j ← i
        while j > 0 do
            print(i, j)
            j ← j/2
        end while
    end for
```

6. Solve the recurrence: $T(n) = 3T(n/3) + n \log n$

7. A recursive algorithm makes 4 recursive calls, each on a problem of size $n/2$, and does $\mathcal{O}(n^2)$ work outside the recursive calls. What is its time complexity?

Implementation Challenges

8. Implement and analyze an algorithm that finds the kth smallest element in an unsorted array.

9. Design a data structure that supports insert and find-median operations. Analyze the amortized complexity of your operations.

10. Write a recursive algorithm to generate all permutations of n distinct elements. Analyze its time complexity.

Advanced Problems

11. Prove that any comparison-based algorithm for finding both minimum and maximum of n elements requires at least $\lceil 3n/2 \rceil - 2$ comparisons.

12. Consider a stack that supports push, pop, and find-min (returns minimum element currently in stack) all in $\mathcal{O}(1)$ time. Explain the data structure and prove the complexity bounds.

13. Analyze the expected number of comparisons in randomized quicksort.

4.9 Further Reading

- Cormen, T. H., Leiserson, C. E., Rivest, R. L., & Stein, C. (2009). *Introduction to Algorithms* (3rd ed.), Chapters 2-4.
- Sedgewick, R., & Wayne, K. (2011). *Algorithms* (4th ed.), Chapter 1.4.
- Kleinberg, J., & Tardos, É. (2005). *Algorithm Design*, Chapter 2.
- Tarjan, R. E. (1985). "Amortized computational complexity." *SIAM Journal on Algebraic Discrete Methods*, 6(2), 306-318.

Chapter 5

Space Complexity Analysis

While time complexity often receives the most attention in algorithm analysis, space complexity is equally important in many practical scenarios. This chapter explores how we measure and analyze the memory requirements of algorithms, providing you with the tools to understand and optimize space usage in your programs.

5.1 Understanding Space Complexity

5.1.1 Definition and Importance

Space complexity measures the amount of memory an algorithm requires as a function of its input size. Just as we use Big O notation for time complexity, we apply the same asymptotic notations to describe how memory usage grows with input size.

Definition 5.1.1 (Space Complexity)**.** The space complexity of an algorithm is the total amount of memory space required by the algorithm, expressed as a function of the input size n.

Space complexity becomes critical in several scenarios:

- **Embedded systems** with limited memory
- **Large-scale data processing** where memory is a bottleneck
- **Mobile applications** with memory constraints
- **Real-time systems** where memory allocation affects performance

5.1.2 Components of Space Complexity

When analyzing space complexity, we consider two main components:

1. **Fixed Space Requirements:** Memory needed for program code, simple variables, and constants. This is typically $\mathcal{O}(1)$ and independent of input size.
2. **Variable Space Requirements:** Memory that depends on the input size, including:
   - Input data storage
   - Auxiliary data structures
   - Stack space for recursion
   - Temporary variables in loops

5.1.3 Measuring Space Complexity

To measure space complexity, we count memory units rather than time units. The basic approach involves:

1. **Identifying all variables** and data structures used
2. **Determining their sizes** based on input
3. **Accounting for dynamic allocations** during execution
4. **Considering the maximum space** used at any point

Example 5.1.1 (Simple Array Processing).

```
def find_max(arr):
    # Fixed space: O(1) for max_val and i
    max_val = arr[0]
    for i in range(1, len(arr)):
        if arr[i] > max_val:
            max_val = arr[i]
    return max_val
```

Space complexity: $\mathcal{O}(1)$ auxiliary space (not counting input array)

Example 5.1.2 (Creating a Copy).

```
def reverse_array(arr):
    n = len(arr)
    # Variable space: O(n) for new array
    reversed_arr = [0] * n
    for i in range(n):
        reversed_arr[i] = arr[n - 1 - i]
    return reversed_arr
```

Space complexity: $\mathcal{O}(n)$ for the new array

5.1.4 Platform-Specific Considerations

Different programming languages and platforms affect actual memory usage:

- **Primitive data types** vary in size (int: 4 bytes, double: 8 bytes typically)
- **Object overhead** in object-oriented languages
- **Memory alignment** and padding
- **Garbage collection** overhead in managed languages

While these factors affect real memory usage, we typically abstract them away in complexity analysis, focusing on the growth rate rather than exact byte counts.

5.2 Auxiliary Space vs. Total Space

5.2.1 Distinguishing Between Space Measures

Understanding the distinction between auxiliary space and total space is crucial for accurate complexity analysis.

Definition 5.2.1 (Total Space)**.** The total space complexity includes all memory used by the algorithm, including the space needed to store the input.

Definition 5.2.2 (Auxiliary Space)**.** The auxiliary space complexity is the extra space or temporary space used by an algorithm, excluding the space needed for inputs.

5.2.2 Why Auxiliary Space Matters

In many contexts, auxiliary space is more relevant than total space because:

1. **Input is given:** The input already exists in memory
2. **Algorithm efficiency:** We want to measure the additional overhead
3. **In-place operations:** Algorithms that modify input directly are space-efficient

Example 5.2.1 (In-place vs. Out-of-place Sorting)**.**

```python
# In-place sorting (auxiliary space: O(1))
def bubble_sort(arr):
    n = len(arr)
    for i in range(n):
        for j in range(0, n-i-1):
            if arr[j] > arr[j+1]:
                arr[j], arr[j+1] = arr[j+1], arr[j]
    # Modifies arr directly, no extra array needed

# Out-of-place sorting (auxiliary space: O(n))
def merge_sort(arr):
    if len(arr) <= 1:
        return arr

    mid = len(arr) // 2
    left = merge_sort(arr[:mid])  # Creates new arrays
    right = merge_sort(arr[mid:])

    # Merge operation creates additional space
    return merge(left, right)
```

5.2.3 Analyzing Different Algorithm Categories

Different types of algorithms have characteristic space patterns:

Iterative Algorithms: Usually have $\mathcal{O}(1)$ auxiliary space. May use temporary variables but not proportional to input.

Divide and Conquer: Often require $\mathcal{O}(n)$ auxiliary space for combining results. Recursive calls add stack space overhead.

Dynamic Programming: Typically trade space for time. Memoization tables often require $\mathcal{O}(n)$ to $\mathcal{O}(n^2)$ space.

Graph Algorithms: Visited arrays: $\mathcal{O}(V)$ where V is number of vertices. Adjacency representations affect total space.

5.2.4 Best Practices for Space Analysis

When analyzing auxiliary space:

1. **Identify all allocations** that depend on input size
2. **Track maximum concurrent usage**, not cumulative
3. **Consider reusable space** in iterative processes
4. **Account for hidden allocations** (string concatenation, list slicing)

5.3 Space-Time Tradeoffs

5.3.1 The Fundamental Tradeoff

One of the most important principles in algorithm design is the space-time tradeoff: we can often reduce time complexity by using more memory, or save memory by accepting slower execution.

Principle 5.3.1 (Space-Time Tradeoff). For many problems, there exists an inverse relationship between the time and space complexity of solutions.

5.3.2 Classic Examples of Space-Time Tradeoffs

Example 5.3.1 (Fibonacci Calculation).

```
# Approach 1: Recursive (Time: O(2^n), Space: O(n))
def fib_recursive(n):
    if n <= 1:
        return n
    return fib_recursive(n-1) + fib_recursive(n-2)

# Approach 2: Dynamic Programming (Time: O(n), Space: O(n))
def fib_dp(n):
    if n <= 1:
        return n
    dp = [0] * (n + 1)
    dp[0], dp[1] = 0, 1
    for i in range(2, n + 1):
        dp[i] = dp[i-1] + dp[i-2]
    return dp[n]

# Approach 3: Space-Optimized (Time: O(n), Space: O(1))
def fib_optimized(n):
    if n <= 1:
        return n
    prev, curr = 0, 1
    for i in range(2, n + 1):
        prev, curr = curr, prev + curr
    return curr
```

5.3.3 Techniques for Managing Tradeoffs

Memoization and Caching

- Store computed results to avoid recalculation
- Space cost: $\mathcal{O}(n)$ to $\mathcal{O}(n^2)$ typically
- Time benefit: Exponential to polynomial reduction

Preprocessing and Lookup Tables

- Precompute results for fast queries
- Example: Prime sieves, trigonometric tables
- Space cost: Depends on range of inputs
- Time benefit: $\mathcal{O}(1)$ lookup vs. computation

Data Structure Choice

- Arrays vs. Linked Lists
- Hash tables vs. Balanced trees
- Compressed vs. Uncompressed representations

Example 5.3.2 (Substring Search).

```
# Naive approach: O(1) space, O(nm) time
def naive_search(text, pattern):
    for i in range(len(text) - len(pattern) + 1):
        if text[i:i+len(pattern)] == pattern:
            return i
    return -1

# KMP with preprocessing: O(m) space, O(n+m) time
def kmp_search(text, pattern):
    # Build failure function (uses O(m) space)
    failure = build_failure_function(pattern)
    # Search using failure function
    return search_with_failure(text, pattern, failure)
```

5.3.4 Decision Factors

When choosing between space and time tradeoffs, consider:

1. **Hardware constraints:** Available memory vs. processing power
2. **Usage patterns:** Frequency of operations
3. **Real-time requirements:** Response time constraints
4. **Scalability needs:** How the solution scales with growth
5. **Cost considerations:** Memory vs. computation costs in cloud environments

5.3.5 Theoretical Bounds and Tradeoffs

Some problems have proven space-time tradeoff lower bounds:

Theorem 5.3.1 (Sorting Lower Bound). *Any comparison-based sorting algorithm that uses S bits of extra space requires $\Omega\left(n^2/S\right)$ comparisons in the worst case.*

This theorem tells us that to sort in $\mathcal{O}(n \log n)$ time, we need at least $\Omega(\log n)$ bits of extra space.

5.4 Memory Hierarchy Considerations

5.4.1 Understanding Memory Hierarchy

Modern computer systems have a hierarchical memory structure that significantly impacts actual performance:

1. **CPU Registers:** Fastest, smallest (bytes)
2. **L1 Cache:** Very fast, small (KB)
3. **L2/L3 Cache:** Fast, moderate (MB)
4. **Main Memory (RAM):** Moderate speed, large (GB)
5. **Disk/SSD:** Slow, very large (TB)

5.4.2 Cache-Aware Algorithm Design

While traditional complexity analysis assumes uniform memory access, cache effects can dominate performance in practice.

Principle 5.4.1 (Locality of Reference). Algorithms that access memory in predictable patterns and keep working sets small perform better due to cache efficiency.

Types of Locality:

1. **Temporal Locality:** Recently accessed data is likely to be accessed again
2. **Spatial Locality:** Data near recently accessed data is likely to be accessed

Example 5.4.1 (Matrix Multiplication and Cache Performance).

```
# Cache-unfriendly (poor spatial locality)
def matrix_mult_naive(A, B, n):
    C = [[0] * n for _ in range(n)]
    for i in range(n):
        for j in range(n):
            for k in range(n):
                C[i][j] += A[i][k] * B[k][j]  # B accessed column-wise
    return C

# Cache-friendly (better spatial locality)
def matrix_mult_cached(A, B, n):
    C = [[0] * n for _ in range(n)]
    # Transpose B first for row-wise access
    B_T = [[B[j][i] for j in range(n)] for i in range(n)]
    for i in range(n):
        for j in range(n):
            for k in range(n):
                C[i][j] += A[i][k] * B_T[j][k]  # Both accessed row-wise
    return C
```

5.4.3 Working Set and Page Faults

Definition 5.4.1 (Working Set)**.** The set of memory pages accessed by an algorithm during a specific time interval.

When the working set exceeds available RAM, the system experiences page faults, causing dramatic performance degradation.

Strategies for Managing Working Set:

1. **Block/Tile algorithms:** Process data in cache-sized blocks
2. **Data structure layout:** Organize data for sequential access
3. **Loop tiling:** Restructure loops to improve locality

5.4.4 External Memory Algorithms

For data too large for main memory, we need external memory algorithms:

I/O Complexity Model:

- Measure transfers between disk and RAM
- Block size B, memory size M, problem size N
- Goal: Minimize I/O operations

Example 5.4.2 (External Sorting).

```
def external_merge_sort(input_file, output_file, memory_limit):
    # Phase 1: Create sorted runs that fit in memory
    runs = create_sorted_runs(input_file, memory_limit)

    # Phase 2: Merge runs using limited memory
    while len(runs) > 1:
        runs = merge_runs(runs, memory_limit)

    # Final run is the sorted output
    rename(runs[0], output_file)
```

I/O Complexity: $\mathcal{O}\left(\right)\left(\frac{N}{B}\log_{M/B}\frac{N}{B}\right)$ where N is file size, B is block size, M is memory size.

5.4.5 Practical Guidelines

1. **Prefer sequential access** over random access
2. **Minimize pointer chasing** in data structures
3. **Use cache-oblivious algorithms** when possible
4. **Profile actual memory access patterns** in critical code
5. **Consider memory bandwidth** not just latency

5.5 Analyzing Recursive Space Usage

5.5.1 Stack Space in Recursion

Recursive algorithms use the call stack to maintain state, which contributes to space complexity. Each recursive call adds a stack frame containing:

- Function parameters
- Local variables
- Return address
- Saved registers

Definition 5.5.1 (Recursion Depth). The maximum number of recursive calls on the call stack at any point during execution.

5.5.2 Computing Recursive Space Complexity

The space complexity of a recursive algorithm depends on:

1. **Maximum recursion depth:** How deep the call stack grows
2. **Space per call:** Memory used by each stack frame
3. **Auxiliary space:** Additional data structures used

Formula:

$$\text{Total Space} = \text{Recursion Depth} \times \text{Space per Call} + \text{Auxiliary Space} \quad (5.1)$$

Example 5.5.1 (Binary Tree Traversal).

```
class TreeNode:
    def __init__(self, val=0, left=None, right=None):
        self.val = val
        self.left = left
        self.right = right

# Recursive traversal
def inorder_recursive(root):
    if not root:
        return []
    result = []

    def traverse(node):
        if node:
            traverse(node.left)
            result.append(node.val)
            traverse(node.right)

    traverse(root)
    return result
    # Space: O(h) where h is tree height
    # Worst case (skewed tree): O(n)
    # Best case (balanced tree): O(log n)

# Iterative traversal (explicit stack)
def inorder_iterative(root):
    result = []
    stack = []
    current = root

    while stack or current:
        while current:
            stack.append(current)
            current = current.left
        current = stack.pop()
```

```
            result.append(current.val)
            current = current.right

    return result
    # Space: O(h) - same as recursive
```

5.5.3 Tail Recursion and Optimization

Definition 5.5.2 (Tail Recursion). A recursive call is tail recursive if it's the last operation in the function.

Tail recursive functions can be optimized to use $\mathcal{O}(1)$ space through tail call optimization (TCO), though not all languages support this.

Example 5.5.2 (Factorial Computation).

```
# Non-tail recursive: O(n) space
def factorial(n):
    if n <= 1:
        return 1
    return n * factorial(n - 1)  # Multiplication after
    recursive call

# Tail recursive: O(1) space with TCO
def factorial_tail(n, accumulator=1):
    if n <= 1:
        return accumulator
    return factorial_tail(n - 1, n * accumulator)  # Recursive
    call is last

# Iterative equivalent: O(1) space guaranteed
def factorial_iterative(n):
    result = 1
    for i in range(2, n + 1):
        result *= i
    return result
```

5.5.4 Analyzing Complex Recursive Patterns

Divide and Conquer Space Analysis:

For algorithms that make multiple recursive calls:

```
def merge_sort(arr):
    if len(arr) <= 1:
        return arr

    mid = len(arr) // 2
    left = merge_sort(arr[:mid])    # First recursive call
    right = merge_sort(arr[mid:])   # Second recursive call
```

```

    return merge(left, right)
```

Space complexity analysis:

- Recursion depth: $\mathcal{O}(\log n)$
- Space per level: $\mathcal{O}(n)$ for array slices
- Total space: $\mathcal{O}(n)$ because slices at each level don't overlap in time

Tree Recursion Space Analysis:

```
def generate_parentheses(n):
    def backtrack(current, open_count, close_count):
        if len(current) == 2 * n:
            result.append(current)
            return

        if open_count < n:
            backtrack(current + "(", open_count + 1, close_count
)
        if close_count < open_count:
            backtrack(current + ")", open_count, close_count +
1)

    result = []
    backtrack("", 0, 0)
    return result
```

Space complexity:

- Maximum recursion depth: $\mathcal{O}(n)$
- Space per call: $\mathcal{O}(n)$ for string
- Total space: $\mathcal{O}(n^2)$ considering string concatenation

5.5.5 Stack Overflow Prevention

Strategies to prevent stack overflow in recursive algorithms:

1. **Iteration conversion:** Replace recursion with explicit stack
2. **Tail recursion optimization:** When language supports it
3. **Trampolining:** For mutual recursion
4. **Depth limiting:** Add maximum depth parameter
5. **Memoization:** Reduce redundant recursive calls

Example 5.5.3 (Preventing Stack Overflow).

```
# Depth-limited recursion
def dfs_limited(graph, start, max_depth=1000):
    def dfs_helper(node, visited, depth):
        if depth > max_depth:
            raise RecursionError("Maximum depth exceeded")

        visited.add(node)
        for neighbor in graph[node]:
            if neighbor not in visited:
                dfs_helper(neighbor, visited, depth + 1)

    visited = set()
    dfs_helper(start, visited, 0)
    return visited

# Iterative alternative
def dfs_iterative(graph, start):
    visited = set()
    stack = [start]

    while stack:
        node = stack.pop()
        if node not in visited:
            visited.add(node)
            stack.extend(graph[node])

    return visited
```

5.5.6 Best Practices for Recursive Space Management

1. **Analyze recursion depth** before implementing
2. **Consider iterative alternatives** for deep recursion
3. **Use tail recursion** when possible
4. **Share data structures** instead of copying
5. **Clear unnecessary references** in long-running recursions
6. **Monitor stack usage** in production systems

Chapter Summary

Space complexity analysis is essential for understanding and optimizing algorithm memory usage. Key takeaways include:

- **Space complexity measures** both auxiliary and total memory requirements
- **Space-time tradeoffs** are fundamental to algorithm design
- **Memory hierarchy** significantly impacts real-world performance
- **Recursive algorithms** require careful analysis of stack space usage
- **Practical considerations** often differ from theoretical analysis

Understanding these concepts enables you to:

- Choose appropriate algorithms for memory-constrained environments
- Optimize programs for cache performance
- Balance space and time requirements effectively
- Prevent memory-related failures in production systems

In the next chapter, we'll explore techniques for solving recurrence relations, which are crucial for analyzing both time and space complexity of recursive algorithms.

Exercises

Theoretical Exercises

1. Prove that any comparison-based sorting algorithm using $\mathcal{O}(1)$ auxiliary space requires $\Omega(n \log n)$ comparisons.
2. Analyze the space complexity of quicksort with different pivot selection strategies.
3. Show that converting any recursive algorithm to iterative form doesn't change its space complexity class.
4. Derive the space complexity of the Strassen matrix multiplication algorithm.

Programming Exercises

1. Implement a space-efficient algorithm to find the kth largest element in an array using $\mathcal{O}(1)$ extra space.
2. Design a cache-friendly matrix transpose algorithm and measure its performance against a naive implementation.
3. Convert a recursive tree traversal algorithm to use an explicit stack and compare space usage.
4. Implement a memory-efficient solution for the longest common subsequence problem using $\mathcal{O}(\min(m, n))$ space instead of $\mathcal{O}(mn)$.

Analysis Exercises

1. Compare the space complexity of different graph representations (adjacency matrix, adjacency list, edge list) for various graph operations.
2. Analyze the space-time tradeoff in dynamic programming solutions for the knapsack problem.
3. Investigate the impact of string immutability on space complexity in different programming languages.
4. Profile a recursive algorithm to measure actual stack space usage and compare with theoretical analysis.

Further Reading

- Knuth, D.E. *The Art of Computer Programming, Volume 1: Fundamental Algorithms* - Classic treatment of space complexity
- Aggarwal, A., and Vitter, J.S. "The Input/Output Complexity of Sorting and Related Problems" - External memory algorithms
- Blelloch, G.E. "Space-Efficient Dynamic Programming" - Advanced space optimization techniques
- Frigo, M., et al. "Cache-Oblivious Algorithms" - Algorithms that perform well regardless of memory hierarchy

Chapter 6

Solving Recurrence Relations

Introduction

Recurrence relations are fundamental tools in the analysis of recursive algorithms. When we analyze a recursive algorithm, we often express its running time as a function that depends on the running time of smaller instances of the same problem. This chapter provides comprehensive techniques for solving these recurrence relations to obtain closed-form expressions for algorithm complexity.

6.1 Types of Recurrence Relations

6.1.1 Linear Recurrences

Linear recurrences are the most common type encountered in algorithm analysis. They have the general form:

$$T(n) = a_1 T(n-1) + a_2 T(n-2) + \cdots + a_k T(n-k) + f(n) \tag{6.1}$$

where the a_i are constants and $f(n)$ is a function of n.

Example 6.1.1 (Fibonacci Sequence). The Fibonacci sequence is defined by the recurrence:

$$F(n) = F(n-1) + F(n-2) \tag{6.2}$$

$$F(0) = 0, \quad F(1) = 1 \tag{6.3}$$

6.1.2 Divide-and-Conquer Recurrences

These arise from algorithms that divide the problem into smaller subproblems:

$$T(n) = aT\left(\frac{n}{b}\right) + f(n) \tag{6.4}$$

where:

- $a \geq 1$ is the number of subproblems
- n/b is the size of each subproblem
- $f(n)$ is the cost of dividing and combining

Example 6.1.2 (Merge Sort)**.** The time complexity of merge sort satisfies:

$$T(n) = 2T\left(\frac{n}{2}\right) + \mathcal{O}\left(()\, n\right) \tag{6.5}$$

6.1.3 Full History Recurrences

These depend on all previous values:

$$T(n) = \sum_{i=1}^{n-1} T(i) + f(n) \tag{6.6}$$

Example 6.1.3 (Dynamic Programming)**.** Certain dynamic programming algorithms exhibit full history recurrences:

$$T(n) = \sum_{i=1}^{n-1} T(i) + \mathcal{O}\left(()\, 1\right) \tag{6.7}$$

6.1.4 Non-Linear Recurrences

Less common but important in certain analyses:

$$T(n) = T(\sqrt{n}) + \mathcal{O}\left(()\, 1\right) \tag{6.8}$$
$$T(n) = T(n-1) \cdot T(n-2) \tag{6.9}$$

6.2 The Substitution Method

The substitution method, also known as the method of mathematical induction, involves two steps:

1. **Guess** the form of the solution
2. **Verify** using mathematical induction

6.2.1 Basic Technique

Step 1: Make an Educated Guess

Examine the recurrence pattern and make an informed guess about the solution's form.

Step 2: Prove by Induction

- **Base Case**: Verify for initial values
- **Inductive Step**: Assume true for all $k < n$, prove for n

6.2.2 Example: Binary Search

Consider the recurrence:

$$T(n) = T\left(\frac{n}{2}\right) + c \tag{6.10}$$

$$T(1) = c \tag{6.11}$$

Guess: $T(n) = \mathcal{O}(() \log n)$
More precisely, we guess $T(n) \leq d \log n$ for some constant d.

Proof by Induction. We modify our guess to $T(n) \leq d \log(n+1)$
Base case: $T(1) = c \leq d \log 2$, true for $d \geq c/\log 2$
Inductive step: Assume $T(k) \leq d \log(k+1)$ for all $k < n$

$$\begin{aligned} T(n) &= T(n/2) + c && (6.12)\\ &\leq d \log(n/2 + 1) + c && (6.13)\\ &\leq d \log(n+1) - d \log 2 + c && (6.14)\\ &= d \log(n+1) - d + c && (6.15)\\ &\leq d \log(n+1) \quad (\text{when } d \geq c) && (6.16) \end{aligned}$$

Therefore, $T(n) = \mathcal{O}(() \log n)$.

6.2.3 Handling Subtleties

Boundary Conditions

Sometimes we need to adjust our guess to handle boundary conditions properly.

Example 6.2.1. For $T(n) = 2T(n/2) + n$
Initial guess: $T(n) \leq cn \log n$
This fails at the boundary. Solution: Subtract a lower-order term.
Refined guess: $T(n) \leq cn \log n - cn$

6.3 The Recursion Tree Method

The recursion tree method provides a visual and intuitive approach to solving recurrences by:

1. Drawing a tree representing the recursive calls
2. Summing the costs at each level
3. Summing across all levels

6.3.1 Construction Process

1. Draw the root representing the initial problem of size n
2. Add children for each recursive call
3. Label each node with its non-recursive cost
4. Continue until reaching base cases

6.3.2 Example: Merge Sort Analysis

For $T(n) = 2T(n/2) + cn$:

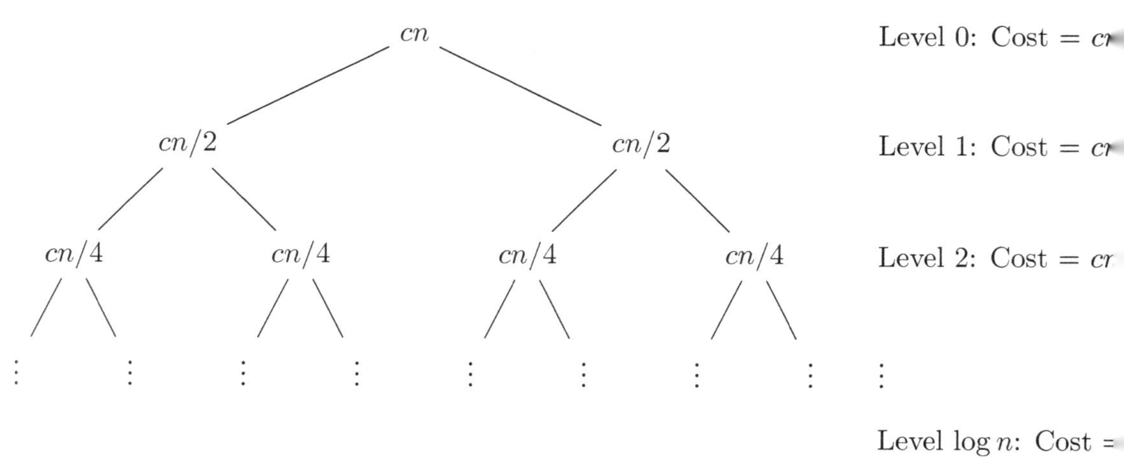

Analysis:

- Number of levels: $\log_2 n + 1$
- Cost per level: cn
- Total cost: $cn(\log_2 n + 1) = \mathcal{O}\left(()\, n \log n\right)$

6.3.3 Unbalanced Trees

For $T(n) = T(n/3) + T(2n/3) + cn$:
The tree is unbalanced, with:

- Shortest path to leaf: $\log_3 n$
- Longest path to leaf: $\log_{3/2} n$

Cost Analysis:

- Each level k has cost at most cn
- Maximum depth: $\log_{3/2} n$
- Total: $\mathcal{O}(n \log n)$

6.3.4 Geometric Series in Trees

When the work decreases geometrically:
For $T(n) = 3T(n/4) + cn^2$:

$$\text{Level } 0 : cn^2 \tag{6.17}$$

$$\text{Level } 1 : 3 \cdot \left(\frac{cn^2}{16}\right) = \frac{3cn^2}{16} \tag{6.18}$$

$$\text{Level } 2 : 9 \cdot \left(\frac{cn^2}{256}\right) = \frac{9cn^2}{256} \tag{6.19}$$

$$\vdots \tag{6.20}$$

Sum $= cn^2 \sum_{i=0}^{\infty} \left(\frac{3}{16}\right)^i = cn^2 \cdot \frac{16}{13} = \mathcal{O}\left(()\, n^2\right)$

6.4 The Master Theorem

The Master Theorem provides a direct solution for recurrences of the form:

$$T(n) = aT\left(\frac{n}{b}\right) + f(n) \tag{6.21}$$

where $a \geq 1$, $b > 1$ are constants, and $f(n)$ is asymptotically positive.

6.4.1 Statement of the Theorem

Theorem 6.4.1 (Master Theorem). *Let $T(n) = aT(n/b)+f(n)$ where $a \geq 1$, $b > 1$, and $f(n)$ is asymptotically positive. Compare $f(n)$ with $n^{\log_b a}$:*

1. ***Case 1:** If $f(n) = \mathcal{O}\left(()\, n^{\log_b a-\varepsilon}\right)$ for some constant $\varepsilon > 0$, then:*

$$T(n) = \Theta\left(()\, n^{\log_b a}\right)$$

2. ***Case 2:** If $f(n) = \Theta\left(()\, n^{\log_b a}\right)$, then:*

$$T(n) = \Theta\left(()\, n^{\log_b a} \cdot \log n\right)$$

3. ***Case 3:** If $f(n) = \Omega\left(()\, n^{\log_b a+\varepsilon}\right)$ for some constant $\varepsilon > 0$, and if $af(n/b) \leq cf(n)$ for some constant $c < 1$ and sufficiently large n, then:*

$$T(n) = \Theta\left(()\, f(n)\right)$$

6.4.2 Application Examples

Example 6.4.1. $T(n) = 9T(n/3) + n$

- $a = 9,\ b = 3,\ f(n) = n$
- $n^{\log_b a} = n^{\log_3 9} = n^2$
- $f(n) = n = \mathcal{O}\left(()\, n^{2-\varepsilon}\right)$ for $\varepsilon = 1$
- **Case 1 applies**: $T(n) = \Theta\left(()\, n^2\right)$

Example 6.4.2. $T(n) = T(2n/3) + 1$

- $a = 1,\ b = 3/2,\ f(n) = 1$
- $n^{\log_b a} = n^0 = 1$
- $f(n) = 1 = \Theta\left(()\, 1\right)$
- **Case 2 applies**: $T(n) = \Theta\left(()\, \log n\right)$

Example 6.4.3. $T(n) = 3T(n/4) + n \log n$

- $a = 3,\ b = 4,\ f(n) = n \log n$
- $n^{\log_b a} = n^{\log_4 3} \approx n^{0.793}$
- $f(n) = n \log n = \Omega\left(()\, n^{0.793+\varepsilon}\right)$
- Regularity check: $3(n/4)\log(n/4) \leq cn \log n$ for $c = 3/4$
- **Case 3 applies**: $T(n) = \Theta\left(()\, n \log n\right)$

6.4.3 Limitations and Gaps

The Master Theorem doesn't cover all cases:

- **Gap between cases**: When $f(n)$ is between cases, e.g., $f(n) = n^{\log_b a} / \log n$
- **Irregular $f(n)$**: When $f(n)$ doesn't have polynomial growth
- **Non-standard forms**: $T(n) = aT(n/b) + cT(n/d) + f(n)$

6.5 Advanced Techniques for Complex Recurrences

6.5.1 The Akra-Bazzi Method

Generalizes the Master Theorem for:

$$T(n) = \sum_{i=1}^{k} a_i T\left(\frac{n}{b_i}\right) + f(n) \tag{6.22}$$

Find p such that $\sum_{i=1}^{k} \frac{a_i}{b_i^p} = 1$
Then:

$$T(n) = \Theta\left(\right)\left(n^p\left(1 + \int_1^n \frac{f(u)}{u^{p+1}} du\right)\right) \tag{6.23}$$

6.5.2 Variable Substitution

For non-standard forms, substitution can simplify:

Example 6.5.1. $T(n) = 2T(\sqrt{n}) + \log n$
Let $m = \log n$, so $n = 2^m$
$S(m) = T(2^m) = 2T(2^{m/2}) + m = 2S(m/2) + m$
Now apply Master Theorem: $S(m) = \Theta\left(()\, m \log m\right)$
Therefore: $T(n) = \Theta\left(()\log n \cdot \log\log n\right)$

6.5.3 Domain Transformation

For recurrences with floors and ceilings:

$$T(n) = T\left(\left\lfloor\frac{n}{2}\right\rfloor\right) + T\left(\left\lceil\frac{n}{2}\right\rceil\right) + n \tag{6.24}$$

Approach: Prove $T(n) \leq cn \log n$ for appropriately chosen c

6.5.4 Characteristic Equation Method

For linear homogeneous recurrences:

$$T(n) = a_1T(n-1) + a_2T(n-2) + \cdots + a_kT(n-k) \tag{6.25}$$

Steps:

1. Form characteristic equation: $x^k - a_1x^{k-1} - \cdots - a_k = 0$
2. Find roots $r_1, r_2, \ldots, r_k$
3. General solution: $T(n) = c_1r_1^n + c_2r_2^n + \cdots + c_kr_k^n$
4. Use initial conditions to find constants

Example 6.5.2 (Fibonacci). $F(n) = F(n-1) + F(n-2)$
Characteristic equation: $x^2 - x - 1 = 0$
Roots: $r_1 = \frac{1+\sqrt{5}}{2}$, $r_2 = \frac{1-\sqrt{5}}{2}$
Solution: $F(n) = c_1\left(\frac{1+\sqrt{5}}{2}\right)^n + c_2\left(\frac{1-\sqrt{5}}{2}\right)^n$

6.6 Generating Functions Approach

Generating functions provide a powerful algebraic method for solving recurrences.

6.6.1 Ordinary Generating Functions

For sequence $\{a_n\}$, the ordinary generating function is:

$$G(x) = \sum_{n=0}^{\infty} a_nx^n \tag{6.26}$$

6.6.2 Method Overview

1. Write the recurrence relation
2. Multiply by x^n and sum over all n
3. Manipulate to isolate $G(x)$
4. Find closed form for $G(x)$
5. Extract coefficients to find a_n

6.6.3 Example: Fibonacci Numbers

Recurrence: $F(n) = F(n-1) + F(n-2)$, $F(0) = 0$, $F(1) = 1$
Let $G(x) = \sum_{n=0}^{\infty} F(n)x^n$
Multiply recurrence by x^n and sum:

$$\sum_{n\geq 2} F(n)x^n = \sum_{n\geq 2} F(n-1)x^n + \sum_{n\geq 2} F(n-2)x^n \tag{6.27}$$

$$G(x) - x = xG(x) + x^2G(x) \tag{6.28}$$

Solving for $G(x)$:

$$G(x) = \frac{x}{1-x-x^2} \tag{6.29}$$

Using partial fractions:

$$G(x) = \frac{1}{\sqrt{5}} \cdot \left[\frac{1}{1-\phi x} - \frac{1}{1-\psi x}\right] \tag{6.30}$$

where $\phi = \frac{1+\sqrt{5}}{2}$ and $\psi = \frac{1-\sqrt{5}}{2}$
Expanding:

$$F(n) = \frac{\phi^n - \psi^n}{\sqrt{5}} \tag{6.31}$$

6.6.4 Exponential Generating Functions

For certain recurrences, exponential generating functions are more appropriate:

$$E(x) = \sum_{n=0}^{\infty} a_n \frac{x^n}{n!} \tag{6.32}$$

Application: Useful for recurrences involving factorials or permutations.

6.6.5 Solving Non-Homogeneous Recurrences

For $T(n) = aT(n-1) + f(n)$:

1. Find generating function $F(x)$ for $f(n)$
2. Set up equation: $G(x) = axG(x) + F(x) + \text{initial terms}$
3. Solve: $G(x) = \frac{F(x)+\text{initial terms}}{1-ax}$

6.6.6 Multivariate Generating Functions

For recurrences with multiple parameters:
$T(n,k) = T(n-1,k) + T(n-1,k-1)$
Use $G(x,y) = \sum_{n,k} T(n,k)x^n y^k$

Summary and Best Practices

Choosing the Right Method

1. **Simple linear recurrences**: Use characteristic equation
2. **Divide-and-conquer with polynomial $f(n)$**: Apply Master Theorem
3. **Visual understanding needed**: Use recursion tree
4. **Verification of guess**: Apply substitution method
5. **Complex or non-standard**: Try domain transformation or generating functions
6. **Multiple recursive terms with different bases**: Use Akra-Bazzi

Common Pitfalls to Avoid

1. **Forgetting base cases** in substitution method
2. **Misidentifying Master Theorem cases**
3. **Ignoring regularity condition** in Case 3
4. **Arithmetic errors** in recursion trees
5. **Wrong characteristic equation** formation

Key Takeaways

- Multiple methods exist; choose based on recurrence structure
- Master Theorem provides quick solutions for common cases
- Recursion trees offer intuitive understanding
- Generating functions provide systematic algebraic approach
- Practice recognizing patterns to select appropriate techniques

Exercises

Basic Exercises

1. Solve $T(n) = 2T(n/2) + n^2$ using all applicable methods

2. Find the solution to $T(n) = T(n-1) + T(n-2) + 1$

3. Apply Master Theorem to $T(n) = 4T(n/2) + n\sqrt{n}$

Intermediate Exercises

4. Solve $T(n) = 2T(\sqrt{n}) + 1$ using substitution

5. Use generating functions for $T(n) = 3T(n-1) - 2T(n-2) + 2^n$

6. Analyze $T(n) = T(n/3) + T(2n/3) + n$ using recursion tree

Advanced Exercises

7. Prove that $T(n) = T(n/2) + T(n/4) + n$ has solution $T(n) = \Theta(()\, n)$

8. Solve the full history recurrence $T(n) = \sum_{i=1}^{n-1} T(i) + n$

9. Apply Akra-Bazzi to $T(n) = 2T(n/2) + 3T(n/3) + n \log n$

Further Reading

- Cormen, Leiserson, Rivest, Stein: *Introduction to Algorithms*, Chapter 4

- Graham, Knuth, Patashnik: *Concrete Mathematics*, Chapters 7-8

- Sedgewick, Flajolet: *An Introduction to the Analysis of Algorithms*

- Wilf: *Generatingfunctionology*

- Purdom, Brown: *The Analysis of Algorithms*

Part III

Complexity Classes and Theory

Chapter 7

Decision Problems and Complexity Classes

Introduction

Computational complexity theory provides a framework for classifying computational problems based on their inherent difficulty. This chapter introduces the fundamental complexity classes that form the backbone of theoretical computer science. We begin by transforming optimization problems into decision problems, then explore the classes P and NP, and conclude with the foundational theory of NP-completeness.

7.1 From Optimization to Decision Problems

7.1.1 Understanding the Transformation

Many computational problems we encounter in practice are **optimization problems**—we seek to find the best solution among many possibilities. However, complexity theory primarily focuses on **decision problems**—problems with yes/no answers. This simplification, surprisingly, doesn't lose generality and makes the theory more tractable.

Definition 7.1.1 (Optimization Problem). An optimization problem consists of:

- An input instance I
- A set of feasible solutions $S(I)$
- An objective function $f : S(I) \to \mathbb{R}$

- A goal: minimize or maximize f

Definition 7.1.2 (Decision Problem)**.** A decision problem is a problem that, given an input, outputs either "yes" or "no".

7.1.2 The Transformation Process

Consider the **Traveling Salesman Problem (TSP)**:

- **Optimization version**: Given a complete graph with edge weights, find the minimum-weight Hamiltonian cycle.
- **Decision version**: Given a complete graph with edge weights and a threshold k, does there exist a Hamiltonian cycle with total weight $\leq k$?

The decision version captures the essential difficulty of the optimization problem. If we can solve the decision version efficiently, we can solve the optimization version through binary search on the threshold value.

Theorem 7.1.1. *If the decision version of an optimization problem can be solved in polynomial time, then the optimization version can be solved in polynomial time with at most a logarithmic factor overhead.*

Proof sketch. For minimization problems with integer costs bounded by M, we can binary search the optimal value using $\mathcal{O}(\log M)$ calls to the decision problem solver.

7.1.3 Language Formulation

In complexity theory, we formalize decision problems as **languages**:

Definition 7.1.3 (Language)**.** A language L is a subset of Σ^*, where Σ is a finite alphabet (typically $\{0, 1\}$).

A decision problem becomes: "Given input x, is $x \in L$?"

Example 7.1.1. The language $\mathsf{HAM-CYCLE} = \{\langle G \rangle \mid G \text{ is a graph containing a Hamiltonian cycle}\}$, where $\langle G \rangle$ denotes an encoding of graph G as a binary string.

7.2 The Class P

7.2.1 Definition and Intuition

Definition 7.2.1 (Class P)**.** P is the class of languages decidable by a deterministic Turing machine in polynomial time. Formally:

$$\mathsf{P} = \{L \mid \exists \text{ a deterministic TM } M \text{ and polynomial } p \text{ such that}$$
$$\forall x : M(x) \text{ accepts iff } x \in L, \text{ and } M(x) \text{ halts within } p(|x|) \text{ steps}\}$$

7.2.2 Why P Represents "Efficient" Computation

The class P captures problems we consider **tractable** or **efficiently solvable**:

1. **Closure properties**: P is closed under composition—combining polynomial-time algorithms yields a polynomial-time algorithm
2. **Model independence**: Problems in P remain in P across reasonable computation models (RAM, multi-tape TMs, etc.)
3. **Practical correlation**: Most polynomial-time algorithms have reasonable degree polynomials (n^2, n^3, rarely n^{100})

7.2.3 Examples of Problems in P

Well-known problems in P include:

1. **SORTED**: Is the input array sorted?
   - Time: $\mathcal{O}(n)$
2. **CONNECTED**: Is the input graph connected?
   - Time: $\mathcal{O}(|V| + |E|)$ using BFS/DFS
3. **2-SAT**: Is the given 2-CNF formula satisfiable?
   - Time: $\mathcal{O}(n + m)$ where $n =$ variables, $m =$ clauses
4. **LINEAR-PROGRAMMING**: Does the given LP have a feasible solution with objective $\geq k$?
   - Time: Polynomial via ellipsoid or interior point methods
5. **PRIMALITY**: Is the input number prime?
   - Time: $\mathcal{O}(\log^3 n)$ via AKS algorithm (2002)

7.2.4 Proving Membership in P

To prove $L \in \mathsf{P}$, we must:

1. Describe a deterministic algorithm A
2. Prove A correctly decides L
3. Analyze A's runtime and show it's polynomial

Example 7.2.1 (EULER-PATH $\in \mathsf{P}$). .

- **Algorithm**: Check if graph has exactly 0 or 2 vertices of odd degree
- **Correctness**: Follows from Euler's theorem
- **Runtime**: $\mathcal{O}(|V| + |E|)$ to count degrees

7.3 Nondeterministic Polynomial Time (NP)

7.3.1 Intuitive Understanding

The class NP captures problems where:

- Solutions might be hard to find
- But solutions are easy to verify

Think of NP as problems with **efficiently verifiable certificates** or **short proofs**.

7.3.2 Formal Definition

Definition 7.3.1 (Class NP - Verifier-based). NP is the class of languages with polynomial-time verifiers. Formally:

$L \in \mathsf{NP}$ iff $\exists$ a polynomial p and polynomial-time algorithm V such that:

- If $x \in L$, then $\exists$ certificate y with $|y| \leq p(|x|)$ such that $V(x, y)$ accepts
- If $x \notin L$, then $\forall$ certificate y with $|y| \leq p(|x|)$, $V(x, y)$ rejects

Definition 7.3.2 (Alternative: NP - Machine-based). NP is the class of languages decidable by a nondeterministic Turing machine in polynomial time.

7.3.3 The Power of Nondeterminism

A nondeterministic TM can be viewed as:

1. Making "lucky guesses" at each step
2. Exploring all computational paths in parallel
3. Accepting if any path accepts

Key insight: Nondeterminism doesn't violate physics—it's a mathematical abstraction that captures the notion of verification.

7.3.4 Examples of Problems in NP

1. **SAT** (Boolean Satisfiability):
    - Instance: Boolean formula ϕ
    - Question: Is ϕ satisfiable?
    - Certificate: Truth assignment
    - Verification: Evaluate ϕ under assignment (polynomial time)
2. **HAMILTONIAN-CYCLE**:
    - Instance: Graph G
    - Question: Does G have a Hamiltonian cycle?
    - Certificate: Sequence of vertices
    - Verification: Check if sequence forms a valid cycle visiting each vertex once
3. **COMPOSITE**:
    - Instance: Integer n
    - Question: Is n composite?
    - Certificate: Factors p, q where $n = p \times q$
    - Verification: Multiply $p \times q$ and check equality
4. **GRAPH-ISOMORPHISM**:
    - Instance: Graphs G_1, G_2
    - Question: Are G_1 and G_2 isomorphic?
    - Certificate: Bijection $f : V_1 \to V_2$
    - Verification: Check if f preserves adjacency

7.3.5 Relationship Between P and NP

Theorem 7.3.1. $\mathsf{P} \subseteq \mathsf{NP}$

Proof. If $L \in \mathsf{P}$, then there exists a polynomial-time algorithm A that decides L. We can construct a verifier V that ignores the certificate and runs A on the input. This verifier witnesses that $L \in \mathsf{NP}$.

Open Question: Is $\mathsf{P} = \mathsf{NP}$ or $\mathsf{P} \neq \mathsf{NP}$?

7.4 The P vs NP Problem

7.4.1 Statement of the Problem

The **P vs NP problem** asks whether every problem whose solution can be verified in polynomial time can also be solved in polynomial time.

Formal Question: Does $\mathsf{P} = \mathsf{NP}$?

This is arguably the most important open problem in computer science and mathematics, with a $1 million Clay Millennium Prize for its resolution.

7.4.2 Philosophical Implications

The P vs NP question has profound implications:

1. **Creativity vs Verification**: Is finding a proof fundamentally harder than checking one?

2. **Search vs Decision**: Can every efficient verification procedure be converted to an efficient search procedure?

3. **Cryptography**: Modern cryptography assumes $\mathsf{P} \neq \mathsf{NP}$ (one-way functions exist)

4. **Artificial Intelligence**: If $\mathsf{P} = \mathsf{NP}$, many AI problems become tractable

7.4.3 Evidence for $\mathbf{P} \neq \mathbf{NP}$

While unproven, most experts believe $\mathsf{P} \neq \mathsf{NP}$ based on:

1. **Decades of failure**: No polynomial algorithms for NP-complete problems despite intensive effort

2. **Natural complexity**: Many NP problems seem to require exhaustive search

3. **Relativization barriers**: There exist oracles A and B where $\mathsf{P}^A = \mathsf{NP}^A$ and $\mathsf{P}^B \neq \mathsf{NP}^B$

4. **Circuit lower bounds**: Related problems in circuit complexity remain difficult

7.4.4 Consequences if P = NP

If $\mathsf{P} = \mathsf{NP}$, the implications would be revolutionary:

Positive consequences:

- Optimal solutions to logistics, scheduling, and optimization problems
- Automated theorem proving and program synthesis
- Perfect protein folding prediction
- Efficient learning algorithms for any concept class

Negative consequences:

- Current cryptographic systems would be broken
- Digital signatures and secure communication compromised
- Need for information-theoretic security

7.4.5 Intermediate Possibilities

Between $\mathsf{P} = \mathsf{NP}$ and $\mathsf{P} \neq \mathsf{NP}$, there are nuanced possibilities:

- NP problems might be solvable in quasi-polynomial time ($2^{\text{polylog}(n)}$)
- Average-case complexity might differ from worst-case
- Quantum computers might provide advantages for some NP problems

7.5 NP-Completeness Theory

7.5.1 Motivation and Intuition

Since we can't prove $\mathsf{P} \neq \mathsf{NP}$, we seek to identify the **hardest problems in NP**. These are the NP-complete problems—if any one of them has a polynomial-time algorithm, then $\mathsf{P} = \mathsf{NP}$.

7.5.2 Polynomial-Time Reductions

Definition 7.5.1 (Polynomial-time reduction)**.** Language L_1 is polynomial-time reducible to L_2 (written $L_1 \leq_p L_2$) if there exists a polynomial-time computable function f such that:

$$\forall x : x \in L_1 \Leftrightarrow f(x) \in L_2$$

Properties of reductions:

1. **Transitivity**: If $L_1 \leq_p L_2$ and $L_2 \leq_p L_3$, then $L_1 \leq_p L_3$
2. **Preservation**: If $L_1 \leq_p L_2$ and $L_2 \in \mathsf{P}$, then $L_1 \in \mathsf{P}$
3. **Hardness transfer**: If $L_1 \leq_p L_2$, then L_2 is at least as hard as L_1

7.5.3 Definition of NP-Completeness

Definition 7.5.2 (NP-hard)**.** A language L is NP-hard if every language in NP reduces to L in polynomial time:

$$\forall L' \in \mathsf{NP} : L' \leq_p L$$

Definition 7.5.3 (NP-complete)**.** A language L is NP-complete if:

1. $L \in \mathsf{NP}$ (membership)
2. L is NP-hard (hardness)

7.5.4 Properties of NP-Complete Problems

Theorem 7.5.1. *If any* NP*-complete problem is in* P*, then* $\mathsf{P} = \mathsf{NP}$.

Proof. Let L be NP-complete and suppose $L \in \mathsf{P}$. For any $L' \in \mathsf{NP}$, we have $L' \leq_p L$ by NP-hardness. Since $L \in \mathsf{P}$ and reductions preserve polynomial time, $L' \in \mathsf{P}$. Therefore $\mathsf{NP} \subseteq \mathsf{P}$, and since $\mathsf{P} \subseteq \mathsf{NP}$, we have $\mathsf{P} = \mathsf{NP}$.

Theorem 7.5.2. *If* $\mathsf{P} \neq \mathsf{NP}$*, then no* NP*-complete problem is in* P.

7.5.5 Proving NP-Completeness

To prove a language L is NP-complete:

1. **Step 1**: Show $L \in \mathsf{NP}$ (provide a polynomial-time verifier)
2. **Step 2**: Show L is NP-hard by either:
   - (First problem) Reduce from every problem in NP
   - (Subsequent problems) Reduce from a known NP-complete problem

7.5.6 The Web of NP-Complete Problems

Once we establish one NP-complete problem, we can prove others by reduction:

$$\mathsf{SAT} \rightarrow \mathsf{3SAT} \rightarrow \text{VERTEX-COVER} \rightarrow \text{HAMILTONIAN-CYCLE} \rightarrow \text{TSP}$$

Each arrow represents a polynomial-time reduction, building a vast web of interconnected NP-complete problems spanning diverse domains:

- Logic and satisfiability
- Graph theory
- Number theory
- Scheduling and optimization
- Computational geometry
- Games and puzzles

7.6 Cook-Levin Theorem

7.6.1 Historical Context

In 1971, Stephen Cook (and independently Leonid Levin in the USSR) proved the first NP-completeness result, establishing SAT as NP-complete. This foundational result launched the field of NP-completeness.

7.6.2 Statement of the Theorem

Theorem 7.6.1 (Cook-Levin). SAT *is* NP-*complete.*

Where $\mathsf{SAT} = \{\langle\phi\rangle \mid \phi \text{ is a satisfiable Boolean formula}\}$

7.6.3 Proof Overview

The proof proceeds by showing:

1. $\mathsf{SAT} \in \mathsf{NP}$ (straightforward)
2. Every language in NP reduces to SAT (the challenging part)

7.6.4 Detailed Proof of NP-Hardness

Let L be an arbitrary language in NP. We must show $L \leq_p$ SAT.

Since $L \in$ NP, there exists a nondeterministic TM M that decides L in polynomial time $p(n)$.

Key idea: For input x, construct a Boolean formula ϕ_x that is satisfiable iff M accepts x.

The Formula Construction:

Variables encode the computation of M on x:

- $Q[i, q]$: At time i, M is in state q
- $H[i, j]$: At time i, the tape head is at position j
- $T[i, j, \sigma]$: At time i, tape cell j contains symbol σ

The formula $\phi_x = \phi_{\text{start}} \wedge \phi_{\text{move}} \wedge \phi_{\text{accept}}$ where:

1. ϕ_{start}: Encodes the initial configuration
   - Machine starts in initial state q_0
   - Tape contains input x followed by blanks
   - Head at position 0
2. ϕ_{move}: Encodes valid transitions
   - For each time step i, the configuration at $i + 1$ follows from i according to M's transition function
   - Ensures exactly one state, one head position, one symbol per cell
   - Non-head cells remain unchanged
3. ϕ_{accept}: Encodes acceptance
   - At some time $i \leq p(|x|)$, machine enters accept state

Size Analysis:

- Number of variables: $\mathcal{O}(p(n)^2)$
- Number of clauses: $\mathcal{O}(p(n)^3)$
- Formula size: polynomial in $|x|$

Correctness:

- If $x \in L$: M accepts x, so there's an accepting computation that satisfies ϕ_x
- If $x \notin L$: M rejects x on all paths, so no assignment satisfies ϕ_x

7.6.5 Significance and Impact

The Cook-Levin theorem:

1. **Established the P vs NP framework**: Provided concrete evidence that some problems might be inherently difficult
2. **Unified complexity theory**: Showed that diverse problems share fundamental difficulty
3. **Guided algorithm design**: Knowing a problem is NP-complete suggests looking for approximations or heuristics
4. **Created a research program**: Launched decades of work on complexity classes, reductions, and the P vs NP question

7.6.6 From SAT to 3-SAT

Corollary 7.6.2. *3SAT is NP-complete, where 3SAT restricts SAT to formulas in 3-CNF form.*

Proof sketch. Transform arbitrary Boolean formula to 3-CNF while preserving satisfiability:

1. Convert to CNF using distributivity (may cause exponential blowup)
2. Better: Introduce auxiliary variables to keep size polynomial
3. Break long clauses into multiple 3-clauses with new variables
4. Pad short clauses by repeating literals

This establishes 3SAT as a convenient starting point for proving other NP-completeness results.

Chapter Summary

This chapter introduced the fundamental framework of computational complexity theory:

1. **Decision problems** provide a clean mathematical formulation for studying computational difficulty
2. **Class** P captures efficiently solvable problems—those with polynomial-time algorithms

3. **Class** NP captures problems with efficiently verifiable solutions
4. **The P vs NP problem** asks whether verification is fundamentally easier than finding solutions
5. NP**-completeness** identifies the hardest problems in NP—solving any one efficiently would solve them all
6. **The Cook-Levin theorem** establishes SAT as the first NP-complete problem, launching the theory

These concepts form the foundation for understanding computational intractability and guide practical algorithm design. When faced with an NP-complete problem, we know to seek approximations, heuristics, or special cases rather than exact polynomial-time algorithms.

Exercises

Exercise 7.6.1. Convert the following optimization problems to decision problems:

1. Find the maximum clique in a graph
2. Find the shortest path between two vertices
3. Minimize the makespan in job scheduling

Exercise 7.6.2. Prove that the following languages are in P:

1. PALINDROME $= \{w \mid w \text{ reads the same forwards and backwards}\}$
2. BIPARTITE $= \{\langle G \rangle \mid G \text{ is a bipartite graph}\}$

Exercise 7.6.3. Show that the following problems are in NP by describing polynomial-time verifiers:

1. SUBSET-SUM: Given integers and target, is there a subset summing to the target?
2. GRAPH-3-COLORING: Can the vertices be colored with 3 colors such that no edge connects same-colored vertices?

Exercise 7.6.4. Prove that NP is closed under union and intersection.

Exercise 7.6.5. If we could solve HAMILTONIAN-CYCLE in polynomial time, show how to find an actual Hamiltonian cycle (not just decide existence) in polynomial time.

Exercise 7.6.6. Explain why the following argument is flawed: "Since we can verify a Sudoku solution in polynomial time, and generating a Sudoku puzzle is harder than solving it, $\mathsf{P} \neq \mathsf{NP}$."

Exercise 7.6.7. Consider the language COMPOSITE. Show that both COMPOSITE and its complement are in NP. What does this tell us about the relationship between NP and co-NP?

Exercise 7.6.8. Trace through the Cook-Levin construction for a simple NTM that decides $\{0^n 1^n \mid n \geq 0\}$ on input "0011".

Further Reading

- Cook, S. (1971). "The complexity of theorem-proving procedures"
- Garey & Johnson (1979). "Computers and Intractability: A Guide to the Theory of NP-Completeness"
- Arora & Barak (2009). "Computational Complexity: A Modern Approach"
- Papadimitriou (1994). "Computational Complexity"
- Sipser (2012). "Introduction to the Theory of Computation"

Chapter 8

Reductions and NP-Completeness

Having established the fundamental complexity classes P and NP in the previous chapter, we now turn our attention to one of the most powerful tools in computational complexity theory: the concept of polynomial-time reductions. This chapter explores how reductions allow us to establish relationships between problems, prove NP-completeness, and understand the landscape of computational difficulty. By the end of this chapter, you will understand how to prove that a problem is NP-complete and appreciate why thousands of naturally occurring problems share the same computational difficulty.

8.1 Polynomial-time Reductions

8.1.1 The Concept of Reduction

At its core, a reduction is a transformation that converts instances of one problem into instances of another problem. If we can efficiently transform problem A into problem B, and we know how to solve B, then we can solve A by first performing the transformation and then solving the resulting instance of B. This simple yet powerful idea forms the foundation of complexity theory.

Definition 8.1.1 (Polynomial-time Reduction). A *polynomial-time reduction* from decision problem A to decision problem B, denoted $A \leq_p B$, is a function $f : \{0,1\}^* \to \{0,1\}^*$ such that:

1. f is computable by a polynomial-time algorithm
2. For all $x \in \{0,1\}^*$, $x \in A$ if and only if $f(x) \in B$

The notation $A \leq_p B$ is read as "A reduces to B" or "A is polynomial-time reducible to B." Intuitively, this means that B is at least as hard as A, since any algorithm for B can be used to solve A with only polynomial overhead.

8.1.2 Properties of Polynomial-time Reductions

Polynomial-time reductions possess several important properties that make them particularly useful for complexity analysis:

Proposition 8.1.1 (Transitivity). *If $A \leq_p B$ and $B \leq_p C$, then $A \leq_p C$.*

This property allows us to chain reductions together, establishing relationships between problems that may not have obvious direct connections.

Proposition 8.1.2 (Preservation of Polynomial Time). *If $A \leq_p B$ and $B \in \mathsf{P}$, then $A \in \mathsf{P}$.*

This follows directly from the definition: we can solve A by first applying the polynomial-time reduction to transform the instance, then solving the resulting instance of B in polynomial time.

Proposition 8.1.3 (Closure under Reductions). *The class NP is closed under polynomial-time reductions. That is, if $A \leq_p B$ and $B \in \mathsf{NP}$, then $A \in \mathsf{NP}$.*

This property is crucial for understanding the structure of NP-complete problems.

8.1.3 Types of Reductions

While we focus primarily on polynomial-time many-one reductions (also called Karp reductions), it's important to understand that other types of reductions exist:

- **Many-one Reductions:** These are the standard reductions we've defined above, where each instance of problem A is mapped to exactly one instance of problem B.
- **Turing Reductions:** Also known as Cook reductions, these allow an algorithm for A to make multiple queries to an oracle for B. While more general than many-one reductions, they are less commonly used in NP-completeness proofs.
- **Logspace Reductions:** These are reductions computable using only logarithmic space. They provide finer distinctions between problems within P.

8.1.4 Example: Reducing Independent Set to Clique

To illustrate the concept of reduction, let's consider two classic graph problems:

Definition 8.1.2 (Independent Set (IS)). Given a graph $G = (V, E)$ and an integer k, does G contain an independent set of size at least k? (An independent set is a subset of vertices with no edges between them.)

Definition 8.1.3 (Clique). Given a graph $G = (V, E)$ and an integer k, does G contain a clique of size at least k? (A clique is a subset of vertices where every pair is connected by an edge.)

Theorem 8.1.4. $\mathsf{IS} \leq_p \mathsf{CLIQUE}$

Proof. Given an instance (G, k) of Independent Set where $G = (V, E)$, we construct an instance of Clique as follows:

Reduction function: Define $f((G, k)) = (\bar{G}, k)$ where $\bar{G} = (V, \bar{E})$ is the complement graph with $\bar{E} = \{(u, v) : u, v \in V, u \neq v, (u, v) \notin E\}$.

Correctness: We must show that G has an independent set of size k if and only if $\bar{G}$ has a clique of size k.

($\Rightarrow$) Suppose $S \subseteq V$ is an independent set of size k in G. Then for any distinct $u, v \in S$, we have $(u, v) \notin E$, which means $(u, v) \in \bar{E}$. Therefore, S forms a clique in $\bar{G}$.

($\Leftarrow$) Suppose $S \subseteq V$ is a clique of size k in $\bar{G}$. Then for any distinct $u, v \in S$, we have $(u, v) \in \bar{E}$, which means $(u, v) \notin E$. Therefore, S is an independent set in G.

Efficiency: Computing the complement graph takes $\mathcal{O}(|V|^2)$ time, which is polynomial in the input size.

8.2 Proving NP-Completeness

8.2.1 The Definition of NP-Completeness

A problem is NP-complete if it is both in NP and is at least as hard as every problem in NP.

Definition 8.2.1 (NP-Completeness). A decision problem L is *NP-complete* if:

1. $L \in \mathsf{NP}$ (membership condition)
2. For every $A \in \mathsf{NP}$, $A \leq_p L$ (hardness condition)

The second condition states that L is *NP-hard*. Thus, NP-complete problems are precisely those that are both NP-hard and in NP.

8.2.2 The First NP-Complete Problem

Proving the first NP-complete problem required showing that every problem in NP reduces to it—a seemingly insurmountable task given the infinite number of problems in NP. This breakthrough was achieved independently by Stephen Cook and Leonid Levin in the early 1970s.

Theorem 8.2.1 (Cook-Levin Theorem)**.** *The Boolean Satisfiability Problem (*SAT*) is NP-complete.*

The proof involves showing that any computation of a nondeterministic Turing machine can be encoded as a Boolean formula that is satisfiable if and only if the machine accepts. The key insight is that the configuration of a polynomial-time NTM at any time step can be described using polynomially many Boolean variables, and the transition relations can be encoded as Boolean constraints.

8.2.3 The Standard Method for Proving NP-Completeness

Once we have one NP-complete problem, proving NP-completeness for other problems becomes much more manageable.

Theorem 8.2.2. *If L' is NP-complete and $L' \leq_p L$, then L is NP-hard. If additionally $L \in \mathsf{NP}$, then L is NP-complete.*

This gives us the standard two-step approach for proving NP-completeness:

1. **Show membership in NP:** Provide a polynomial-time verifier for the problem. This typically involves describing what constitutes a certificate and showing that it can be verified in polynomial time.

2. **Show NP-hardness:** Choose a known NP-complete problem L' and construct a polynomial-time reduction from L' to L. The choice of L' is crucial—select a problem whose structure naturally relates to your target problem.

8.2.4 Example: Proving 3-SAT is NP-Complete

Let's demonstrate this method by proving that 3-SAT (SAT restricted to clauses with exactly three literals) is NP-complete.

Definition 8.2.2 (3-SAT)**.** Given a Boolean formula ϕ in conjunctive normal form where each clause contains exactly three literals, is ϕ satisfiable?

Theorem 8.2.3. 3SAT *is NP-complete.*

Proof. **Step 1:** $\mathsf{3SAT} \in \mathsf{NP}$

Given a Boolean formula in 3-CNF and a truth assignment σ, we can verify in polynomial time whether σ satisfies the formula by evaluating each clause. This takes $\mathcal{O}(m)$ time where m is the number of clauses.

Step 2: $\mathsf{SAT} \leq_p \mathsf{3SAT}$

Given an arbitrary Boolean formula ϕ in CNF, we transform it to an equivalent 3-CNF formula ϕ'. For each clause C in ϕ:

- **Clauses with exactly 3 literals:** Keep unchanged.
- **Clauses with 1 literal** (a): Introduce new variables y, z and replace with:
$$(a \vee y \vee z) \wedge (a \vee y \vee \bar{z}) \wedge (a \vee \bar{y} \vee z) \wedge (a \vee \bar{y} \vee \bar{z})$$
- **Clauses with 2 literals** $(a \vee b)$: Introduce new variable y and replace with:
$$(a \vee b \vee y) \wedge (a \vee b \vee \bar{y})$$
- **Clauses with $k > 3$ literals** $(l_1 \vee l_2 \vee \cdots \vee l_k)$: Introduce $k-3$ new variables $y_1, \ldots, y_{k-3}$ and replace with:
$$\begin{aligned}
&(l_1 \vee l_2 \vee y_1) \wedge \\
&(\bar{y}_1 \vee l_3 \vee y_2) \wedge \\
&(\bar{y}_2 \vee l_4 \vee y_3) \wedge \\
&\quad \vdots \\
&(\bar{y}_{k-4} \vee l_{k-2} \vee y_{k-3}) \wedge \\
&(\bar{y}_{k-3} \vee l_{k-1} \vee l_k)
\end{aligned}$$

The transformation preserves satisfiability and runs in polynomial time, as we add at most $\mathcal{O}(n)$ new variables and $\mathcal{O}(m \cdot k_{max})$ new clauses, where n is the number of variables, m is the number of clauses, and k_{max} is the maximum clause length in ϕ.

8.3 Classic NP-Complete Problems

8.3.1 The Canonical NP-Complete Problems

Through decades of research, thousands of problems have been proven NP-complete. Here we examine several fundamental problems that frequently serve as starting points for NP-completeness proofs.

Definition 8.3.1 (Vertex Cover (VC)). **Input:** A graph $G = (V, E)$ and integer k
Question: Is there a set $S \subseteq V$ with $|S| \leq k$ such that every edge has at least one endpoint in S?

Definition 8.3.2 (Hamiltonian Cycle (HAM-CYCLE)). **Input:** An undirected graph $G = (V, E)$
Question: Does G contain a cycle that visits each vertex exactly once?

Definition 8.3.3 (3-Colorability (3-COL)). **Input:** An undirected graph $G = (V, E)$
Question: Can the vertices be colored using three colors such that no adjacent vertices share the same color?

8.3.2 Problems from Different Domains

NP-complete problems arise naturally across various domains:

Number Theory and Arithmetic

Definition 8.3.4 (Subset Sum). **Input:** Integers $a_1, \ldots, a_n$ and target t
Question: Is there a subset $S \subseteq \{1, \ldots, n\}$ such that $\sum_{i \in S} a_i = t$?

Definition 8.3.5 (Partition). **Input:** A set of integers $A = \{a_1, \ldots, a_n\}$
Question: Can A be partitioned into two subsets with equal sum?

Scheduling and Resource Allocation

Definition 8.3.6 (Bin Packing). **Input:** Items with sizes $s_1, \ldots, s_n \in (0, 1]$ and integer k
Question: Can the items be packed into at most k bins of capacity 1?

8.3.3 The Web of Reductions

The NP-complete problems form an intricate web of reductions. Common reduction paths include:

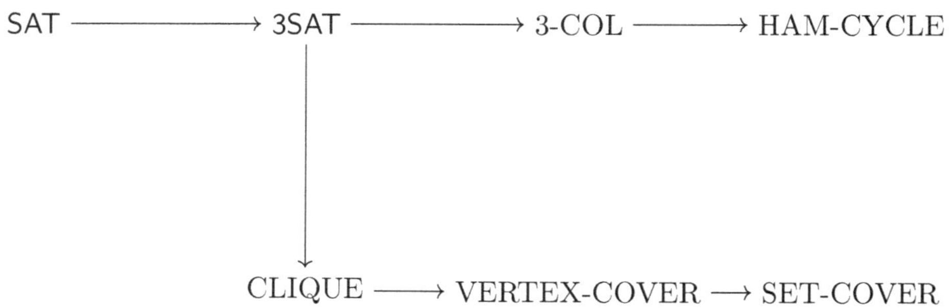

8.4 Techniques for Reduction Proofs

8.4.1 Gadget Construction

One of the most powerful techniques in reduction proofs is the use of *gadgets*—small substructures that encode specific constraints or behaviors.

- **Variable Gadgets:** Encode Boolean variables and their truth values. For example, in reducing 3SAT to 3-COL, we might use a triangle gadget where two vertices represent true and false values.
- **Clause Gadgets:** Represent logical constraints. These gadgets typically interact with variable gadgets to ensure that satisfiability conditions are met.
- **Consistency Gadgets:** Ensure that related parts of the construction maintain consistent values.

Example 8.4.1 (3-SAT to 3-COL Gadgets)**.** In the classic reduction from 3SAT to 3-COL, we use:

- A base triangle with vertices colored with three colors: TRUE, FALSE, and BASE
- Variable gadgets: pairs of vertices for each variable, one representing the positive literal and one the negative
- Clause gadgets: 5-vertex subgraphs that can be properly 3-colored if and only if at least one literal in the clause is true

8.4.2 Local Replacement

Local replacement involves transforming problem instances by replacing local structures with equivalent structures from the target problem.

Steps in Local Replacement:

1. Identify the basic units in the source problem
2. Design replacement structures in the target problem
3. Prove that the replacement preserves the essential properties
4. Show that the transformation can be done in polynomial time

8.4.3 Component Design

Component design involves building specialized structures that interact in controlled ways to encode the constraints of the source problem.

Key Principles:

- **Modularity:** Design components that can be combined without unexpected interactions
- **Locality:** Ensure that constraints are enforced locally within components
- **Composability:** Allow components to be connected in flexible ways

8.4.4 Common Pitfalls and How to Avoid Them

1. **Non-polynomial Blowup:** Ensure that the size of the constructed instance is polynomial in the size of the original instance. Watch for exponential gadget constructions or number encodings.
2. **Incorrect Direction:** Remember that to prove L is NP-hard, you must reduce FROM a known NP-complete problem TO L, not the other way around.
3. **Incomplete Equivalence:** Verify both directions of the equivalence: the source instance is yes if and only if the constructed instance is yes.
4. **Hidden Assumptions:** Make all assumptions explicit, particularly about input formats and problem definitions.

8.5 NP-Hardness and Optimization Problems

8.5.1 From Decision to Optimization

While NP-completeness is defined for decision problems, many practical problems are naturally formulated as optimization problems.

Definition 8.5.1 (NP-hard Optimization)**.** An optimization problem is *NP-hard* if its decision version is NP-complete.

For example, the optimization version of Vertex Cover asks for the minimum size vertex cover, while the decision version asks whether a vertex cover of size at most k exists.

8.5.2 Function Problems and FNP

Definition 8.5.2 (FNP)**.** The class FNP (Function NP) consists of function problems where:

- Given input x, find y such that $R(x, y)$ holds, where R is a polynomial-time computable relation
- The length of y is polynomially bounded in the length of x

FNP captures the computational complexity of finding witnesses for NP problems, not just deciding their existence.

8.5.3 Approximation and Inapproximability

For NP-hard optimization problems, we often seek approximate solutions. The complexity of approximation leads to refined classifications:

- APX: Problems admitting constant-factor polynomial-time approximation algorithms
- PTAS: Problems admitting polynomial-time approximation schemes
- APX-hard: Problems for which no PTAS exists unless $\mathsf{P} = \mathsf{NP}$

8.5.4 Parameterized Complexity

Parameterized complexity provides another lens for understanding NP-hard problems by considering additional problem parameters.

Definition 8.5.3 (Fixed-Parameter Tractability)**.** A problem is FPT with respect to parameter k if it can be solved in time $f(k) \cdot n^{\mathcal{O}(1)}$, where f is any computable function.

Example 8.5.1. Vertex Cover is FPT with respect to the solution size k, solvable in $\mathcal{O}(2^k \cdot n)$ time, despite being NP-complete in general.

Chapter Summary

This chapter has explored the fundamental concept of polynomial-time reductions and their application to proving NP-completeness. We've seen how reductions allow us to establish relationships between problems and build a rich theory of computational complexity. The technique of proving NP-completeness through reduction from known NP-complete problems has become a standard tool in computer science, helping us identify and understand computationally intractable problems.

Key concepts to remember:

- Polynomial-time reductions preserve efficient solvability and establish relative problem difficulty
- NP-complete problems form the "hardest" problems in NP, and thousands of natural problems fall into this category
- Gadget construction and component design are powerful techniques for building reductions
- NP-hardness extends naturally to optimization problems, though approximability varies widely
- Understanding the landscape of NP-complete problems helps in recognizing intractability and choosing appropriate algorithmic approaches

The theory of NP-completeness has profound practical implications. When faced with an NP-complete problem, we know to adjust our expectations: instead of seeking exact polynomial-time algorithms, we might pursue approximation algorithms, heuristics, or algorithms for special cases. The next chapter will explore complexity classes beyond NP, revealing even more structure in the hierarchy of computational problems.

Exercises

Conceptual Exercises

Exercise 8.5.1. Prove that the reduction relation $\leq_p$ is transitive but not symmetric.

Exercise 8.5.2. Show that if $\mathsf{P} = \mathsf{NP}$, then every non-trivial problem in P is NP-complete under polynomial-time reductions. (A problem is trivial if it is always yes or always no.)

Exercise 8.5.3. Explain why we cannot prove NP-completeness using reductions that run in exponential time.

Reduction Exercises

Exercise 8.5.4. Prove that the Dominating Set problem is NP-complete by reduction from Vertex Cover.

Exercise 8.5.5. Show that the Longest Path problem (finding a simple path of length at least k) is NP-complete.

Exercise 8.5.6. Prove that the Graph Isomorphism problem is in NP. (Note: It is not known whether this problem is NP-complete.)

Advanced Exercises

Exercise 8.5.7. Design a reduction from 3SAT to the Traveling Salesman Problem (TSP).

Exercise 8.5.8. Prove that the following variant of SAT is NP-complete: Given a Boolean formula where each variable appears at most three times, is it satisfiable?

Exercise 8.5.9. Show that if there exists an NP-complete problem in P, then P = NP.

Exercise 8.5.10. Prove that the optimization version of an NP-complete decision problem is NP-hard.

Further Reading

- Garey, M. R., & Johnson, D. S. (1979). *Computers and Intractability: A Guide to the Theory of NP-Completeness.* The definitive reference for NP-complete problems and reduction techniques.
- Papadimitriou, C. H. (1994). *Computational Complexity.* Chapter 8 provides extensive coverage of reductions and completeness.
- Arora, S., & Barak, B. (2009). *Computational Complexity: A Modern Approach.* Chapters 2-3 offer a modern treatment of NP-completeness with recent developments.
- Kleinberg, J., & Tardos, É. (2006). *Algorithm Design.* Chapter 8 provides an accessible introduction to NP-completeness with practical emphasis.
- Sipser, M. (2012). *Introduction to the Theory of Computation.* Chapter 7 presents NP-completeness from a theoretical computer science perspective.

Chapter 9

Beyond NP: Other Complexity Classes

While P and NP capture many fundamental computational problems, the landscape of computational complexity extends far beyond these two classes. This chapter explores the rich hierarchy of complexity classes that arise when we consider different computational resources, models of computation, and acceptance criteria. These classes help us understand the subtle gradations of computational difficulty and reveal deep connections between seemingly disparate areas of theoretical computer science.

9.1 The Polynomial Hierarchy

The polynomial hierarchy (PH) generalizes the relationship between P and NP to create an infinite hierarchy of complexity classes. Just as NP can be viewed as problems solvable in polynomial time with one level of nondeterministic quantification, the polynomial hierarchy extends this to multiple alternating levels of quantification.

9.1.1 Defining the Hierarchy

The polynomial hierarchy consists of three equivalent formulations:

Definition 9.1.1 (Oracle-Based Definition). The polynomial hierarchy is defined inductively as:

$$\Sigma_0^{\mathsf{P}} = \Pi_0^{\mathsf{P}} = \mathsf{P} \tag{9.1}$$

$$\Sigma_{k+1}^{\mathsf{P}} = \mathsf{NP}^{\Sigma_k^{\mathsf{P}}} \text{ (NP with a } \Sigma_k^{\mathsf{P}} \text{ oracle)} \tag{9.2}$$

$$\Pi_{k+1}^{\mathsf{P}} = \mathsf{coNP}^{\Sigma_k^{\mathsf{P}}} \text{ (coNP with a } \Sigma_k^{\mathsf{P}} \text{ oracle)} \tag{9.3}$$

Definition 9.1.2 (Alternating Quantifier Definition)**.** A language L is in Σ_k^{P} if there exists a polynomial-time verifier V and polynomial p such that:

$$x \in L \iff \exists y_1 \forall y_2 \exists y_3 \cdots Q_k y_k : V(x, y_1, \ldots, y_k) = 1$$

where $|y_i| \leq p(|x|)$ and Q_k is $\exists$ if k is odd, $\forall$ if k is even.

Definition 9.1.3 (Alternating Turing Machine Definition)**.** Σ_k^{P} consists of languages decidable by alternating Turing machines in polynomial time with at most k alternations, starting in an existential state.

9.1.2 Key Properties and Relationships

The polynomial hierarchy exhibits several fundamental properties:

Theorem 9.1.1 (Basic Properties of PH)**.** *For all $k \geq 0$:*

1. ***Complementation:*** $\Pi_k^{\mathsf{P}} = \text{co-}\Sigma_k^{\mathsf{P}}$
2. ***Containment:*** $\Sigma_k^{\mathsf{P}} \cup \Pi_k^{\mathsf{P}} \subseteq \Sigma_{k+1}^{\mathsf{P}} \cap \Pi_{k+1}^{\mathsf{P}}$
3. ***Union:*** $\mathsf{PH} = \bigcup_{k\geq 0} \Sigma_k^{\mathsf{P}} = \bigcup_{k\geq 0} \Pi_k^{\mathsf{P}}$

9.1.3 Complete Problems

Each level of the hierarchy has complete problems that capture its computational essence:

Example 9.1.1 (Σ_2^{P}-complete: Minimum Circuit)**.** Given a Boolean circuit C and integer k, does there exist a circuit C' with at most k gates such that for all inputs x, $C(x) = C'(x)$?

Example 9.1.2 (Π_2^{P}-complete: Circuit Equivalence)**.** Given two Boolean circuits C_1 and C_2, do they compute the same function on all inputs?

9.1.4 Collapse Theorems

The polynomial hierarchy is conjectured to be infinite, but several results show conditions under which it would collapse:

Theorem 9.1.2 (Karp-Lipton)**.** *If* $\mathsf{NP} \subseteq \mathsf{P/poly}$, *then* $\mathsf{PH} = \Sigma_2^{\mathsf{P}}$.

Theorem 9.1.3. *If* $\Sigma_k^{\mathsf{P}} = \Pi_k^{\mathsf{P}}$ *for some k, then* $\mathsf{PH} = \Sigma_k^{\mathsf{P}}$.

These collapse results provide evidence that certain separations (like $\mathsf{P} \neq \mathsf{NP}$) are likely true, as their failure would have surprising consequences.

9.2 PSPACE and PSPACE-Completeness

PSPACE represents the class of problems solvable using polynomial space, regardless of time complexity. This class captures many problems involving games, planning, and verification.

9.2.1 Formal Definition

Definition 9.2.1 (PSPACE).

$$\mathsf{PSPACE} = \mathsf{SPACE}(n^{\mathcal{O}(1)}) = \bigcup_{k \geq 0} \mathsf{SPACE}(n^k)$$

A language L is in PSPACE if there exists a deterministic Turing machine that decides L using space polynomial in the input size.

9.2.2 Fundamental Results

Theorem 9.2.1 (Savitch's Theorem). PSPACE = NPSPACE

Proof Sketch. Given an NPSPACE machine using space $s(n)$, we can simulate it deterministically by exploring all possible computation paths using a recursive procedure that requires only $\mathcal{O}(s^2(n))$ space.

Theorem 9.2.2 (PH vs PSPACE). $\mathsf{PH} \subseteq \mathsf{PSPACE}$

Every level of the polynomial hierarchy is contained in PSPACE, as we can simulate alternating quantifiers by exhaustive search in polynomial space.

9.2.3 PSPACE-Complete Problems

Definition 9.2.2 (Quantified Boolean Formula (QBF)). Given a quantified Boolean formula

$$\phi = Q_1 x_1 Q_2 x_2 \cdots Q_n x_n \psi(x_1, \ldots, x_n)$$

where $Q_i \in \{\exists, \forall\}$, is ϕ true?

Theorem 9.2.3. *QBF is* PSPACE*-complete.*

Example 9.2.1 (Other PSPACE-Complete Problems).

- **Generalized Geography:** Given a directed graph and starting vertex, does the first player have a winning strategy?
- **Regular Expression Equivalence:** Given two regular expressions with intersection and complement operators, do they describe the same language?

9.2.4 Interactive Proof Characterization

Theorem 9.2.4 (Shamir, 1990). $\mathsf{IP} = \mathsf{PSPACE}$

This shows that the problems solvable with polynomial space are exactly those that have interactive proof systems with polynomial rounds of interaction.

9.3 Exponential Time Classes

When polynomial resources aren't sufficient, we enter the realm of exponential complexity classes.

9.3.1 Basic Exponential Classes

Definition 9.3.1 (Exponential Time Classes).

$$\mathsf{EXP} = \mathsf{DTIME}(2^{n^{\mathcal{O}(1)}}) \tag{9.4}$$

$$\mathsf{NEXP} = \mathsf{NTIME}(2^{n^{\mathcal{O}(1)}}) \tag{9.5}$$

$$\text{2-}\mathsf{EXP} = \mathsf{DTIME}(2^{2^{n^{\mathcal{O}(1)}}}) \tag{9.6}$$

$$\mathsf{EXPSPACE} = \mathsf{SPACE}(2^{n^{\mathcal{O}(1)}}) \tag{9.7}$$

9.3.2 Separation Results

Unlike the polynomial world, we have provable separations:

Theorem 9.3.1 (Time Hierarchy Theorem). $\mathsf{P} \subsetneq \mathsf{EXP}$

Theorem 9.3.2 (Space Hierarchy Theorem). $\mathsf{PSPACE} \subsetneq \mathsf{EXPSPACE}$

Theorem 9.3.3 (Nondeterministic Time Hierarchy). $\mathsf{NP} \subsetneq \mathsf{NEXP}$

9.3.3 Complete Problems

Example 9.3.1 (EXP-complete: Succinct Circuit Value). Given a succinctly represented Boolean circuit (size 2^n described in n bits) and input, determine the output.

Example 9.3.2 (NEXP-complete: Succinct 3-SAT). Given a succinctly represented 3-CNF formula, is it satisfiable?

9.3.4 Connections to Lower Bounds

Theorem 9.3.4. *If* $\mathsf{EXP} \not\subseteq \mathsf{P/poly}$, *then there exist problems in* EXP *requiring superpolynomial circuit size.*

This connection motivates the study of circuit complexity as an approach to proving lower bounds.

9.4 Probabilistic Complexity Classes

Incorporating randomness into computation yields new complexity classes that capture the power of randomized algorithms.

9.4.1 Bounded-Error Probabilistic Classes

Definition 9.4.1 (BPP - Bounded-Error Probabilistic Polynomial Time)**.** $L \in \mathsf{BPP}$ if there exists a probabilistic polynomial-time algorithm A such that:

- If $x \in L$: $\Pr[A(x) = 1] \geq 2/3$
- If $x \notin L$: $\Pr[A(x) = 1] \leq 1/3$

The error probability $1/3$ can be reduced to 2^{-n} through amplification.

Definition 9.4.2 (RP - Randomized Polynomial Time)**.** One-sided error version where:

- If $x \in L$: $\Pr[A(x) = 1] \geq 1/2$
- If $x \notin L$: $\Pr[A(x) = 1] = 0$

Definition 9.4.3 (ZPP - Zero-Error Probabilistic Polynomial Time)**.** $\mathsf{ZPP} = \mathsf{RP} \cap \mathsf{coRP}$

9.4.2 Relationships and Open Problems

Theorem 9.4.1 (Known Relationships)**.** *1.* $\mathsf{P} \subseteq \mathsf{ZPP} \subseteq \mathsf{RP} \subseteq \mathsf{BPP}$

2. $\mathsf{BPP} \subseteq \mathsf{P/poly}$ *(BPP has polynomial-size circuits)*

3. $\mathsf{BPP} \subseteq \Sigma_2^{\mathsf{P}} \cap \Pi_2^{\mathsf{P}}$

Remark 9.4.1 (Major Open Problem). Is $\mathsf{P} = \mathsf{BPP}$? Many believe this equality holds, suggesting randomness doesn't fundamentally increase computational power for decision problems.

9.4.3 Derandomization

Theorem 9.4.2 (Hardness vs. Randomness). *If certain hard problems exist (e.g., problems in* EXP *requiring exponential-size circuits), then* $\mathsf{BPP} = \mathsf{P}$.

9.4.4 Probabilistic Proof Systems

Definition 9.4.4 (Additional Probabilistic Classes).

- **PP (Probabilistic Polynomial Time):** Accept if probability $> 1/2$ (no gap requirement)
- **MA (Merlin-Arthur):** NP with probabilistic verification
- **AM (Arthur-Merlin):** Probabilistic verifier sends random challenge, prover responds

Theorem 9.4.3. $\mathsf{MA} \subseteq \mathsf{AM} = \mathsf{AM}[2]$ *(two-round AM equals constant-round AM)*

9.5 Interactive Proofs and IP = PSPACE

Interactive proof systems revolutionized our understanding of proof and verification.

9.5.1 The Interactive Proof Model

Definition 9.5.1 (Interactive Proof System). An interactive proof system consists of:

- **Prover** P**:** Computationally unbounded, potentially dishonest
- **Verifier** V**:** Polynomial-time probabilistic algorithm
- **Interaction:** Polynomial rounds of communication

$L \in \mathsf{IP}$ if there exists a polynomial-time verifier V such that:

- **Completeness:** If $x \in L$, $\exists P : \Pr[(P, V)(x) \text{ accepts}] \geq 2/3$
- **Soundness:** If $x \notin L$, $\forall P^* : \Pr[(P^*, V)(x) \text{ accepts}] \leq 1/3$

9.5.2 The Power of Interaction

Example 9.5.1 (Graph Non-Isomorphism). Graph Non-Isomorphism $\in$ IP: The verifier randomly permutes one of two graphs and challenges the prover to identify which one. This problem is not known to be in NP.

Example 9.5.2 (#SAT). #SAT $\in$ IP: The exact number of satisfying assignments can be verified interactively.

9.5.3 The IP = PSPACE Theorem

Theorem 9.5.1 (Shamir, 1990). IP = PSPACE

Proof Outline.

1. IP $\subseteq$ PSPACE: Simulate all possible interactions in polynomial space
2. PSPACE $\subseteq$ IP: Arithmetize QBF formulas and use algebraic techniques

The proof introduces arithmetization, converting Boolean formulas to polynomials.

9.5.4 Implications and Extensions

Definition 9.5.2 (Extensions).

- **MIP (Multi-Prover Systems):** MIP = NEXP
- **Zero-Knowledge Proofs:** Proofs revealing nothing beyond validity
- **PCPs (Probabilistically Checkable Proofs):** Verify by reading constant bits

9.6 Quantum Complexity Classes

Quantum computation introduces fundamentally new complexity classes based on quantum mechanical principles.

9.6.1 Quantum Computational Model

Quantum computers manipulate quantum bits (qubits) using:

- **Superposition:** Qubits exist in combinations of $|0\rangle$ and $|1\rangle$
- **Entanglement:** Correlated quantum states
- **Unitary Evolution:** Reversible quantum operations
- **Measurement:** Probabilistic collapse to classical states

9.6.2 Basic Quantum Classes

Definition 9.6.1 (BQP - Bounded-Error Quantum Polynomial Time). $L \in \mathsf{BQP}$ if there exists a polynomial-time uniform family of quantum circuits $\{C_n\}$ such that:

- If $x \in L$: $\Pr[C_n(x) = 1] \geq 2/3$
- If $x \notin L$: $\Pr[C_n(x) = 1] \leq 1/3$

Theorem 9.6.1 (Key Properties).

1. $\mathsf{P} \subseteq \mathsf{BPP} \subseteq \mathsf{BQP} \subseteq \mathsf{PSPACE}$
2. BQP *likely incomparable with* NP
3. *Factoring* $\in \mathsf{BQP}$ *(Shor's algorithm)*
4. *Unstructured search:* $\sqrt{n}$ *speedup (Grover's algorithm)*

9.6.3 Quantum Proof Systems

Definition 9.6.2 (QMA - Quantum Merlin-Arthur). NP with quantum proofs and quantum verification.

Theorem 9.6.2 (Properties of QMA).

- $\mathsf{NP} \subseteq \mathsf{MA} \subseteq \mathsf{QMA}$
- *QMA-complete: Local Hamiltonian Problem*
- QMA *likely strictly contains* NP

Definition 9.6.3 (QIP - Quantum Interactive Proofs). Interactive proofs with quantum communication.

Theorem 9.6.3 (Breakthrough Result). $\mathsf{QIP} = \mathsf{PSPACE}$

Quantum interaction doesn't increase power beyond classical interaction!

9.6.4 Quantum Supremacy and Complexity

Definition 9.6.4 (Quantum Supremacy). Demonstrating quantum computers solving problems intractable for classical computers.

Theorem 9.6.4 (Complexity-Theoretic Evidence).

- *Relative to oracle:* $\mathsf{BQP} \not\subseteq \mathsf{PH}$
- *If* PH *infinite:* $\mathsf{BQP} \not\subseteq \mathsf{PH}$
- *Sampling problems exhibiting quantum advantage*

9.6.5 Error Correction and Fault Tolerance

Theorem 9.6.5 (Threshold Theorem). *Quantum computation is possible with imperfect gates if error rate is below threshold.*

Remark 9.6.1 (Implications for Complexity). BQP is robust under reasonable noise models.

9.7 Summary and Perspectives

This chapter has explored the rich landscape of complexity classes beyond P and NP. We've seen how:

1. **The Polynomial Hierarchy** creates a fine-grained classification of problems with alternating quantifiers
2. **PSPACE** captures problems requiring polynomial memory, including game-playing and planning
3. **Exponential Classes** demonstrate provable separations and connections to circuit complexity
4. **Probabilistic Classes** formalize the power of randomness in computation
5. **Interactive Proofs** revolutionize our notion of verification through the IP = PSPACE theorem
6. **Quantum Complexity** introduces fundamentally new computational possibilities

These classes reveal that computational complexity forms a rich hierarchy with subtle relationships and deep mathematical structure. Many fundamental questions remain open:

- Does the polynomial hierarchy collapse?
- Is P = BPP? (Can we derandomize efficiently?)
- What is the exact power of quantum computation?
- How do these classes relate under various resource bounds?

Understanding these complexity classes is essential for:

- Identifying the computational requirements of problems

- Choosing appropriate algorithmic approaches
- Understanding the limits of efficient computation
- Advancing theoretical computer science

The study of these classes continues to yield surprises, from the collapse of IP to PSPACE to the recent proof that $\mathsf{MIP}^* = \mathsf{RE}$, showing that quantum entanglement enables verification of undecidable problems.

9.8 Exercises

Exercise 9.8.1. Prove that if $\mathsf{P} = \mathsf{NP}$, then the polynomial hierarchy collapses to P.

Exercise 9.8.2. Show that TQBF (True Quantified Boolean Formulas) is PSPACE-complete by reduction from the acceptance problem for polynomial-space Turing machines.

Exercise 9.8.3. Prove that BPP is closed under complement.

Exercise 9.8.4. Design an interactive proof protocol for Graph Non-Isomorphism.

Exercise 9.8.5. Show that any problem in BQP can be solved in PSPACE on a classical computer.

Exercise 9.8.6. Prove that if $\Sigma_k^{\mathsf{P}} = \Pi_k^{\mathsf{P}}$ for some $k \geq 1$, then $\mathsf{PH} = \Sigma_k^{\mathsf{P}}$.

Exercise 9.8.7. Demonstrate the amplification lemma: show how to reduce the error probability in BPP from $1/3$ to 2^{-n}.

Exercise 9.8.8. Prove Savitch's theorem for the special case of $\mathsf{NSPACE}(\log n) \subseteq \mathsf{SPACE}(\log^2 n)$.

Exercise 9.8.9. Show that PP is closed under intersection and union.

Exercise 9.8.10. Design a zero-knowledge proof for graph 3-coloring.

9.9 Further Reading

- Arora, S., & Barak, B. (2009). *Computational Complexity: A Modern Approach.* Cambridge University Press.
- Goldreich, O. (2008). *Computational Complexity: A Conceptual Perspective.* Cambridge University Press.

- Papadimitriou, C. H. (1994). *Computational Complexity.* Addison-Wesley.
- Nielsen, M. A., & Chuang, I. L. (2010). *Quantum Computation and Quantum Information.* Cambridge University Press.
- Sipser, M. (2012). *Introduction to the Theory of Computation* (3rd ed.). Cengage Learning.

Part IV

Advanced Analysis Techniques

Chapter 10

Amortized Analysis

Introduction

In traditional worst-case analysis, we examine the maximum time required for any single operation. However, this approach can be overly pessimistic when operations vary significantly in cost and expensive operations occur rarely. Amortized analysis provides a more accurate picture by considering the average performance of each operation in the worst case over a sequence of operations.

Unlike average-case analysis, which relies on probabilistic assumptions about input distribution, amortized analysis guarantees performance bounds for any sequence of operations. This chapter explores three fundamental techniques for amortized analysis and their applications to important data structures.

10.1 The Aggregate Method

10.1.1 Fundamental Concept

The aggregate method is the simplest approach to amortized analysis. We analyze the total cost of a sequence of n operations and divide by n to obtain the amortized cost per operation. If the worst-case cost of n operations is $T(n)$, then the amortized cost per operation is $T(n)/n$.

Definition 10.1.1 (Aggregate Method)**.** Given a sequence of n operations with total worst-case cost $T(n)$, the amortized cost per operation is:

$$\hat{c} = \frac{T(n)}{n}$$

10.1.2 Stack with Multipop Operation

Consider a stack supporting three operations:

- `PUSH`(S, x): Push element x onto stack S (cost: 1)
- `POP`(S): Pop the top element from S (cost: 1)
- `MULTIPOP`(S, k): Pop $\min(k, |S|)$ elements from S

Worst-case analysis

- `PUSH`: $\mathcal{O}(1)$
- `POP`: $\mathcal{O}(1)$
- `MULTIPOP`: $\mathcal{O}(n)$ where n is the stack size

Amortized analysis using aggregate method

Theorem 10.1.1. *For a sequence of n stack operations starting with an empty stack, the amortized cost per operation is $\mathcal{O}(1)$.*

Proof. For a sequence of n operations starting with an empty stack:

- Each element can be pushed at most once
- Each element can be popped at most once
- Total number of `POP` operations (including those in `MULTIPOP`) $\leq n$

Therefore, the total cost of n operations is at most $2n$, giving an amortized cost of $\mathcal{O}(1)$ per operation.

10.1.3 Binary Counter Increment

Consider a k-bit binary counter initialized to 0, supporting only the `INCREMENT` operation.

Example 10.1.1 (Bit flip analysis).

Counter Transition	Bits Flipped
$0000 \to 0001$	1
$0001 \to 0010$	2
$0010 \to 0011$	1
$0011 \to 0100$	3
$0100 \to 0101$	1
$0101 \to 0110$	2
$0110 \to 0111$	1
$0111 \to 1000$	4

Lemma 10.1.2 (Bit Flip Pattern). *In a binary counter:*

- *Bit 0 flips every increment: n times*
- *Bit 1 flips every 2 increments: $n/2$ times*
- *Bit 2 flips every 4 increments: $n/4$ times*
- *Bit i flips every 2^i increments: $n/2^i$ times*

Theorem 10.1.3. *The amortized cost of* **`INCREMENT`** *operation is $\mathcal{O}(1)$.*

Proof. Total cost for n increments:

$$T(n) = \sum_{i=0}^{k-1} \left\lfloor \frac{n}{2^i} \right\rfloor < n \times \sum_{i=0}^{\infty} \frac{1}{2^i} = 2n$$

Therefore, amortized cost $= T(n)/n = \mathcal{O}(1)$ per increment.

10.2 The Accounting Method

10.2.1 Credit System

In the accounting method, we assign different charges to different operations. Some operations are charged more than their actual cost (building credit), while others are charged less (using credit).

Definition 10.2.1 (Credit Invariant). Let c_i be the actual cost of the i-th operation and $\hat{c}_i$ be the amortized cost. The credit after n operations must satisfy:

$$\sum_{i=1}^{n} (\hat{c}_i - c_i) \geq 0$$

10.2.2 Stack Example Revisited

Theorem 10.2.1. *Using the accounting method, stack operations have $\mathcal{O}(1)$ amortized cost.*

Proof. Assign amortized costs:

- `PUSH`: $\hat{c} = 2$ (actual cost: 1, stores 1 credit)
- `POP`: $\hat{c} = 0$ (actual cost: 1, uses stored credit)
- `MULTIPOP`(k): $\hat{c} = 0$ (actual cost: k', uses k' stored credits)

Credit invariant: Each element in the stack has 1 credit associated with it.

Verification:

- When we `PUSH`, we pay 2: 1 for the push operation, 1 credit stored with the element
- When we `POP` or `MULTIPOP`, each popped element uses its stored credit
- Credit never becomes negative

10.2.3 Dynamic Table Doubling

Consider a dynamic table that doubles in size when full.

Algorithm 7 Dynamic Table Insert with Doubling

```
procedure INSERT(T, x)
    if size[T] = capacity[T] then
        new_table ← ALLOCATE(2 × capacity[T])
        for i = 1 size[T] do
            new_table[i] ← T[i]
        end for
        T ← new_table
        capacity[T] ← 2 × capacity[T]
    end if
    size[T] ← size[T] + 1
    T[size[T]] ← x
end procedure
```

Theorem 10.2.2. *The amortized cost of `INSERT` in a dynamic table with doubling is $\mathcal{O}(1)$.*

Proof. Amortized cost assignment for `INSERT`: $\hat{c} = 3$

- 1 for inserting the element
- 1 credit for future move of this element
- 1 credit for future move of one existing element

When doubling from size m to $2m$:

- Cost of doubling: m (copying m elements)

- Credits available: m (one per element)
- Credits exactly cover the doubling cost

10.3 The Potential Method

10.3.1 Potential Functions

The potential method uses a potential function Φ that maps each data structure state to a real number, representing stored energy that can pay for future operations.

Definition 10.3.1 (Potential Method Framework). Let D_i be the data structure state after operation i, and $\Phi(D_i)$ be the potential after operation i. For operation i with actual cost c_i:

$$\hat{c}_i = c_i + \Phi(D_i) - \Phi(D_{i-1})$$

where $\hat{c}_i$ is the amortized cost.

Theorem 10.3.1 (Potential Method Correctness). *If $\Phi(D_0) = 0$ and $\Phi(D_i) \geq 0$ for all i, then:*

$$\sum_{i=1}^{n} c_i \leq \sum_{i=1}^{n} \hat{c}_i$$

Proof.

$$\sum_{i=1}^{n} \hat{c}_i = \sum_{i=1}^{n} [c_i + \Phi(D_i) - \Phi(D_{i-1})] \quad (10.1)$$

$$= \sum_{i=1}^{n} c_i + \Phi(D_n) - \Phi(D_0) \quad (10.2)$$

$$= \sum_{i=1}^{n} c_i + \Phi(D_n) \quad (10.3)$$

$$\geq \sum_{i=1}^{n} c_i \quad (10.4)$$

Since $\Phi(D_n) \geq 0$ by assumption.

10.3.2 Stack Analysis with Potential Method

Definition 10.3.2 (Stack Potential Function). $\Phi(S) = |S|$ (number of elements in stack S)

Theorem 10.3.2. *Using the potential method with $\Phi(S) = |S|$, all stack operations have amortized cost $\mathcal{O}(1)$.*

Proof. Amortized costs:

- **PUSH:**

$$\hat{c} = c + \Delta\Phi \tag{10.5}$$
$$= 1 + 1 = 2 = \mathcal{O}(1) \tag{10.6}$$

- **POP:**

$$\hat{c} = c + \Delta\Phi \tag{10.7}$$
$$= 1 + (-1) = 0 = \mathcal{O}(1) \tag{10.8}$$

- **MULTIPOP(k):** Let $k' = \min(k, |S|)$

$$\hat{c} = c + \Delta\Phi \tag{10.9}$$
$$= k' + (-k') = 0 = \mathcal{O}(1) \tag{10.10}$$

10.3.3 Binary Counter with Potential Method

Definition 10.3.3 (Binary Counter Potential). $\Phi(\text{counter}) = b(\text{counter})$ where b is the number of 1s in the binary representation.

Theorem 10.3.3. *The amortized cost of* `INCREMENT` *is $\mathcal{O}(1)$ using the potential method.*

Proof. Let t_i = number of 1s after i-th increment. If increment flips k bits from 1 to 0 and 1 bit from 0 to 1:

$$\hat{c} = c + \Delta\Phi \tag{10.11}$$
$$= (k + 1) + [t_i - t_{i-1}] \tag{10.12}$$
$$= (k + 1) + [(-k) + 1] \tag{10.13}$$
$$= 2 = \mathcal{O}(1) \tag{10.14}$$

10.3.4 Choosing Good Potential Functions

Remark 10.3.1 (Guidelines for Potential Function Design).

1. Should be 0 initially and non-negative always
2. Should increase before expensive operations
3. Should decrease during expensive operations to offset their cost
4. Should be simple enough to analyze
5. Should capture the essential state that determines future costs

10.4 Applications to Data Structures

10.4.1 Union-Find Data Structure

Algorithm 8 Union-Find with Path Compression and Union by Rank

```
procedure FIND(x)
    if x ≠ parent[x] then
        parent[x] ← FIND(parent[x])                ▷ Path compression
    end ifreturn parent[x]
end procedure
procedure UNION(x, y)
    r_x ← FIND(x)
    r_y ← FIND(y)
    if rank[r_x] > rank[r_y] then
        parent[r_y] ← r_x
    else if rank[r_x] < rank[r_y] then
        parent[r_x] ← r_y
    else
        parent[r_y] ← r_x
        rank[r_x] ← rank[r_x] + 1
    end if
end procedure
```

Theorem 10.4.1 (Union-Find Complexity). *A sequence of m operations on n elements takes $\mathcal{O}(m \cdot \alpha(n))$ time, where $\alpha(n)$ is the inverse Ackermann function.*

10.4.2 Fibonacci Heaps

Definition 10.4.1 (Fibonacci Heap Potential).

$$\Phi(H) = t(H) + 2m(H)$$

where $t(H)$ is the number of trees in heap H and $m(H)$ is the number of marked nodes.

Theorem 10.4.2 (Fibonacci Heap Operations). *Amortized costs:*

- *INSERT:* $\mathcal{O}(1)$
- *FIND-MIN:* $\mathcal{O}(1)$
- *UNION:* $\mathcal{O}(1)$
- *EXTRACT-MIN:* $\mathcal{O}(\log n)$
- *DECREASE-KEY:* $\mathcal{O}(1)$
- *DELETE:* $\mathcal{O}(\log n)$

10.4.3 Scapegoat Trees

Scapegoat trees are self-balancing BSTs with:

- No balance information stored in nodes
- Rebuilding subtrees when they become unbalanced
- Amortized $\mathcal{O}(\log n)$ for insertions and deletions
- Worst-case $\mathcal{O}(\log n)$ for searches

10.5 Dynamic Arrays and Hash Tables

10.5.1 Dynamic Array Expansion

Growth Strategies Comparison

Theorem 10.5.1 (Growth Factor Analysis). *For a dynamic array with growth factor $\alpha > 1$:*

- *Amortized insertion cost:* $\mathcal{O}(1)$ *if* $\alpha > 1$
- *Space efficiency after expansion:* $1/\alpha$
- *Total cost for n insertions:* $\mathcal{O}(n)$

Proof. For growth factor α, capacity sequence: $1, \alpha, \alpha^2, \alpha^3, \ldots$

Total copy cost for n insertions:

$$\sum_{i=0}^{\lfloor \log_\alpha n \rfloor} \alpha^i = \frac{\alpha^{\lfloor \log_\alpha n \rfloor + 1} - 1}{\alpha - 1} = \mathcal{O}(n)$$

Amortized cost per insertion: $\mathcal{O}(n)/n = \mathcal{O}(1)$

10.5.2 Dynamic Array Shrinking

Definition 10.5.1 (Correct Shrinking Strategy).

- Expand when $size = capacity$
- Shrink when $size = capacity/4$ (to $capacity/2$)
- Maintains $size \in [capacity/4, capacity]$

Definition 10.5.2 (Shrinking Potential Function).

$$\Phi(D) = \begin{cases} 2 \times size - capacity & \text{if } size \geq capacity/2 \\ capacity/2 - size & \text{if } size < capacity/2 \end{cases}$$

10.5.3 Hash Table Resizing

Algorithm 9 Hash Table with Dynamic Resizing

```
procedure INSERT(key, value)
    if load_factor > 0.75 then
        RESIZE(2 × capacity)
    end if
    INSERT-INTO-TABLE(key, value)
end procedure
procedure DELETE(key)
    DELETE-FROM-TABLE(key)
    if load_factor < 0.25 then
        RESIZE(capacity/2)
    end if
end procedure
```

Theorem 10.5.2. *Hash table operations with resizing have $\mathcal{O}(1)$ amortized cost.*

10.6 Splay Trees Case Study

10.6.1 Splay Tree Operations

Splay trees are self-adjusting BSTs where accessed nodes are moved to root via splaying.

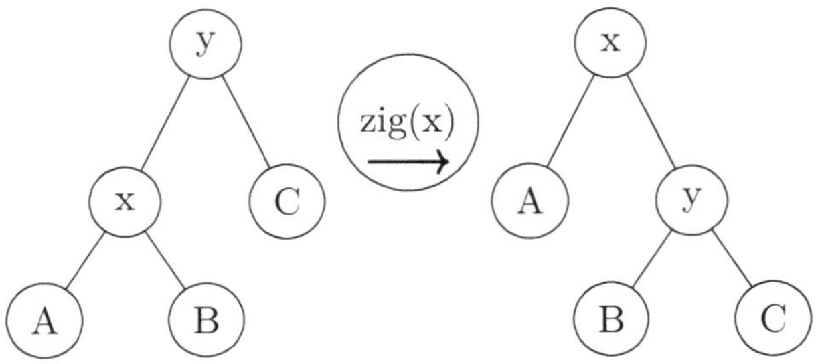

Figure 10.1: Zig operation in splay tree

10.6.2 Access Lemma

Definition 10.6.1 (Rank Function). For a node x in tree T, define:

- $size(x)$ = number of nodes in subtree rooted at x
- $rank(x) = \log(size(x))$

Definition 10.6.2 (Splay Tree Potential).

$$\Phi(T) = \sum_{x \in T} rank(x) = \sum_{x \in T} \log(size(x))$$

Lemma 10.6.1 (Access Lemma). *The amortized cost of splaying node x to root in tree with root t is at most:*

$$3(rank(t) - rank(x)) + 1 = 3(\log(size(t)) - \log(size(x))) + 1$$

Proof Sketch.

1. Analyze potential change for each rotation type:
   - Zig: $\Delta\Phi \leq 3(rank'(x) - rank(x))$
   - Zig-Zig: $\Delta\Phi \leq 3(rank'(x) - rank(x)) - 2$
   - Zig-Zag: $\Delta\Phi \leq 3(rank'(x) - rank(x)) - 2$
2. Telescope the sum over all rotations
3. Most terms cancel, leaving the stated bound

10.6.3 Consequences of Access Lemma

Theorem 10.6.2 (Sequential Access Theorem). *Accessing all n nodes in symmetric order takes $\mathcal{O}(n)$ time total.*

Proof. When accessing node i in increasing order:

- Initial rank of node $i \leq \log(n - i + 1)$
- Amortized cost: $3\log(n/(n - i + 1)) + 1$
- Total amortized cost:

$$\sum_{i=1}^{n} 3\log\left(\frac{n}{n-i+1}\right) + 1 = \sum_{i=1}^{n} 3\log\left(\frac{n}{i}\right) + 1 = \mathcal{O}(n)$$

Theorem 10.6.3 (Working Set Theorem). *Let $w(x)$ be the number of distinct items accessed since last access to x. The amortized access cost for x is $\mathcal{O}(\log(w(x)))$.*

Theorem 10.6.4 (Dynamic Finger Theorem). *The amortized cost to access y after accessing x is $\mathcal{O}(\log|rank(x) - rank(y)|)$.*

10.6.4 Other Properties

Theorem 10.6.5 (Static Optimality). *Splay trees are $\mathcal{O}(\log\log n)$-competitive with the optimal static BST.*

Conjecture 10.6.6 (Dynamic Optimality Conjecture). *Splay trees are $\mathcal{O}(1)$-competitive with the optimal offline BST algorithm.*

Note: The Dynamic Optimality Conjecture remains open as of 2025.

Summary

Amortized analysis provides powerful techniques for analyzing data structures where operation costs vary significantly. The three methods—aggregate, accounting, and potential—offer different perspectives on the same fundamental idea: expensive operations are rare and can be paid for by the savings from many cheap operations.

Key takeaways:

1. The **aggregate method** is simplest but sometimes insufficient
2. The **accounting method** provides intuitive credit-based reasoning

3. The **potential method** offers the most flexibility and mathematical rigor

4. Amortized bounds are worst-case guarantees, not average-case

5. Many practical data structures rely on amortized analysis for efficiency

The techniques learned in this chapter are essential for understanding advanced data structures like Fibonacci heaps, splay trees, and union-find, as well as for analyzing the true cost of operations in practical applications.

Exercises

1. **Two-Stack Queue:** Analyze a queue implemented with two stacks, where `ENQUEUE` pushes onto stack 1, and `DEQUEUE` pops from stack 2 (transferring all elements from stack 1 if stack 2 is empty). Show that both operations have $\mathcal{O}(1)$ amortized cost.

2. **Potential Design:** Design a potential function for the two-stack queue and prove the same amortized bounds using the potential method.

3. **Binary Counter with Decrement:** Consider a binary counter that supports both `INCREMENT` and `DECREMENT`. Show that the amortized cost per operation is still $\mathcal{O}(1)$.

4. **Alternative Growth Factor:** Analyze a dynamic array that grows by a factor of 1.5 instead of 2. What is the amortized cost of insertion? What are the trade-offs?

5. **Splay Tree Insertion:** Prove that in a splay tree, the amortized cost of inserting n items in sorted order is $\mathcal{O}(n)$.

6. **Extract-Median:** Design a data structure supporting `INSERT` and `EXTRACT-MEDIAN` with $\mathcal{O}(\log n)$ amortized cost per operation.

7. **Pop-Half Stack:** Consider a stack that supports `PUSH` and `POP-HALF` (removes $\lceil n/2 \rceil$ elements). Analyze the amortized cost of each operation.

8. **Double-Ended Queue:** Implement and analyze a deque (double-ended queue) with dynamic resizing at both ends. What potential function works best?

References and Further Reading

1. Tarjan, R. E. (1985). "Amortized Computational Complexity." *SIAM Journal on Algebraic Discrete Methods*, 6(2), 306-318.

2. Sleator, D. D., & Tarjan, R. E. (1985). "Self-adjusting binary search trees." *Journal of the ACM*, 32(3), 652-686.

3. Cormen, T. H., Leiserson, C. E., Rivest, R. L., & Stein, C. (2022). *Introduction to Algorithms* (4th ed.), Chapter 17: Amortized Analysis.

4. Kozen, D. C. (1992). *The Design and Analysis of Algorithms*, Chapter 8: Amortized Analysis.

5. Okasaki, C. (1998). *Purely Functional Data Structures* – Extensive use of amortized analysis in functional setting.

Chapter 11

Probabilistic Analysis

Introduction

While worst-case analysis provides important guarantees about algorithm performance, it can sometimes be overly pessimistic. Many algorithms that perform poorly in the worst case actually perform quite well in practice. Probabilistic analysis offers a more nuanced view by incorporating randomness into our complexity models, either through random inputs or randomized algorithm design. This chapter explores the fundamental techniques for analyzing algorithms from a probabilistic perspective, providing the mathematical tools necessary to understand and analyze randomized algorithms that have become increasingly important in modern computing.

11.1 Expected Running Time

11.1.1 Foundations of Expected Value Analysis

The expected running time of an algorithm represents the average performance over all possible executions, weighted by their probabilities. For a discrete random variable T representing running time:

Definition 11.1.1 (Expected Running Time). The expected running time $\mathbb{E}[T]$ is defined as:

$$\mathbb{E}[T] = \sum_{t} t \cdot \Pr[T = t] \tag{11.1}$$

where the sum is taken over all possible running times t.

For continuous distributions, we use the integral:

$$\mathbb{E}[T] = \int_{-\infty}^{\infty} t \cdot f(t)\, dt \tag{11.2}$$

where $f(t)$ is the probability density function.

11.1.2 Linearity of Expectation

One of the most powerful tools in probabilistic analysis is the linearity of expectation, which holds even when random variables are not independent.

Theorem 11.1.1 (Linearity of Expectation). *For any random variables $X_1, X_2, \ldots, X_n$ and constants $a_1, a_2, \ldots, a_n$:*

$$\mathbb{E}\left[\sum_{i=1}^{n} a_i X_i\right] = \sum_{i=1}^{n} a_i \mathbb{E}[X_i] \tag{11.3}$$

Example 11.1.1 (Analyzing Linear Search). Consider searching for an element in an unsorted array of n elements. Let X be the number of comparisons:

- If the element is at position i: $X = i$ comparisons
- Assuming uniform distribution: $\Pr[\text{position} = i] = \frac{1}{n}$
- $\mathbb{E}[X] = \sum_{i=1}^{n} i \cdot \frac{1}{n} = \frac{1}{n} \cdot \sum_{i=1}^{n} i = \frac{n+1}{2}$

11.1.3 Indicator Random Variables

Indicator random variables simplify the analysis of complex algorithms by breaking them into simple binary events.

Definition 11.1.2 (Indicator Random Variable). An indicator random variable X_i for event A_i is:

$$X_i = \begin{cases} 1 & \text{if } A_i \text{ occurs} \\ 0 & \text{otherwise} \end{cases} \tag{11.4}$$

Key Property: $\mathbb{E}[X_i] = \Pr[A_i]$

Example 11.1.2 (Expected Inversions in Random Permutation). For a random permutation of n elements, the expected number of inversions:

- Define $X_{ij} = 1$ if elements at positions $i < j$ are inverted
- Total inversions: $X = \sum_{i<j} X_{ij}$
- $\mathbb{E}[X_{ij}] = \Pr[\text{inversion at } (i,j)] = \frac{1}{2}$
- $\mathbb{E}[X] = \sum_{i<j} \mathbb{E}[X_{ij}] = \binom{n}{2} \cdot \frac{1}{2} = \frac{n(n-1)}{4}$

11.1.4 Variance and Standard Deviation

Understanding the spread of running times is crucial for practical performance guarantees.

Definition 11.1.3 (Variance). The variance of running time T is:

$$\mathrm{Var}[T] = \mathbb{E}[(T - \mathbb{E}[T])^2] = \mathbb{E}[T^2] - (\mathbb{E}[T])^2 \tag{11.5}$$

The standard deviation $\sigma = \sqrt{\mathrm{Var}[T]}$ provides a measure of typical deviation from the mean.

11.2 Randomized Algorithms

11.2.1 Sources of Randomization

Randomized algorithms introduce randomness through:

1. **Random choices during execution** (e.g., pivot selection in quicksort)
2. **Random preprocessing** (e.g., random hash functions)
3. **Random sampling** (e.g., randomized selection algorithms)

11.2.2 Advantages of Randomization

Simplicity: Randomized algorithms often have simpler implementations than their deterministic counterparts.

Efficiency: Many randomized algorithms achieve better expected time complexity than the best known deterministic algorithms.

Robustness: Performance doesn't depend on specific input patterns, eliminating adversarial worst cases.

11.2.3 Randomized Algorithm Design Paradigms

Random Sampling

Select a random subset to make decisions about the whole:

```
def randomized_median(A, k):
    # Sample O(n^(3/4)) elements
    sample = random.sample(A, int(n**0.75))
    sample.sort()
    # Use sample to partition effectively
```

Listing 11.1: Randomized Median Selection

Random Perturbation

Add random noise to break symmetries:

```
def randomized_incremental_hull(points):
    # Random shuffle breaks worst-case orderings
    random.shuffle(points)
    return incremental_convex_hull(points)
```

Listing 11.2: Randomized Incremental Convex Hull

Random Rounding

Convert fractional solutions to integer solutions:

```
def randomized_rounding(fractional_solution):
    return [1 if random.random() < x else 0
            for x in fractional_solution]
```

Listing 11.3: Randomized Rounding

11.2.4 Derandomization

Some randomized algorithms can be converted to deterministic ones using:

- Method of conditional expectations
- Pessimistic estimators
- Explicit constructions replacing random choices

11.3 Las Vegas vs Monte Carlo Algorithms

11.3.1 Las Vegas Algorithms

Definition 11.3.1 (Las Vegas Algorithm)**.** A Las Vegas algorithm always produces the correct answer but has randomized running time.

Characteristics:

- Output is always correct
- Running time is a random variable
- May not terminate (with probability 0)

Example 11.3.1 (Randomized Quicksort)**.**

```
def randomized_quicksort(A):
    if len(A) <= 1:
        return A
    pivot = A[random.randint(0, len(A)-1)]
    left = [x for x in A if x < pivot]
    middle = [x for x in A if x == pivot]
    right = [x for x in A if x > pivot]
    return randomized_quicksort(left) + middle +
   randomized_quicksort(right)
```

- Always produces correctly sorted output
- Expected time: $O(n \log n)$
- Worst case: $O(n^2)$ (but with negligible probability)

11.3.2 Monte Carlo Algorithms

Definition 11.3.2 (Monte Carlo Algorithm)**.** A Monte Carlo algorithm has bounded running time but may produce incorrect results with some probability.

Types:

1. **One-sided error:** Error only on one type of input (e.g., primality testing)
2. **Two-sided error:** May err on any input (e.g., randomized min-cut)

Example 11.3.2 (Randomized Primality Testing (Miller-Rabin))**.**

```
def is_prime_monte_carlo(n, k):
    # k iterations, each reduces error probability by 1/4
    for _ in range(k):
        a = random.randint(2, n-2)
        if not miller_rabin_test(n, a):
            return False  # Definitely composite
    return True  # Probably prime, error <= (1/4)^k
```

11.3.3 Amplification Techniques

For Monte Carlo algorithms:

- Run algorithm k times independently
- One-sided error: Return TRUE if any run returns TRUE

- Two-sided error: Take majority vote

Error probability reduction:

- Original error: ε
- After k independent runs: ε^k (one-sided) or exponentially small (two-sided by Chernoff bounds)

11.3.4 Converting Between Types

Las Vegas to Monte Carlo:

- Add timeout mechanism
- Return "failure" if timeout exceeded
- Bounded time, but may fail

Monte Carlo to Las Vegas (when verification is easy):

```
def monte_carlo_to_las_vegas(monte_carlo_alg, verify):
    while True:
        result = monte_carlo_alg()
        if verify(result):
            return result
```

11.4 Concentration Inequalities

11.4.1 Markov's Inequality

The most basic concentration inequality, requiring only non-negativity.

Theorem 11.4.1 (Markov's Inequality). *For non-negative random variable X and $a > 0$:*

$$\Pr[X \geq a] \leq \frac{\mathbb{E}[X]}{a} \tag{11.6}$$

Application: Bounding probability of excessive running time

- If expected time is μ, then $\Pr[T \geq k\mu] \leq \frac{1}{k}$

11.4.2 Chebyshev's Inequality

Uses variance information for tighter bounds.

Theorem 11.4.2 (Chebyshev's Inequality). *For random variable X with mean μ and variance σ^2:*

$$\Pr[|X - \mu| \geq k\sigma] \leq \frac{1}{k^2} \tag{11.7}$$

Example 11.4.1 (Load Balancing).

- n balls thrown into n bins uniformly at random
- Expected load per bin: $\mu = 1$
- Variance per bin: $\sigma^2 = 1 - \frac{1}{n} \approx 1$
- $\Pr[\text{bin load} \geq k] \leq \frac{1}{k^2}$ by Chebyshev

11.4.3 Moment Generating Functions

Powerful technique for deriving exponential concentration bounds.

Definition 11.4.1 (Moment Generating Function). The moment generating function of X is:

$$M_X(t) = \mathbb{E}[e^{tX}] \tag{11.8}$$

Key Property: For independent $X_1, \ldots, X_n$:

$$M_{\sum X_i}(t) = \prod M_{X_i}(t) \tag{11.9}$$

11.4.4 Hoeffding's Inequality

For bounded independent random variables.

Theorem 11.4.3 (Hoeffding's Inequality). *If $X_1, \ldots, X_n$ are independent with $X_i \in [a_i, b_i]$, and $S = \sum X_i$:*

$$\Pr[|S - \mathbb{E}[S]| \geq t] \leq 2\exp\left(-\frac{2t^2}{\sum_{i=1}^{n}(b_i - a_i)^2}\right) \tag{11.10}$$

Application: Randomized Algorithms with Bounded Steps

- Each step contributes bounded amount to total
- Deviation from expected decreases exponentially

11.4.5 Azuma's Inequality

Extension to martingales (dependent but "fair" sequences).

Theorem 11.4.4 (Azuma's Inequality). *For martingale sequence with bounded differences $|X_i - X_{i-1}| \leq c_i$:*

$$\Pr[|X_n - X_0| \geq t] \leq 2\exp\left(-\frac{t^2}{2\sum_{i=1}^{n} c_i^2}\right) \tag{11.11}$$

11.5 Chernoff Bounds and Applications

11.5.1 The Chernoff Bound

The tightest general concentration inequality for sums of independent random variables.

Theorem 11.5.1 (Chernoff Bound). *For independent random variables $X_1, \ldots, X_n \in \{0, 1\}$, let $X = \sum X_i$ and $\mu = \mathbb{E}[X]$. Then:*

Upper tail *($\delta > 0$):*

$$\Pr[X \geq (1+\delta)\mu] \leq \exp\left(-\frac{\delta^2\mu}{2+\delta}\right) \tag{11.12}$$

Lower tail *($0 < \delta < 1$):*

$$\Pr[X \leq (1-\delta)\mu] \leq \exp\left(-\frac{\delta^2\mu}{2}\right) \tag{11.13}$$

Simplified forms:

- For $\delta \geq 2e - 1$: $\Pr[X \geq (1+\delta)\mu] \leq 2^{-(1+\delta)\mu}$
- For $0 < \delta < 1$: $\Pr[X \leq (1-\delta)\mu] \leq e^{-\delta^2\mu/2}$

11.5.2 Proof Technique

The proof uses the moment generating function method:

1. Apply Markov's inequality to e^{tX}
2. Bound $M_X(t)$ using independence
3. Optimize over parameter t

Detailed proof for upper tail:

$$\Pr[X \geq (1+\delta)\mu] = \Pr[e^{tX} \geq e^{t(1+\delta)\mu}] \tag{11.14}$$

$$\leq \frac{\mathbb{E}[e^{tX}]}{e^{t(1+\delta)\mu}} \quad \text{(Markov)} \tag{11.15}$$

$$= \frac{\prod_{i=1}^{n} \mathbb{E}[e^{tX_i}]}{e^{t(1+\delta)\mu}} \quad \text{(Independence)} \tag{11.16}$$

Optimizing over t yields the bound.

11.5.3 Applications to Algorithm Analysis

Application 1: Randomized Routing

- n packets, each choosing random path
- Expected load on any edge: μ
- $\Pr[\text{edge load} > (1+\delta)\mu] \leq \exp(-\delta^2\mu/3)$
- Setting $\delta = \sqrt{3 \ln n/\mu}$ gives high probability bound

Application 2: Hash Table Chains

```
def analyze_hash_table(n, m):
    # n items, m buckets
    mu = n/m  # expected chain length
    # Probability any chain exceeds (1+delta)*mu
    prob_long_chain = m * exp(-delta**2 * mu/3)
    # Choose delta to make this o(1)
    return sqrt(3*log(m)/mu)
```

Application 3: Random Sampling

- Sample s items from population of n
- Fraction of items with property P is p
- Expected in sample: sp
- $\Pr[|\text{sample count} - sp| > \varepsilon sp] \leq 2\exp(-\varepsilon^2 sp/3)$

11.5.4 Multiplicative Forms

Sometimes more convenient for relative error analysis.

Theorem 11.5.2 (Multiplicative Chernoff). *For $X = \sum X_i$ with $X_i \in \{0, 1\}$ independent:*

$$\Pr[X > (1+\varepsilon)\mu] \leq \left(\frac{e^{\varepsilon}}{(1+\varepsilon)^{1+\varepsilon}}\right)^{\mu} \tag{11.17}$$

$$\Pr[X < (1-\varepsilon)\mu] \leq \left(\frac{e^{-\varepsilon}}{(1-\varepsilon)^{1-\varepsilon}}\right)^{\mu} \tag{11.18}$$

11.5.5 Extensions and Variants

Negative Association: Chernoff bounds hold for negatively associated variables (e.g., sampling without replacement).

Bounded Range Variables: For $X_i \in [0, 1]$ (not just $\{0, 1\}$), same bounds apply.

Poisson Approximation: When events are rare (p small), Poisson distribution provides good approximation.

11.6 Analysis of Randomized Quicksort

11.6.1 Algorithm Description

Randomized quicksort achieves excellent expected performance by randomly selecting pivots.

Algorithm 10 Randomized Quicksort

```
Require: Array A, indices left, right
if left < right then
    pivot_index ← RANDOM(left, right)
    pivot ← A[pivot_index]
    i ← PARTITION(A, left, right, pivot)
    RANDOMIZED-QUICKSORT(A, left, i − 1)
    RANDOMIZED-QUICKSORT(A, i + 1, right)
end if
```

11.6.2 Expected Number of Comparisons

Theorem 11.6.1. *The expected number of comparisons in randomized quicksort is $2n \ln n + O(n)$.*

Proof using indicator random variables. Let the sorted array be $a_1 < a_2 < \cdots < a_n$.

Define indicator: $X_{ij} = 1$ if a_i and a_j are compared, 0 otherwise.

Total comparisons: $X = \sum_{i<j} X_{ij}$

Key Observation: a_i and a_j are compared iff one of them is chosen as pivot before any element between them.

Probability calculation:

$$\Pr[X_{ij} = 1] = \Pr[a_i \text{ or } a_j \text{ chosen first from } \{a_i, a_{i+1}, \ldots, a_j\}] = \frac{2}{j-i+1} \tag{11.19}$$

Expected comparisons:

$$\mathbb{E}[X] = \sum_{i<j} \mathbb{E}[X_{ij}] = \sum_{i<j} \frac{2}{j-i+1} \tag{11.20}$$

$$= \sum_{i=1}^{n-1} \sum_{j=i+1}^{n} \frac{2}{j-i+1} \tag{11.21}$$

$$= \sum_{i=1}^{n-1} \sum_{k=2}^{n-i+1} \frac{2}{k} \quad (\text{where } k = j-i+1) \tag{11.22}$$

$$\leq 2n \sum_{k=2}^{n} \frac{1}{k} \tag{11.23}$$

$$= 2n(H_n - 1) \tag{11.24}$$

$$\approx 2n \ln n \tag{11.25}$$

11.6.3 Concentration of Running Time

While expected time is $O(n \log n)$, we can prove the algorithm rarely deviates significantly.

Theorem 11.6.2 (High Probability Bound). *With probability at least $1 - \frac{1}{n^2}$, randomized quicksort runs in $O(n \log n)$ time.*

Proof sketch.

1. Define "good" pivot: splits array in ratio at least $1:3$
2. Probability of good pivot $\geq \frac{1}{2}$
3. After $O(\log n)$ good pivots, recursion depth is $O(1)$

4. Use Chernoff bound to show we get enough good pivots

Detailed analysis of recursion depth: Let $D(n)$ be the recursion depth for n elements.

- Each good pivot reduces problem size by at least $\frac{1}{4}$
- After k good pivots: size $\leq n \cdot \left(\frac{3}{4}\right)^k$
- Need $k = \log_{4/3} n$ good pivots to reach base case

Let Y_i = number of pivots to get i-th good pivot.

- $\mathbb{E}[Y_i] = 2$ (geometric distribution with $p = \frac{1}{2}$)
- Total pivots $Y = \sum Y_i$
- $\mathbb{E}[Y] = 2 \log_{4/3} n$

By Chernoff bound:

$$\Pr[Y > 4 \log_{4/3} n] \leq \exp\left(-\frac{\log_{4/3} n}{3}\right) \leq \frac{1}{n^2} \tag{11.26}$$

11.6.4 Comparison with Deterministic Algorithms

Advantages of Randomized Quicksort:

1. Simple implementation (no need for median-of-three or other heuristics)
2. Optimal cache performance due to good locality
3. In-place sorting with $O(\log n)$ expected stack space
4. No worst-case inputs (adversarial or accidental)

Comparison with other $O(n \log n)$ algorithms:

- **Heapsort:** Worse cache performance, not stable
- **Mergesort:** Requires $O(n)$ extra space (or complex in-place version)
- **Introsort:** More complex, falls back to heapsort

11.6.5 Tail Bounds and Worst Case

Theorem 11.6.3 (Exponential Tail Bound). *For any constant $c > 2e$:*

$$\Pr[comparisons > cn \ln n] \leq \frac{1}{n^{c-1}} \tag{11.27}$$

This shows that the probability of significantly exceeding expected time decreases polynomially with n.

True worst case: Even with random pivots, worst case is still $O(n^2)$ when:

- Every pivot is minimum or maximum
- Probability: $\left(\frac{2}{n}\right)^{n-1}$ = exponentially small

11.6.6 Practical Optimizations

Hybrid approaches maintaining randomization benefits:

```
def optimized_randomized_quicksort(A, left, right):
    # Small arrays: use insertion sort
    if right - left < CUTOFF:
        insertion_sort(A, left, right)
        return

    # Three-way partitioning for duplicates
    pivot = A[random.randint(left, right)]
    lt, gt = three_way_partition(A, left, right, pivot)

    # Tail recursion optimization
    randomized_quicksort(A, left, lt-1)
    randomized_quicksort(A, gt+1, right)
```

Summary and Key Takeaways

Main Concepts Covered

1. **Expected Running Time Analysis**
   - Linearity of expectation as a fundamental tool
   - Indicator random variables for simplifying complex analyses
   - Variance for understanding performance spread
2. **Randomized Algorithm Types**
   - Las Vegas: always correct, randomized time

   - Monte Carlo: bounded time, probabilistic correctness
   - Trade-offs and conversion techniques

3. **Concentration Inequalities**
   - Hierarchy: Markov $\rightarrow$ Chebyshev $\rightarrow$ Chernoff
   - Exponential bounds for rare events
   - Applications to algorithm analysis

4. **Chernoff Bounds**
   - Tight bounds for sums of independent variables
   - Multiplicative forms for relative error
   - Wide applicability in randomized algorithms

5. **Case Study: Randomized Quicksort**
   - Expected $O(n \log n)$ with simple random pivot
   - High probability bounds using concentration inequalities
   - Practical advantages over deterministic alternatives

When to Use Probabilistic Analysis

- Input is genuinely random or unknown
- Algorithm makes random choices
- Worst-case is too pessimistic for practical use
- Need to analyze average behavior over many executions
- Dealing with large-scale systems where statistical behavior dominates

Common Pitfalls and Misconceptions

1. **Independence assumptions:** Many analyses assume independence; verify this holds
2. **Expected vs. typical:** Expected value may not be typical (e.g., bimodal distributions)
3. **Tail behavior matters:** Rare bad events can dominate in critical systems

4. **Randomness quality:** Theoretical analysis assumes perfect randomness

5. **Adversarial inputs:** Randomization helps only if adversary can't predict random choices

Exercises

1. **Basic Probability:** Analyze expected comparisons in randomized binary search tree insertion.

2. **Las Vegas Design:** Convert the Monte Carlo primality test to a Las Vegas algorithm given a certificate verifier.

3. **Chernoff Application:** In a hash table with n items and n buckets, bound the probability that any bucket has more than $\frac{\log n}{\log \log n}$ items.

4. **Quicksort Variant:** Analyze randomized quicksort with "median-of-three" random pivots.

5. **Concentration Challenge:** Prove that for randomized quicksort, $\Pr[\text{time} > 10n \ln n] < \frac{1}{n^9}$.

Further Reading

- Motwani & Raghavan: *Randomized Algorithms* – Comprehensive treatment
- Mitzenmacher & Upfal: *Probability and Computing* – Modern approach with applications
- Dubhashi & Panconesi: *Concentration of Measure for the Analysis of Randomized Algorithms*
- Original papers: Hoare (1961) on quicksort, Rabin (1980) on primality testing

Historical Notes

The probabilistic analysis of algorithms began with the average-case analysis of sorting algorithms in the 1960s. The development of Las Vegas and Monte Carlo algorithm classifications emerged from the study of primality testing in the 1970s. The systematic use of concentration inequalities in algorithm analysis was pioneered by researchers in the 1980s and 1990s, with Chernoff bounds becoming a standard tool. The analysis of randomized quicksort presented here combines classical techniques from Hoare and modern probabilistic tools, demonstrating the evolution of the field.

Chapter 12

Smoothed Analysis

Introduction

Traditional complexity analysis has long relied on worst-case bounds to provide guarantees about algorithm performance. However, many algorithms that perform exceptionally well in practice exhibit poor worst-case complexity. This discrepancy between theoretical predictions and practical observations has motivated the development of alternative analytical frameworks. Smoothed analysis, introduced by Spielman and Teng in 2001, offers a compelling middle ground between worst-case and average-case analysis, providing insights into why certain algorithms work well in practice despite pessimistic worst-case bounds.

12.1 Limitations of Worst-Case Analysis

12.1.1 The Pessimism Problem

Worst-case analysis, while providing absolute guarantees, often yields overly pessimistic bounds that fail to reflect typical algorithm behavior. Consider the simplex algorithm for linear programming: despite its exponential worst-case complexity, it routinely solves problems with millions of variables in practice. This disconnect reveals fundamental limitations in worst-case analysis:

1. Pathological Inputs Are Rare The inputs that trigger worst-case behavior are often highly contrived and unlikely to occur in practical applications. For instance, the exponential examples for simplex require carefully constructed constraint matrices that are virtually impossible to encounter naturally.

2. Ignoring Input Distribution Worst-case analysis makes no assumptions about input distribution, treating all inputs as equally likely. In reality, practical inputs often exhibit structure and patterns that algorithms can exploit effectively.

3. Brittle Complexity Bounds Small perturbations to worst-case inputs often dramatically improve performance, suggesting that the worst-case scenarios occupy an insignificantly small portion of the input space.

12.1.2 Examples of Misleading Worst-Case Bounds

- **Quicksort:** Despite $\mathcal{O}(n^2)$ worst-case time complexity, quicksort's $\mathcal{O}(n \log n)$ expected performance and excellent cache behavior make it the sorting algorithm of choice in many standard libraries.
- ***k*-means Clustering:** The Lloyd's algorithm for k-means can require exponentially many iterations in the worst case, yet typically converges within a polynomial number of iterations on real data.
- **Interior Point Methods:** While theoretically requiring $\mathcal{O}(n^3)$ operations per iteration, practical implementations often converge much faster due to problem structure.

12.1.3 The Need for Alternative Frameworks

These limitations motivate the search for analytical frameworks that:

- Provide meaningful performance guarantees
- Explain practical algorithm behavior
- Avoid the pessimism of worst-case analysis
- Maintain mathematical rigor

12.2 Introduction to Smoothed Analysis

12.2.1 Core Concept

Smoothed analysis measures algorithm performance on slightly perturbed versions of worst-case inputs. Given an input x, we add small random perturbations to obtain $\tilde{x}$, then analyze the expected running time over these perturbations. This approach captures the intuition that real-world data contains small amounts of random noise that prevent worst-case behavior.

12.2.2 Mathematical Framework

Definition 12.2.1 (Smoothed Complexity)**.** Let A be an algorithm with input space $\mathcal{X}$. For any input $x \in \mathcal{X}$ and perturbation parameter $\sigma > 0$, the smoothed complexity of A is:

$$\text{smoothed-complexity}(n, \sigma) = \max_{x \in \mathcal{X}} \mathbb{E}[T(A, \tilde{x})]$$

where $\tilde{x}$ is obtained by perturbing x with noise of magnitude σ, and $T(A, \tilde{x})$ denotes the running time of A on input $\tilde{x}$.

Perturbation Models

1. **Gaussian Perturbations:** Each component of x is perturbed by adding Gaussian noise:

$$\tilde{x}_i = x_i + \mathcal{N}(0, \sigma^2)$$

2. **Relative Perturbations:** Components are multiplied by random factors:

$$\tilde{x}_i = x_i \cdot (1 + \epsilon_i)$$

   where ϵ_i is drawn uniformly from $[-\sigma, \sigma]$.

3. **Discrete Perturbations:** For combinatorial problems, flip each bit with probability σ or swap elements with probability proportional to σ.

12.2.3 Properties of Smoothed Analysis

Interpolation Property Smoothed complexity interpolates between worst-case and average-case:

- As $\sigma \to 0$: Smoothed complexity approaches worst-case complexity
- As $\sigma \to \infty$: Smoothed complexity approaches average-case complexity

Stability Under Perturbation Algorithms with good smoothed complexity are robust to small input changes, explaining their practical reliability.

Realistic Modeling The perturbation model captures measurement errors, rounding errors, and natural variability in real-world data.

12.2.4 Smoothed Analysis Techniques

1. Probabilistic Arguments

Analyze the probability that perturbed inputs retain worst-case properties:

$$\mathbb{P}[\tilde{x} \text{ is bad}] \leq \epsilon(\sigma)$$

where $\epsilon(\sigma)$ decreases rapidly with σ.

2. Geometric Arguments

Exploit the geometry of the input space to show that worst-case inputs form low-dimensional manifolds easily avoided by perturbations.

3. Condition Number Analysis

Relate algorithm performance to problem conditioning, then bound the probability of ill-conditioning under perturbation.

12.3 Simplex Algorithm Case Study

12.3.1 Background: The Simplex Method

The simplex algorithm solves linear programs of the form:

$$\begin{aligned} \text{maximize} \quad & c^T x && (12.1) \\ \text{subject to} \quad & Ax \leq b && (12.2) \\ & x \geq 0 && (12.3) \end{aligned}$$

Despite Klee-Minty examples showing exponential worst-case behavior, simplex typically requires only $\mathcal{O}(m)$ to $\mathcal{O}(m^2)$ pivots for m constraints in practice.

12.3.2 Smoothed Analysis of Simplex

Theorem 12.3.1 (Spielman-Teng 2004). *For the shadow vertex simplex algorithm with Gaussian perturbations of variance σ^2 to the constraint matrix A and objective vector c, the expected number of pivot steps is polynomial in n, m, and $1/\sigma$.*

Proof Sketch. 1. **Geometric Interpretation:** The simplex algorithm traces edges of the feasible polyhedron. Worst-case examples create polyhedra with exponentially many edges visited by the algorithm.

2. **Perturbation Effect:** Small perturbations to constraints slightly shift hyperplane positions, dramatically altering the polyhedron's combinatorial structure.

3. **Shadow Projection:** The shadow vertex method projects the polyhedron onto a 2D plane defined by the original and perturbed objective functions. The number of pivots equals the number of edges in this shadow.

4. **Probabilistic Bound:** Using geometric probability, bound the expected number of shadow edges:

$$\mathbb{E}[\text{number of edges}] \leq \mathcal{O}\left(\right)\left(\frac{m^2 \cdot n \cdot \log(n)}{\sigma}\right)$$

5. **Key Insight:** Degenerate vertices (where many constraints are tight) cause exponential behavior but are destroyed by arbitrarily small perturbations.

12.3.3 Implications for Practice

Pivot Rule Independence Smoothed analysis explains why various pivot rules (Dantzig's rule, steepest edge, random edge) all perform well in practice.

Degeneracy Handling Practical LP solvers use perturbation techniques (like adding small random values to constraints) that essentially implement smoothed analysis insights.

Preprocessing Benefits Standard preprocessing steps (scaling, equilibration) can be viewed as controlled perturbations that improve smoothed complexity.

12.4 Applications and Implications

12.4.1 Successful Applications

1. Local Search Algorithms

- **2-opt for TSP:** Smoothed analysis shows polynomial convergence for Euclidean instances with perturbed coordinates
- **Lloyd's Algorithm for k-means:** Polynomial smoothed complexity explains practical performance

2. **Numerical Linear Algebra**
   - **Gaussian Elimination:** Smoothed analysis of growth factors explains stability without pivoting in practice
   - **Conjugate Gradient Method:** Smoothed condition numbers bound iteration counts
3. **Computational Geometry**
   - **Convex Hull Algorithms:** Smoothed complexity is $\mathcal{O}(n \log n)$ despite $\mathcal{O}(n^2)$ worst case for certain algorithms
   - **Delaunay Triangulation:** Smoothed analysis explains the rarity of degenerate configurations
4. **Machine Learning**
   - **Perceptron Algorithm:** Smoothed margin bounds explain generalization despite worst-case exponential convergence
   - **Support Vector Machines:** Smoothed analysis of kernel matrix conditioning

12.4.2 Theoretical Implications

Complexity Class Connections Smoothed analysis suggests a refined complexity hierarchy where problems may be:

- Hard in the worst case but easy in the smoothed case (like LP)
- Hard in both worst and smoothed cases (likely for NP-complete problems)

Algorithm Design Principles

1. Algorithms robust to perturbations often have good smoothed complexity
2. Randomization can simulate perturbations, converting smoothed to expected complexity
3. Preprocessing that adds controlled noise can improve practical performance

Explaining Heuristic Success Many successful heuristics implicitly exploit smoothed complexity:

- Random restarts escape worst-case configurations
- Noise injection prevents cycling in local search
- Regularization in optimization adds beneficial perturbations

12.4.3 Limitations and Criticisms

1. **Model Selection:** Choosing appropriate perturbation models and magnitudes requires domain knowledge.
2. **Analysis Difficulty:** Smoothed analysis often requires sophisticated probability theory and can be technically challenging.
3. **Worst-Case Guarantees:** For safety-critical applications, worst-case bounds remain necessary despite smoothed analysis insights.
4. **Input Assumptions:** The perturbation model may not apply to highly structured or discrete inputs.

12.5 Comparison with Average-Case Analysis

12.5.1 Fundamental Differences

Input Distribution Assumptions

- **Average-case:** Assumes specific input distribution (often uniform)
- **Smoothed:** Makes minimal assumptions, only requiring small perturbations

Robustness of Results

- **Average-case:** Highly sensitive to distribution choice
- **Smoothed:** Robust across different perturbation models

Adversarial Perspective

- **Average-case:** Nature generates inputs randomly
- **Smoothed:** Adversary chooses worst input, then nature adds small noise

12.5.2 Comparative Analysis Framework

Aspect	Worst-Case	Average-Case	Smoothed
Pessimism	Very High	Very Low	Moderate
Assumptions	None	Strong (distribution)	Weak (perturbation)
Practical Relevance	Low	Variable	High
Analysis Difficulty	Moderate	High	Very High
Guarantee Type	Absolute	Probabilistic	Probabilistic

Table 12.1: Comparison of complexity analysis frameworks

12.5.3 When to Use Each Framework

Worst-Case Analysis

- Safety-critical systems
- Adversarial environments
- Real-time systems with hard deadlines
- Theoretical complexity classifications

Average-Case Analysis

- Well-understood input distributions
- Random input generation
- Cryptographic applications
- Probabilistic algorithms

Smoothed Analysis

- Explaining practical algorithm performance
- Numerical algorithms with measurement error
- Optimization problems with real-world data
- Understanding heuristic effectiveness

12.5.4 Relationships and Hierarchies

Theorem 12.5.1. *For any algorithm A:*

$$\textit{average-case complexity} \leq \textit{smoothed complexity} \leq \textit{worst-case complexity}$$

Separation Examples

1. **Simplex Algorithm:**
   - Worst-case: Exponential
   - Smoothed: Polynomial
   - Average-case: Linear to quadratic
2. **Quicksort with Median-of-Three:**
   - Worst-case: $\mathcal{O}(n^2)$
   - Smoothed: $\mathcal{O}(n \log n)$ with high probability
   - Average-case: $\mathcal{O}(n \log n)$

12.5.5 Hybrid Approaches

Smoothed Average-Case Analyze average performance over smoothed inputs, combining both frameworks' benefits.

Parameterized Smoothed Analysis Vary perturbation magnitude to obtain a complexity spectrum from worst to average case.

Instance-Optimal Smoothed Analysis Find the minimum perturbation needed to achieve good performance for each input.

12.6 Exercises

Theoretical Exercises

Exercise 12.6.1. Prove that for any algorithm with worst-case complexity $W(n)$ and average-case complexity $A(n)$, the smoothed complexity $S(n, \sigma)$ satisfies: $A(n) \leq S(n, \sigma) \leq W(n)$.

Exercise 12.6.2. Consider the following simple sorting algorithm: repeatedly find the minimum element and move it to the front. Analyze its smoothed complexity when each element is perturbed by $\pm\epsilon$ uniformly at random.

Exercise 12.6.3. Show that if an algorithm has polynomial smoothed complexity for Gaussian perturbations, it also has polynomial smoothed complexity for uniform perturbations in a bounded range.

Exercise 12.6.4. Prove that the probability of a random $n \times n$ matrix being singular is 0, explaining why Gaussian elimination rarely needs pivoting in practice.

Applied Exercises

Exercise 12.6.5. Implement the simplex algorithm and experimentally verify its smoothed complexity by running it on perturbed linear programs.

Exercise 12.6.6. Design a perturbation scheme for the Boolean satisfiability problem and analyze the smoothed complexity of the DPLL algorithm.

Exercise 12.6.7. Consider the k-means clustering algorithm. Experimentally investigate how the number of iterations depends on the perturbation magnitude σ.

Exercise 12.6.8. Analyze the smoothed complexity of finding the closest pair of points in 2D when point coordinates are perturbed by Gaussian noise.

Advanced Exercises

Exercise 12.6.9. Develop a smoothed analysis for the traveling salesman problem with the 2-opt local search heuristic.

Exercise 12.6.10. Investigate the relationship between smoothed complexity and the condition number of optimization problems.

Exercise 12.6.11. Propose a perturbation model for graph problems and analyze the smoothed complexity of a graph coloring heuristic.

Exercise 12.6.12. Explore connections between smoothed analysis and regularization in machine learning algorithms.

12.7 Bibliographic Notes

Smoothed analysis was introduced by Spielman and Teng in their seminal 2004 paper "Smoothed Analysis of Algorithms: Why the Simplex Algorithm Usually Takes Polynomial Time" (*Journal of the ACM*, 51(3):385–463). This work earned them the Gödel Prize in 2008 and fundamentally changed how we think about algorithm analysis.

The original motivation came from observing the simplex algorithm's excellent practical performance despite exponential worst-case examples constructed by Klee and Minty (1972). Earlier attempts to explain this phenomenon through average-case analysis by Borgwardt (1982) and Smale (1983) required strong distributional assumptions.

Subsequent developments include:

- Spielman and Teng (2003): Smoothed analysis of condition numbers
- Arthur and Vassilvitskii (2006): Smoothed analysis of k-means algorithm
- Manthey and Reischuk (2007): Smoothed analysis of binary search trees
- Röglin and Vöcking (2007): Smoothed analysis of integer programming

The framework has been extended to multiobjective optimization (Brunsch and Röglin, 2013), online algorithms (Becchetti et al., 2006), and machine learning (Blum and Dunagan, 2002).

For comprehensive surveys, see:

- Spielman and Teng (2009): "Smoothed Analysis: An Attempt to Explain the Behavior of Algorithms in Practice"
- Röglin (2012): "The Complexity of Nash Equilibria, Local Optima, and Pareto-Optimal Solutions"

12.8 Summary

Smoothed analysis provides a powerful framework for understanding the typical behavior of algorithms, bridging the gap between overly pessimistic worst-case bounds and potentially unrealistic average-case assumptions. By analyzing performance on slightly perturbed inputs, it captures the robustness and practical efficiency of algorithms that work well in practice.

Key takeaways:

- Smoothed analysis explains why algorithms like simplex perform well despite poor worst-case complexity
- The framework requires only minimal assumptions about input perturbations
- It provides a mathematical foundation for understanding the success of many heuristics

- The technique has broad applications across algorithms, numerical analysis, and machine learning

As we continue to develop algorithms for increasingly complex real-world problems, smoothed analysis offers valuable insights into which approaches will succeed in practice, beyond what traditional complexity measures alone can provide.

Part V

Complexity in Specific Domains

Chapter 13

Data Structure Complexity

Introduction

Data structures form the backbone of efficient algorithm design. The choice of an appropriate data structure can mean the difference between a solution that scales gracefully and one that becomes impractical for large inputs. This chapter provides a comprehensive analysis of fundamental and advanced data structures, examining their time and space complexity characteristics for various operations.

We'll explore how theoretical complexity bounds translate into practical performance, investigate the tradeoffs between different implementations, and establish lower bounds that inform us about the fundamental limits of what's achievable. By the end of this chapter, you'll have a deep understanding of when and why to choose specific data structures based on their complexity profiles.

13.1 Fundamental Data Structure Operations

13.1.1 Core Operations and Their Significance

Every data structure supports a set of fundamental operations that define its utility. Understanding the complexity of these operations is crucial for making informed design decisions.

Primary Operations:

- **Access/Search**: Retrieving an element by key or value
- **Insertion**: Adding a new element
- **Deletion**: Removing an existing element
- **Update**: Modifying an existing element
- **Traversal**: Visiting all elements in a specific order

Secondary Operations:

- **Merge**: Combining two structures
- **Split**: Dividing a structure into parts
- **Min/Max**: Finding extreme elements
- **Predecessor/Successor**: Finding neighboring elements in an ordering

13.1.2 Complexity Notation and Conventions

When analyzing data structures with n elements:

- **Time Complexity**: Measured in elementary operations (comparisons, assignments, arithmetic)
- **Space Complexity**: Additional memory beyond storing the data itself
- **Amortized Complexity**: Average cost over a sequence of operations

Definition 13.1.1 (Complexity Classifications)**.** For a data structure with n elements:

$$\text{Worst-case: } \mathcal{O}(f(n)) \text{ – Maximum time for any input} \tag{13.1}$$
$$\text{Average-case: } \Theta(g(n)) \text{ – Expected time for random input} \tag{13.2}$$
$$\text{Amortized: } \mathcal{O}(h(n)) \text{ – Average over a sequence of operations} \tag{13.3}$$

13.1.3 The Complexity Tradeoff Triangle

Data structures typically involve tradeoffs between:

1. **Time efficiency** for different operations
2. **Space efficiency**
3. **Implementation simplicity**

No single data structure excels at everything—understanding these tradeoffs is essential for optimal selection.

13.2 Arrays, Lists, and Basic Structures

13.2.1 Static Arrays

Structure: Contiguous memory allocation with fixed size.

Table 13.1: Static Array Complexity Analysis

Operation	Time Complexity	Space Complexity
Access by index	$\mathcal{O}(1)$	–
Search (unsorted)	$\mathcal{O}(n)$	$\mathcal{O}(1)$
Search (sorted)	$\mathcal{O}(\log n)$	$\mathcal{O}(1)$
Insertion at end	$\mathcal{O}(1)$*	–
Insertion at position	$\mathcal{O}(n)$	$\mathcal{O}(1)$
Deletion	$\mathcal{O}(n)$	$\mathcal{O}(1)$

*Assuming space available

Memory Characteristics:

- Cache-friendly due to spatial locality
- Predictable memory access patterns
- Overhead: $\mathcal{O}(1)$ beyond data storage

13.2.2 Dynamic Arrays (Vectors)

Structure: Resizable arrays with geometric growth strategy.

Theorem 13.2.1 (Amortized Insertion Time). *For a dynamic array with growth factor $\alpha > 1$, the amortized time complexity of insertion is $\mathcal{O}(1)$.*

Proof. Using the accounting method: Charge 3 units per insertion.

- 1 unit for actual insertion
- 2 units saved for future copying

When the array of size n is full and must be resized to αn:

- Cost of copying: n units
- Credits accumulated: $2n$ units (from n insertions)
- Net cost: $n - 2n = -n$ units (surplus)

Therefore, each insertion has amortized cost $\mathcal{O}(1)$.

13.2.3 Linked Lists

Singly Linked List

Structure: `Node: [data | next] [data | next] ... null`

Table 13.2: Singly Linked List Complexity

Operation	Time Complexity	Notes
Access at index	$\mathcal{O}(n)$	Sequential traversal required
Search	$\mathcal{O}(n)$	No random access
Insert at head	$\mathcal{O}(1)$	Simple pointer update
Insert at position	$\mathcal{O}(n)$	Requires traversal
Delete at head	$\mathcal{O}(1)$	Update head pointer
Delete at position	$\mathcal{O}(n)$	Requires traversal

Doubly Linked List

Additional backward pointers enable:

- Bidirectional traversal: $\mathcal{O}(1)$ per step
- Deletion given node reference: $\mathcal{O}(1)$
- Space overhead: 2 pointers per node vs. 1

13.2.4 Skip Lists

Structure: Probabilistic data structure with multiple linked list levels.

Theorem 13.2.2 (Skip List Expected Complexity). *For a skip list with n elements and probability parameter $p = 1/2$:*

$$\mathbb{E}[Search] = \mathcal{O}(\log n) \tag{13.4}$$

$$\mathbb{E}[Insert] = \mathcal{O}(\log n) \tag{13.5}$$

$$\mathbb{E}[Delete] = \mathcal{O}(\log n) \tag{13.6}$$

$$\mathbb{E}[Space] = \mathcal{O}(n) \tag{13.7}$$

Analysis:

- Expected number of levels: $\mathcal{O}(\log n)$
- Probability of element at level i: p^i
- Expected nodes per level: $n/2^i$

13.3 Trees: BSTs, AVL, Red-Black Trees

13.3.1 Binary Search Trees (BST)

Table 13.3: BST Complexity Analysis

Operation	Best Case	Average Case	Worst Case
Search	$\mathcal{O}(\log n)$	$\mathcal{O}(\log n)$	$\mathcal{O}(n)$
Insert	$\mathcal{O}(\log n)$	$\mathcal{O}(\log n)$	$\mathcal{O}(n)$
Delete	$\mathcal{O}(\log n)$	$\mathcal{O}(\log n)$	$\mathcal{O}(n)$

Theorem 13.3.1 (Average BST Height). *For a randomly built BST with n nodes, the expected height is $\mathcal{O}(\log n)$.*

13.3.2 AVL Trees

Definition 13.3.1 (AVL Balance Invariant). For every node in an AVL tree, the heights of its left and right subtrees differ by at most 1.

Theorem 13.3.2 (AVL Height Bound). *An AVL tree with n nodes has height h satisfying:*

$$h \leq 1.44 \log_2(n+2) - 0.328$$

Table 13.4: AVL Tree Complexity Guarantees

Operation	Time Complexity	Rotations Required
Search	$\mathcal{O}(\log n)$	0
Insert	$\mathcal{O}(\log n)$	≤ 2
Delete	$\mathcal{O}(\log n)$	$\leq \log n$

13.3.3 Red-Black Trees

Definition 13.3.2 (Red-Black Properties).

1. Every node is either red or black
2. The root is black
3. All leaves (NIL) are black
4. Red nodes have black children

5. All paths from root to leaves have the same black count

Theorem 13.3.3 (Red-Black Height Bound). *A red-black tree with n internal nodes has height at most $2\log_2(n+1)$.*

Proof. Let $bh(x)$ denote the black-height of node x. The subtree rooted at x contains at least $2^{bh(x)} - 1$ internal nodes. Since at least half the nodes on any path from root to leaf are black, $bh(root) \geq h/2$. Therefore:

$$n \geq 2^{h/2} - 1 \implies h \leq 2\log_2(n+1)$$

13.3.4 Splay Trees

Theorem 13.3.4 (Splay Tree Amortized Bound). *The amortized time for any splay tree operation is $\mathcal{O}(\log n)$.*

Potential Function Analysis: Define $\Phi = \sum_{x \in T} \log(\text{size}(x))$
For splay operations:

- Zig: $\mathcal{O}(1)$ amortized
- Zig-zig: $\mathcal{O}(1)$ amortized
- Zig-zag: $\mathcal{O}(1)$ amortized
- Total splay cost: $\mathcal{O}(\log n)$ amortized

13.4 Hash Tables and Collision Resolution

13.4.1 Hash Table Fundamentals

Definition 13.4.1 (Load Factor). For a hash table with n items and m buckets, the load factor is:

$$\alpha = \frac{n}{m}$$

Ideal Complexity (with perfect hash function):

- Search: $\mathcal{O}(1)$ expected
- Insert: $\mathcal{O}(1)$ expected
- Delete: $\mathcal{O}(1)$ expected

13.4.2 Collision Resolution: Chaining

Theorem 13.4.1 (Chaining Performance). *For a hash table with chaining and load factor α:*

$$\mathbb{E}[\textit{Successful search}] = \mathcal{O}\left(1 + \alpha/2\right) \tag{13.8}$$

$$\mathbb{E}[\textit{Unsuccessful search}] = \mathcal{O}\left(1 + \alpha\right) \tag{13.9}$$

With $\alpha = \mathcal{O}(1)$, all operations are $\mathcal{O}(1)$ expected.

13.4.3 Open Addressing

Linear Probing

Probe sequence: $h(k), h(k) + 1, h(k) + 2, \ldots$

Theorem 13.4.2 (Linear Probing Expected Probes). *Under uniform hashing assumption:*

$$\mathbb{E}[\textit{Successful search}] = \frac{1}{2}\left(1 + \frac{1}{1-\alpha}\right) \tag{13.10}$$

$$\mathbb{E}[\textit{Unsuccessful search}] = \frac{1}{2}\left(1 + \frac{1}{(1-\alpha)^2}\right) \tag{13.11}$$

Double Hashing

Probe sequence: $h_1(k) + i \cdot h_2(k) \bmod m$

Theorem 13.4.3 (Double Hashing Performance). *Expected number of probes:*

$$\mathbb{E}[\textit{Successful search}] = \frac{1}{\alpha} \ln\left(\frac{1}{1-\alpha}\right) \tag{13.12}$$

$$\mathbb{E}[\textit{Unsuccessful search}] = \frac{1}{1-\alpha} \tag{13.13}$$

13.4.4 Dynamic Resizing

Algorithm 11 Dynamic Hash Table Resizing

```
if α > 0.75 then
    Allocate new table of size 2m
    Rehash all elements to new table
    Update table reference
else if α < 0.25 then
    Allocate new table of size m/2
    Rehash all elements to new table
    Update table reference
end if
```

Amortized cost: $\mathcal{O}(1)$ per operation

13.4.5 Universal and Perfect Hashing

Definition 13.4.2 (Universal Hash Family)**.** A family $\mathcal{H}$ of hash functions is universal if for any distinct keys x, y:

$$\Pr_{h \in \mathcal{H}}[h(x) = h(y)] \leq \frac{1}{m}$$

Theorem 13.4.4 (Perfect Hashing (FKS))**.** *For a static set of n keys, we can construct a perfect hash table with:*

- *Space:* $\mathcal{O}(n)$
- *Worst-case lookup:* $\mathcal{O}(1)$
- *Expected construction time:* $\mathcal{O}(n)$

13.5 Advanced Structures: B-trees, Tries

13.5.1 B-Trees

Definition 13.5.1 (B-tree of order m)**.** A B-tree of order m satisfies:

1. Each node has at most m children
2. Each internal node has at least $\lceil m/2 \rceil$ children (except root)
3. All leaves are at the same level
4. A node with k children contains $k - 1$ keys

Theorem 13.5.1 (B-tree Height). *A B-tree with n keys and minimum degree $t = \lceil m/2 \rceil$ has height:*

$$h \leq \log_t \left(\frac{n+1}{2} \right)$$

Table 13.5: B-tree Complexity (in disk accesses)

Operation	**Disk Reads**	**Disk Writes**
Search	$\mathcal{O}(\log_m n)$	0
Insert	$\mathcal{O}(\log_m n)$	$\mathcal{O}(\log_m n)$
Delete	$\mathcal{O}(\log_m n)$	$\mathcal{O}(\log_m n)$

13.5.2 B+ Trees

Modifications from B-tree:

- All data stored in leaves
- Internal nodes store only keys
- Leaves linked for sequential access

Advantages:

- Better cache utilization for internal nodes
- Efficient range queries: $\mathcal{O}(\log_m n + k)$ for k results
- Sequential access: $\mathcal{O}(n/B)$ I/Os for full scan

13.5.3 Tries (Prefix Trees)

Theorem 13.5.2 (Standard Trie Complexity). *For n strings of maximum length m over alphabet Σ:*

$$\text{Search: } \mathcal{O}(m) \tag{13.14}$$
$$\text{Insert: } \mathcal{O}(m) \tag{13.15}$$
$$\text{Delete: } \mathcal{O}(m) \tag{13.16}$$
$$\text{Space: } \mathcal{O}(|\Sigma| \cdot n \cdot m) \text{ worst-case} \tag{13.17}$$

13.5.4 Compressed Tries (Patricia Trees)

Space Optimization:

- Compress chains of single-child nodes
- Space: $\mathcal{O}(n)$ nodes for n strings
- Height: $\mathcal{O}(n)$ worst-case, $\mathcal{O}(\log n)$ expected for random strings

13.5.5 Suffix Trees

Theorem 13.5.3 (Suffix Tree Construction). *A suffix tree for a string of length n can be constructed in:*

- *Naive algorithm:* $\mathcal{O}(n^2)$
- *Ukkonen's algorithm:* $\mathcal{O}(n)$
- *Space complexity:* $\mathcal{O}(n)$

Applications and Complexity:

- Pattern matching: $\mathcal{O}(m + occ)$ for pattern of length m
- Longest common substring: $\mathcal{O}(n)$
- All palindromes: $\mathcal{O}(n)$

13.6 Lower Bounds for Comparison-Based Operations

13.6.1 The Decision Tree Model

Theorem 13.6.1 (Decision Tree Lower Bound). *Any comparison-based algorithm for a problem with N possible outcomes requires at least $\lceil \log_2 N \rceil$ comparisons in the worst case.*

Proof. A decision tree representing the algorithm has:

- N leaves (one per outcome)
- Height h with at most 2^h leaves

Therefore: $2^h \geq N \implies h \geq \lceil \log_2 N \rceil$

13.6.2 Searching Lower Bound

Theorem 13.6.2 (Search Lower Bound). *Finding a specific element among n sorted elements requires at least $\lceil \log_2 n \rceil$ comparisons.*

Proof. There are $N = n$ possible positions for the element. By the decision tree lower bound, we need at least $\lceil \log_2 n \rceil$ comparisons. Binary search achieves this bound, hence it is optimal.

13.6.3 Sorting Lower Bound

Theorem 13.6.3 (Sorting Lower Bound). *Sorting n elements using comparisons requires at least $\lceil \log_2(n!) \rceil$ comparisons.*

Proof. Using Stirling's approximation:

$$\log_2(n!) = \sum_{i=1}^{n} \log_2(i) \tag{13.18}$$
$$\geq \int_1^n \log_2(x)\,dx \tag{13.19}$$
$$= n\log_2(n) - n\log_2(e) + \mathcal{O}(1) \tag{13.20}$$
$$\approx n\log_2(n) - 1.443n \tag{13.21}$$

Therefore, $\Omega(n \log n)$ comparisons are required.

13.6.4 Dynamic Predecessor Problem

Theorem 13.6.4 (Cell-Probe Lower Bound). *In the cell-probe model with universe size U and n elements:*

$$\textit{Query time} \times \textit{Update time} = \Omega\left(\frac{\log n}{\log\log n}\right)$$

This establishes a fundamental tradeoff between query and update efficiency.

13.6.5 Lower Bounds for Specific Operations

Membership (Dictionary Problem): Information-theoretic lower bound: $\log_2\binom{U}{n}$ bits required, where $\binom{U}{n}$ is the number of n-subsets of universe U.
Priority Queue Operations:

- Extract-min with comparisons: $\Omega(\log n)$
- Decrease-key in binary heap: $\Omega(\log n)$
- Fibonacci heap achieves $\mathcal{O}(1)$ amortized decrease-key

Summary and Key Insights

This chapter has explored the complexity landscape of fundamental and advanced data structures. Key takeaways include:

1. **No Universal Solution:** Each data structure excels in specific scenarios. Arrays provide $\mathcal{O}(1)$ random access but $\mathcal{O}(n)$ insertion; trees balance operations at $\mathcal{O}(\log n)$; hash tables achieve $\mathcal{O}(1)$ average-case but with no ordering.

2. **Amortized vs. Worst-case:** Dynamic arrays and splay trees demonstrate how amortized analysis reveals efficiency in practice despite occasional expensive operations.

3. **Balance Maintenance Cost:** Self-balancing trees (AVL, Red-Black) trade implementation complexity and constant factors for guaranteed $\mathcal{O}(\log n)$ operations.

4. **Cache Effects Matter:** B-trees optimize for disk access patterns; arrays benefit from CPU cache locality—complexity analysis must consider memory hierarchy.

5. **Theoretical Limits:** Lower bounds prove certain problems have inherent complexity limits, regardless of algorithmic cleverness.

6. **Space-Time Tradeoffs:** Hash tables trade space for time; compressed tries trade preprocessing for query efficiency.

Understanding these complexity characteristics enables informed decisions when selecting data structures for real-world applications. The next chapter will explore how these structures perform in the specific context of sorting and searching algorithms.

Exercises

1. **Analysis Problem:** Prove that in a red-black tree with n internal nodes, the height h satisfies $h \leq 2\log_2(n+1)$.

2. **Design Problem:** Design a data structure supporting insert, delete, and find-median operations, all in $\mathcal{O}(\log n)$ time.

3. **Lower Bound Problem:** Prove that any comparison-based algorithm for finding both minimum and maximum of n elements requires at least $\lceil 3n/2 \rceil - 2$ comparisons.

4. **Implementation Analysis:** Implement a skip list and empirically verify that search time is $\mathcal{O}(\log n)$ with high probability.

5. **Tradeoff Exploration:** For a workload of 70% searches, 20% insertions, and 10% deletions, analyze whether an AVL tree or red-black tree would be more efficient.

Further Reading

- Cormen, T. H., et al. *Introduction to Algorithms* – Comprehensive coverage of data structures
- Tarjan, R. E. "Amortized Computational Complexity" – Foundational work on amortized analysis
- Fredman, M. L., & Saks, M. E. "The cell probe complexity of dynamic data structures" – Lower bounds
- Sleator, D. D., & Tarjan, R. E. "Self-adjusting binary search trees" – Original splay tree paper
- Bayer, R., & McCreight, E. "Organization and maintenance of large ordered indices" – B-tree introduction

Chapter 14

Sorting and Searching Complexity

Sorting and searching form the foundation of algorithmic problem-solving, appearing as subroutines in countless applications from database management to computational geometry. This chapter explores the fundamental limits of these operations, examines algorithms that achieve theoretical bounds, and investigates specialized techniques that exploit problem structure to transcend traditional limitations.

14.1 Comparison-Based Sorting Lower Bound

14.1.1 The Decision Tree Model

Understanding the inherent complexity of sorting requires establishing a computational model that captures the essence of how sorting algorithms operate. The comparison-based model provides this framework.

Definition 14.1.1 (Comparison-Based Sorting). A *comparison-based sorting algorithm* is one that determines the sorted order of input elements solely through pairwise comparisons of the form "is $a[i] \leq a[j]$?" where the only information gained about elements comes from these binary comparisons.

To analyze the fundamental limits of such algorithms, we employ the decision tree model. In this model:

- Each internal node represents a comparison between two elements
- Each edge represents the outcome of a comparison (true or false)
- Each leaf represents a final permutation of the input

- The path from root to leaf traces the sequence of comparisons made for a particular input

Theorem 14.1.1 (Lower Bound for Comparison-Based Sorting). *Any deterministic comparison-based sorting algorithm requires $\Omega(n \log n)$ comparisons in the worst case to sort n distinct elements.*

Proof. Consider a decision tree T representing any comparison-based sorting algorithm for n elements.

1. Since the input can be any of the $n!$ possible permutations, and the algorithm must correctly identify which permutation to output, T must have at least $n!$ leaves.

2. A binary tree of height h has at most 2^h leaves. Therefore:
$$2^h \geq n!$$

3. Taking logarithms of both sides:
$$h \geq \log_2(n!)$$

4. Using Stirling's approximation: $n! \approx \sqrt{2\pi n}\left(\frac{n}{e}\right)^n$, we get:
$$\log_2(n!) = n\log_2(n) - n\log_2(e) + \frac{1}{2}\log_2(2\pi n) \tag{14.1}$$
$$= n\log_2(n) - \Theta(n) \tag{14.2}$$
$$= \Theta(n \log n) \tag{14.3}$$

5. Therefore, $h = \Omega(n \log n)$.

Since the height h represents the maximum number of comparisons (worst-case), any comparison-based sorting algorithm requires $\Omega(n \log n)$ comparisons.

14.1.2 Information-Theoretic Interpretation

The lower bound gains deeper meaning through information theory. Each comparison yields at most one bit of information (binary outcome). To distinguish among $n!$ possible orderings requires:

$$I = \log_2(n!) \approx n\log_2(n) - 1.44n \text{ bits}$$

This information-theoretic necessity establishes that $\Omega(n \log n)$ comparisons are required regardless of the algorithm's cleverness.

14.1.3 Average-Case Analysis

Theorem 14.1.2 (Average-Case Lower Bound). *The average-case complexity of comparison-based sorting is $\Omega(n \log n)$, assuming uniform distribution over all input permutations.*

Proof Sketch. The average path length in a binary tree with L leaves is minimized when the tree is balanced. For $L = n!$ leaves:

- Average path length $\geq \log_2(n!)$
- Expected comparisons $= \Omega(n \log n)$

14.2 Optimal Sorting Algorithms

Having established the $\Omega(n \log n)$ lower bound, we examine algorithms that achieve this optimal complexity.

14.2.1 Merge Sort: The Divide-and-Conquer Paradigm

Merge sort epitomizes the divide-and-conquer strategy, achieving optimal worst-case complexity through perfectly balanced recursion.

Algorithm 12 MergeSort

```
Require: Array A[left..right]
if left < right then
    mid ← ⌊(left + right)/2⌋
    MergeSort(A, left, mid)
    MergeSort(A, mid + 1, right)
    Merge(A, left, mid, right)
end if
```

Complexity Analysis:

- **Time Complexity:** The recurrence relation $T(n) = 2T(n/2) + \Theta(n)$ yields $T(n) = \Theta(n \log n)$ by the Master Theorem
- **Space Complexity:** $\mathcal{O}(n)$ auxiliary space for temporary arrays
- **Stability:** Preserves relative order of equal elements
- **Cache Performance:** Good locality during merging phase

14.2.2 Heap Sort: In-Place Optimal Sorting

Heap sort achieves optimal time complexity with $\mathcal{O}(1)$ auxiliary space, leveraging the heap data structure's efficient selection properties.

Algorithm 13 HeapSort

Require: Array $A[1..n]$
Build-Max-Heap(A) ▷ $\mathcal{O}(n)$ time
for $i = n$ **downto** 2 **do**
  Exchange $A[1]$ with $A[i]$
  Heap-size ← Heap-size -1
  Max-Heapify($A, 1$) ▷ $\mathcal{O}(\log n)$ time
end for

Theorem 14.2.1. *Heap sort runs in $\mathcal{O}(n \log n)$ time using $\mathcal{O}(1)$ auxiliary space.*

Proof.

- Building the initial heap takes $\mathcal{O}(n)$ time (proved separately using amortized analysis)
- Extracting n elements, each requiring $\mathcal{O}(\log n)$ heapify operations, takes $\mathcal{O}(n \log n)$ time
- Total: $\mathcal{O}(n) + \mathcal{O}(n \log n) = \mathcal{O}(n \log n)$

14.2.3 Quick Sort: Average-Case Optimality

Despite $\mathcal{O}(n^2)$ worst-case complexity, quicksort's excellent average-case performance and cache efficiency make it the preferred choice in practice.

Algorithm 14 QuickSort

Require: Array $A[p..r]$
if $p < r$ **then**
  $q \leftarrow$ Partition(A, p, r)
  QuickSort($A, p, q - 1$)
  QuickSort($A, q + 1, r$)
end if

Average-Case Analysis:

- Expected time: $\mathcal{O}(n \log n)$ with random pivot selection
- Worst case: $\mathcal{O}(n^2)$ for already sorted arrays
- Space: $\mathcal{O}(\log n)$ expected stack depth

14.2.4 Introsort: Hybrid Optimality

Modern implementations combine multiple algorithms to achieve robust performance. Introsort begins with quicksort, switches to heapsort when recursion depth exceeds $2\lfloor \log_2 n \rfloor$, and uses insertion sort for small subarrays.

14.3 Non-Comparison Based Sorting

By exploiting additional information about input elements, we can surpass the $\Omega(n \log n)$ barrier.

14.3.1 Counting Sort: Linear Time for Bounded Integers

When input elements are integers in a known range $[0, k)$, counting sort achieves linear time complexity.

Algorithm 15 CountingSort

Require: Array $A[1..n]$ with elements in range $[0, k)$
Ensure: Sorted array $B[1..n]$

Let $C[0..k-1]$ be a new array
for $i = 0$ **to** $k-1$ **do**
    $C[i] \leftarrow 0$
end for
for $j = 1$ **to** n **do**
    $C[A[j]] \leftarrow C[A[j]] + 1$
end for
for $i = 1$ **to** $k-1$ **do**
    $C[i] \leftarrow C[i] + C[i-1]$
end for
for $j = n$ **downto** 1 **do**
    $B[C[A[j]]] \leftarrow A[j]$
    $C[A[j]] \leftarrow C[A[j]] - 1$
end forreturn B

Theorem 14.3.1. *Counting sort runs in $\mathcal{O}(n + k)$ time and space, where n is the number of elements and k is the range.*

14.3.2 Radix Sort: Extending Linear-Time Sorting

Radix sort extends counting sort to larger ranges by processing digits independently.

Theorem 14.3.2. *For n d-digit numbers in base b, radix sort runs in $\mathcal{O}(d(n+b))$ time.*

Proof. Each of d passes uses counting sort with range b, taking $\mathcal{O}(n+b)$ time per pass. Total time: $d \cdot \mathcal{O}(n+b) = \mathcal{O}(d(n+b))$.

For 32-bit integers: $d = 32/\log_2(b)$, yielding $\mathcal{O}(n)$ time when $b = \Theta(n)$.

14.3.3 Bucket Sort: Average-Case Linear Time

When input is uniformly distributed over $[0,1)$, bucket sort achieves expected linear time.

Theorem 14.3.3. *For uniformly distributed input, bucket sort runs in $\mathcal{O}(n)$ expected time.*

Proof Sketch.

- Expected number of elements per bucket: 1
- Expected time to sort each bucket: $\mathcal{O}(1)$
- Total expected time: $\mathcal{O}(n) + n \cdot \mathcal{O}(1) = \mathcal{O}(n)$

14.4 Searching in Various Models

14.4.1 Binary Search: Optimal Comparison-Based Searching

For sorted arrays, binary search achieves optimal $\mathcal{O}(\log n)$ comparison complexity.

Algorithm 16 BinarySearch

Require: Sorted array $A[1..n]$, target value x
Ensure: Index of x in A, or -1 if not found

```
left ← 1, right ← n
while left ≤ right do
    mid ← ⌊(left + right)/2⌋
    if A[mid] = x then return mid
    else if A[mid] < x then
        left ← mid + 1
    else
        right ← mid − 1
    end if
end whilereturn −1
```

Theorem 14.4.1. *Binary search is optimal among comparison-based algorithms for searching sorted arrays, requiring* $\lceil \log_2(n+1) \rceil$ *comparisons in the worst case.*

14.4.2 Interpolation Search: Exploiting Distribution

When data is uniformly distributed, interpolation search improves upon binary search.

Expected Complexity: $\mathcal{O}(\log \log n)$ for uniformly distributed data

14.4.3 Hash Table Search: Expected Constant Time

Hash tables provide $\mathcal{O}(1)$ expected search time without requiring sorted data.

Table 14.1: Hash Table Search Complexity

Collision Resolution	**Expected Search Time**
Chaining	$\mathcal{O}(1+\alpha)$
Open Addressing	$\mathcal{O}(1/(1-\alpha))$
Cuckoo Hashing	$\mathcal{O}(1)$ worst-case

where $\alpha = n/m$ is the load factor (n elements, m slots).

14.4.4 Search in External Memory

When data exceeds main memory, I/O complexity dominates.

B-Tree Search Complexity:

- Height: $\mathcal{O}(\log_B n)$ where B is the branching factor
- I/Os per search: $\mathcal{O}(\log_B n)$
- Optimal for external memory model

14.5 Selection and Order Statistics

Finding the k-th smallest element without full sorting reveals interesting complexity trade-offs.

14.5.1 QuickSelect: Expected Linear Time

Algorithm 17 QuickSelect

Require: Array $A[p..r]$, rank k
Ensure: The k-th smallest element

```
if p = r then return A[p]
end if
q ← Partition(A, p, r)
ℓ ← q − p + 1                          ▷ Number of elements in left partition
if k = ℓ then return A[q]
else if k < ℓ then return QuickSelect(A, p, q − 1, k)
elsereturn QuickSelect(A, q + 1, r, k − ℓ)
end if
```

Complexity Analysis:

- Expected time: $\mathcal{O}(n)$
- Worst case: $\mathcal{O}(n^2)$
- Space: $\mathcal{O}(1)$ auxiliary

14.5.2 Median-of-Medians: Worst-Case Linear Time

The median-of-medians algorithm guarantees linear time selection.

Theorem 14.5.1. *The median-of-medians algorithm finds the k-th smallest element in $\mathcal{O}(n)$ worst-case time.*

Proof Sketch. The recurrence $T(n) = T(n/5) + T(7n/10) + \mathcal{O}(n)$ solves to $T(n) = \mathcal{O}(n)$. The key insight is that the median of medians guarantees eliminating at least $3n/10$ elements.

14.5.3 Heap-Based Selection

For finding k smallest elements, heap-based approaches offer different trade-offs:

Table 14.2: Heap-Based Selection Methods

Method	Time Complexity	Space
Min-heap of size n	$\mathcal{O}(n + k \log n)$	$\mathcal{O}(n)$
Max-heap of size k	$\mathcal{O}(n \log k)$	$\mathcal{O}(k)$
Partial heapsort	$\mathcal{O}(n + k \log n)$	$\mathcal{O}(1)$

14.6 External Sorting Considerations

When data exceeds main memory, I/O operations dominate complexity analysis.

14.6.1 External Merge Sort

The standard approach for external sorting adapts merge sort to minimize I/O operations.

Algorithm 18 External Merge Sort

Require: Input file of size N, memory size M, page size B
Ensure: Sorted output file

```
Phase 1: Create sorted runs
while input data remains do
    Read M elements into memory
    Sort in memory using quicksort
    Write sorted run to disk
end while
Phase 2: Multi-way merge
while more than one run remains do
    Merge up to M/B runs at a time
    Write merged run to disk
end while
```

14.6.2 I/O Complexity Analysis

Theorem 14.6.1. *External merge sort with memory size M and disk page size B requires $\mathcal{O}\left(\frac{n}{B} \log_{M/B} \frac{n}{M}\right)$ I/O operations to sort n elements.*

Proof.

1. Initial run creation: $\mathcal{O}(n/B)$ I/Os to read and write data once
2. Number of merge passes: $\lceil \log_{M/B}(n/M) \rceil$
3. Each pass: $\mathcal{O}(n/B)$ I/Os
4. Total: $\mathcal{O}\left(\frac{n}{B} \log_{M/B} \frac{n}{M}\right)$ I/Os

14.6.3 Optimizations for External Sorting

Replacement Selection: Generates runs of expected length $2M$ using a priority queue, reducing the number of merge passes.

Polyphase Merge: Distributes runs unevenly across tapes/disks to minimize rewind time and optimize merge patterns.

Parallel I/O: Modern systems exploit parallel disk arrays:

- Striping for bandwidth
- Independent disks for concurrent run generation
- Complexity: $\mathcal{O}\left(\frac{n}{PB} \log_{M/B} \frac{n}{M}\right)$ with P disks

14.6.4 Cache-Oblivious Sorting

Cache-oblivious algorithms achieve optimal I/O complexity without knowing memory hierarchy parameters.

Funnel Sort: Achieves $\mathcal{O}\left(\frac{n}{B} \log_{M/B} \frac{n}{B}\right)$ I/Os without knowing M or B.

The algorithm recursively:

1. Divides input into $\sqrt{n}$ segments
2. Sorts each segment recursively
3. Merges using a cache-oblivious k-merger

14.7 Summary and Practical Guidelines

14.7.1 Choosing the Right Sorting Algorithm

Table 14.3: Sorting Algorithm Selection Guide

Scenario	Recommended	Rationale
General purpose	Introsort/Timsort	Robust worst-case, adaptive
Small arrays ($n < 50$)	Insertion sort	Low overhead, cache-friendly
Stable sorting needed	Merge sort	Optimal stable sort
Limited memory	Heap sort	$\mathcal{O}(1)$ auxiliary space
Integer keys	Radix sort	Linear time for fixed range
Nearly sorted data	Timsort	$\mathcal{O}(n)$ on sorted data
External data	External merge sort	Minimizes I/O operations
Parallel systems	Parallel quicksort	Good parallelization

14.7.2 Complexity Trade-offs

The choice of sorting algorithm involves multiple considerations:

1. **Time vs. Space:** Merge sort uses $\mathcal{O}(n)$ space for $\mathcal{O}(n \log n)$ guaranteed time; heap sort trades worse constants for $\mathcal{O}(1)$ space
2. **Average vs. Worst Case:** Quicksort excels in practice despite poor worst-case; introsort provides best of both worlds
3. **Adaptivity:** Algorithms like Timsort exploit existing order, achieving $\mathcal{O}(n)$ on sorted data
4. **Stability Requirements:** Stable sorting may require different algorithms or additional space
5. **Hardware Considerations:**
    - Cache effects favor quicksort's locality
    - Branch prediction favors merge sort's predictable patterns
    - SIMD instructions benefit bitonic sort and sorting networks

14.7.3 Open Problems and Research Directions

Despite extensive study, several questions remain:

1. **Integer Sorting:** Can we sort integers in $o(n \log \log n)$ time with $\mathcal{O}(n)$ space?

2. **Cache-Oblivious Complexity:** Tight bounds for cache-oblivious sorting in practice

3. **Parallel Complexity:** Optimal parallel sorting with minimal communication

4. **Quantum Sorting:** Leveraging quantum parallelism for sub-logarithmic sorting

5. **Learning-Augmented Algorithms:** Using machine learning to predict optimal pivot selection or algorithm choice

The study of sorting complexity continues to reveal deep connections between algorithm design, computer architecture, and theoretical computer science, making it a perpetually relevant topic in complexity analysis.

Chapter 15

Graph Algorithm Complexity

Graphs are among the most versatile and widely-used data structures in computer science, modeling everything from social networks and transportation systems to molecular structures and computational dependencies. The algorithmic complexity of graph problems spans the entire spectrum from linear-time solvable to NP-complete and beyond. This chapter explores the time and space complexity of fundamental graph algorithms, providing both theoretical analysis and practical insights into their behavior on real-world data.

15.1 Graph Representation and Basic Operations

The choice of graph representation fundamentally impacts the complexity of graph operations. Before analyzing specific algorithms, we must understand how representation affects basic operations.

15.1.1 Adjacency Matrix Representation

An adjacency matrix represents a graph $G = (V, E)$ using a $|V| \times |V|$ matrix A where:

- $A[i][j] = 1$ if edge $(i, j) \in E$
- $A[i][j] = 0$ otherwise

For weighted graphs, $A[i][j]$ stores the edge weight, with ∞ or a special value indicating no edge.

Space Complexity: $\Theta(|V|^2)$, regardless of the number of edges.

Time Complexity of Operations:

- Check if edge (u, v) exists: $O(1)$

- Find all neighbors of vertex v: $O(|V|)$
- Add an edge: $O(1)$
- Remove an edge: $O(1)$
- Add a vertex: $O(|V|^2)$ (requires matrix resizing)
- Remove a vertex: $O(|V|^2)$

The adjacency matrix representation is optimal when the graph is dense ($|E| = \Theta(|V|^2)$) or when constant-time edge queries are critical. However, for sparse graphs, it wastes significant space.

15.1.2 Adjacency List Representation

An adjacency list maintains, for each vertex v, a list of its neighbors. This can be implemented using:

- Arrays of linked lists
- Arrays of dynamic arrays (vectors)
- Hash tables mapping vertices to neighbor sets

Space Complexity: $\Theta(|V| + |E|)$
Time Complexity of Operations:

- Check if edge (u, v) exists: $O(\deg(u))$
- Find all neighbors of vertex v: $O(\deg(v))$
- Add an edge: $O(1)$
- Remove an edge: $O(\deg(u))$
- Add a vertex: $O(1)$
- Remove a vertex: $O(|V| + |E|)$ in worst case

For sparse graphs where $|E| = O(|V|)$, adjacency lists provide significant space savings. Most real-world graphs are sparse, making this representation the default choice for many applications.

15.1.3 Edge List Representation

An edge list simply stores all edges as a collection of pairs (or triples for weighted graphs).

Space Complexity: $\Theta(|E|)$

Time Complexity of Operations:

- Check if edge (u, v) exists: $O(|E|)$
- Find all neighbors of vertex v: $O(|E|)$
- Add an edge: $O(1)$
- Remove an edge: $O(|E|)$

Edge lists are primarily useful for algorithms that process edges sequentially, such as Kruskal's minimum spanning tree algorithm.

15.1.4 Implicit Graph Representations

Many graphs arise implicitly from problem constraints rather than explicit edge storage. For example:

- State spaces in puzzle solving
- Configuration graphs in optimization
- Lattice graphs in computational physics

For implicit graphs, the complexity of edge generation becomes a critical factor in overall algorithm complexity.

15.2 Breadth-First and Depth-First Search

Graph traversal algorithms form the foundation for solving more complex graph problems. Both BFS and DFS exhibit linear time complexity but differ in their space requirements and applications.

15.2.1 Breadth-First Search (BFS)

BFS explores vertices in order of their distance from the source, making it ideal for finding shortest paths in unweighted graphs.

Theorem 15.2.1 (BFS Complexity). *Breadth-First Search on a graph $G = (V, E)$ runs in:*

- *Time: $O(|V| + |E|)$ using adjacency lists*

- *Space: $O(|V|)$ for the queue and visited array*

Proof. The time complexity breakdown:

- Each vertex is enqueued and dequeued exactly once: $O(|V|)$
- Each edge is examined exactly once (twice for undirected graphs): $O(|E|)$
- Total: $O(|V| + |E|)$

Key Insight: BFS's level-by-level exploration guarantees that when a vertex is first discovered, the shortest path to it has been found. This property is crucial for many applications:

- Single-source shortest paths in unweighted graphs
- Testing bipartiteness
- Finding connected components
- Computing graph diameter

15.2.2 Depth-First Search (DFS)

DFS explores as far as possible along each branch before backtracking, naturally implemented using recursion or an explicit stack.

Theorem 15.2.2 (DFS Complexity)**.** *Depth-First Search on a graph $G = (V, E)$ runs in:*

- *Time: $O(|V| + |E|)$ using adjacency lists*
- *Space: $O(|V|)$ for the recursion stack in worst case*

The recursive implementation's space complexity depends on the maximum depth of the DFS tree, which can be $O(|V|)$ for a path graph but $O(\log |V|)$ for balanced trees.

Applications and Their Complexity:

- Topological sorting: $O(|V| + |E|)$
- Strongly connected components (Tarjan's algorithm): $O(|V| + |E|)$
- Detecting cycles: $O(|V| + |E|)$
- Finding articulation points and bridges: $O(|V| + |E|)$

15.2.3 Bidirectional Search

For finding paths between two specific vertices, bidirectional search can offer significant improvements:

Theorem 15.2.3 (Bidirectional Search Improvement). *For a graph with branching factor b and distance d between source and target:*

- *Traditional BFS:* $O(b^d)$
- *Bidirectional search:* $O(b^{d/2})$

This represents an exponential improvement for large distances, though the constant factors and implementation complexity must be considered.

15.3 Shortest Path Algorithms

The shortest path problem exhibits a rich complexity landscape depending on graph properties and requirements.

15.3.1 Dijkstra's Algorithm

For graphs with non-negative edge weights, Dijkstra's algorithm finds shortest paths from a single source to all other vertices.

Data Structure	Extract-Min	Decrease-Key	Total Complexity
Array	$O(\|V\|)$	$O(1)$	$O(\|V\|^2)$
Binary Heap	$O(\log \|V\|)$	$O(\log \|V\|)$	$O((\|V\| + \|E\|) \log \|V\|)$
Fibonacci Heap	$O(\log \|V\|)$ amortized	$O(1)$ amortized	$O(\|V\| \log \|V\| + \|E\|)$

Table 15.1: Dijkstra's Algorithm Complexity with Different Priority Queues

The Fibonacci heap implementation achieves the theoretically optimal complexity for this problem, though the constant factors often make binary heaps more practical for moderate-sized graphs.

15.3.2 Bellman-Ford Algorithm

When negative edge weights are present, Bellman-Ford provides a robust solution at the cost of increased complexity.

Theorem 15.3.1 (Bellman-Ford Complexity). *The Bellman-Ford algorithm runs in $O(|V| \cdot |E|)$ time and $O(|V|)$ space.*

The algorithm performs $|V| - 1$ iterations, each examining all $|E|$ edges. The additional $|V|$-th iteration detects negative cycles.

15.3.3 Floyd-Warshall Algorithm

For all-pairs shortest paths, Floyd-Warshall offers simplicity despite its cubic complexity.

Algorithm 19 Floyd-Warshall Algorithm

```
for k = 1 to |V| do
    for i = 1 to |V| do
        for j = 1 to |V| do
            d[i][j] = min(d[i][j], d[i][k] + d[k][j])
        end for
    end for
end for
```

Complexity:

- Time: $O(|V|^3)$
- Space: $O(|V|^2)$

15.3.4 Johnson's Algorithm

For sparse graphs with negative weights, Johnson's algorithm combines Bellman-Ford and Dijkstra to achieve better complexity than Floyd-Warshall.

Theorem 15.3.2 (Johnson's Algorithm Complexity). *Johnson's algorithm runs in $O(|V|^2 \log |V| + |V| \cdot |E|)$ time.*

Proof. The algorithm steps:

1. Add a new vertex with zero-weight edges to all vertices: $O(|V|)$
2. Run Bellman-Ford from this vertex: $O(|V| \cdot |E|)$
3. Reweight edges to eliminate negative weights: $O(|E|)$
4. Run Dijkstra from each vertex: $O(|V| \cdot (|V| \log |V| + |E|))$

Total: $O(|V|^2 \log |V| + |V| \cdot |E|)$

15.4 Minimum Spanning Trees

The minimum spanning tree (MST) problem admits several efficient algorithms with interesting complexity tradeoffs.

15.4.1 Kruskal's Algorithm

Kruskal's algorithm builds the MST by greedily selecting edges in order of weight.

Theorem 15.4.1 (Kruskal's Complexity). *Kruskal's algorithm runs in $O(|E| \log |V|)$ time.*

Proof.

1. Sort edges by weight: $O(|E| \log |E|)$
2. Process edges using Union-Find: $O(|E| \cdot \alpha(|V|))$

where α is the inverse Ackermann function. Since $|E| \leq |V|^2$, we have $\log |E| \leq 2 \log |V|$, hence $O(|E| \log |E|) = O(|E| \log |V|)$.

15.4.2 Prim's Algorithm

Prim's algorithm grows the MST from a starting vertex, similar to Dijkstra's algorithm.

Data Structure	Time Complexity
Array	$O(\|V\|^2)$
Binary Heap	$O((\|V\| + \|E\|) \log \|V\|)$
Fibonacci Heap	$O(\|V\| \log \|V\| + \|E\|)$

Table 15.2: Prim's Algorithm Complexity

15.4.3 Borvka's Algorithm

Borvka's algorithm proceeds in phases where each component adds its minimum-weight outgoing edge.

Theorem 15.4.2 (Borvka's Complexity). *Borvka's algorithm runs in $O(|E| \log |V|)$ time.*

The algorithm performs $O(\log |V|)$ phases, each taking $O(|E|)$ time. This algorithm parallelizes naturally, making it attractive for distributed computing.

15.4.4 Linear-Time MST Algorithms

Theoretical breakthroughs have produced:

- Randomized $O(|E|)$ expected time (Karger, Klein, and Tarjan)
- Deterministic $O(|E| \cdot \alpha(|E|, |V|))$ (Chazelle)

However, these remain primarily of theoretical interest due to large constant factors.

15.5 Network Flow Problems

Network flow problems exhibit polynomial-time complexity but with significant variation based on the specific algorithm and problem parameters.

15.5.1 Ford-Fulkerson Method

The Ford-Fulkerson method's complexity depends critically on the augmenting path selection strategy.

Theorem 15.5.1 (Ford-Fulkerson Complexity). *With integer capacities, Ford-Fulkerson runs in $O(|E| \cdot f^*)$ time, where f^* is the maximum flow value.*

This pseudo-polynomial complexity becomes problematic for large flow values.

15.5.2 Edmonds-Karp Algorithm

By using BFS to find augmenting paths, Edmonds-Karp achieves polynomial complexity independent of flow values.

Theorem 15.5.2 (Edmonds-Karp Complexity). *The Edmonds-Karp algorithm runs in $O(|V| \cdot |E|^2)$ time.*

Proof. BFS ensures the shortest augmenting path, guaranteeing at most $O(|V| \cdot |E|)$ augmentations, each requiring $O(|E|)$ time for BFS.

15.5.3 Dinic's Algorithm

Dinic's algorithm uses level graphs to find multiple augmenting paths simultaneously.

Theorem 15.5.3 (Dinic's Complexity). *Dinic's algorithm runs in:*

- *General graphs:* $O(|V|^2 \cdot |E|)$
- *Unit capacity networks:* $O(\min(|E|^{3/2}, |V|^{2/3} \cdot |E|))$
- *Bipartite matching:* $O(|E| \cdot \sqrt{|V|})$

15.5.4 Push-Relabel Algorithms

Push-relabel algorithms maintain a preflow rather than a valid flow during execution.

Selection Rule	Time Complexity
Generic	$O(\|V\|^2 \cdot \|E\|)$
FIFO	$O(\|V\|^3)$
Highest Label	$O(\|V\|^2\sqrt{\|E\|})$

Table 15.3: Push-Relabel Algorithm Variants

15.5.5 Minimum Cost Flow

Adding costs to edges creates the minimum cost flow problem.

Theorem 15.5.4 (Minimum Cost Flow Complexity)**.** *The successive shortest path algorithm solves minimum cost flow in* $O(|E|\log|V|\cdot(|E|+|V|\log|V|))$ *time.*

Improvements using scaling techniques:

- Capacity scaling: $O(|E|^2\log|V|)$
- Cost scaling: $O(|E|\cdot|V|\cdot\log(|V|\cdot C))$ where C is the maximum cost

15.6 Advanced Graph Problems and Complexity

Many fundamental graph problems are NP-complete, requiring exponential time in the worst case or approximation algorithms.

15.6.1 NP-Complete Graph Problems

Hamiltonian Path/Cycle

- Decision problem: NP-complete
- Best exact algorithm: $O(2^{|V|}\cdot|V|^2)$ using dynamic programming
- No constant-factor approximation unless P = NP

Graph Coloring

- k-coloring for $k \geq 3$: NP-complete
- Chromatic number: NP-hard to approximate within $|V|^{1-\epsilon}$ for any $\epsilon > 0$
- Greedy coloring: $O(|V| + |E|)$ but may use $O(\Delta)$ colors where optimal is $O(1)$

Maximum Clique

- NP-complete for decision version
- Best exact algorithm: $O(2^{0.249|V|})$ (theoretical)
- Hard to approximate within $|V|^{1-\epsilon}$ for any $\epsilon > 0$

Traveling Salesman Problem (TSP)

- NP-hard optimization problem
- Dynamic programming solution: $O(2^{|V|} \cdot |V|^2)$
- Metric TSP: $\frac{3}{2}$-approximation in $O(|V|^3)$ (Christofides)

15.6.2 Fixed-Parameter Tractable Problems

Some NP-hard problems become tractable when certain parameters are small.

Vertex Cover

Theorem 15.6.1 (Vertex Cover FPT). *Vertex Cover with parameter k (cover size) can be solved in $O(2^k \cdot |V|)$ time.*

Kernelization reduces to equivalent instance with $O(k^2)$ vertices.

Graph Minor Testing

Theorem 15.6.2 (Robertson-Seymour). *Testing if H is a minor of G runs in $O(|V|^3)$ time for fixed H.*

Practical algorithms: $O(2^{O(|H|)} \cdot |V|^2)$

15.6.3 Graph Isomorphism

The graph isomorphism problem occupies a unique position in complexity theory.

Theorem 15.6.3 (Babai, 2016). *Graph isomorphism can be solved in quasi-polynomial time:* $2^{O((\log |V|)^3)}$.

Special cases with polynomial-time solutions:

- Trees: $O(|V|)$
- Planar graphs: $O(|V| \log |V|)$
- Bounded degree graphs: $O(|V|^{O(d)})$ for degree d

15.6.4 Dynamic Graph Algorithms

Maintaining graph properties under edge insertions and deletions presents unique complexity challenges.

Dynamic Connectivity:

- Amortized $O(\log^2 |V|)$ per operation
- $O(\log |V| / \log \log |V|)$ for plane graphs

Dynamic Shortest Paths:

- Single-source: $\tilde{O}(|V|^2)$ amortized update
- All-pairs: $\tilde{O}(|V|^{2.5})$ worst-case update

15.6.5 Parallel Graph Algorithms

Parallel complexity introduces work (total operations) and depth (parallel time).

Problem	Work	Depth
Connected Components	$O(\|E\| \cdot \alpha(\|V\|))$	$O(\log \|V\|)$
Shortest Paths	$O(\|V\| \cdot \|E\|)$	$O(\|V\| \cdot \log \|V\|)$
Minimum Spanning Tree	$O(\|E\| \cdot \log \|V\|)$	$O(\log^2 \|V\|)$

Table 15.4: Parallel Graph Algorithm Complexity

15.7 Summary

Graph algorithm complexity spans from elegant linear-time algorithms to intractable NP-complete problems. Key insights from this chapter:

1. **Representation matters:** The choice between adjacency matrices and lists can change an algorithm's complexity by a factor of $|V|$.
2. **Problem structure determines complexity:** Shortest paths range from $O(|V| + |E|)$ for unweighted graphs to $O(|V|^3)$ for all-pairs with negative weights.
3. **Data structures are crucial:** The difference between array, binary heap, and Fibonacci heap implementations can be significant for large graphs.
4. **Many problems are inherently hard:** A large class of graph problems are NP-complete, requiring approximation algorithms or heuristics for practical solutions.
5. **Theoretical vs. practical complexity:** Algorithms with superior asymptotic complexity may have constants that make them impractical.
6. **Parallelization potential varies:** Some graph algorithms parallelize naturally (BFS), while others are inherently sequential (DFS).

Understanding these complexity characteristics enables informed algorithm selection based on graph properties, problem requirements, and computational resources.

15.8 Exercises

1. Prove that any comparison-based algorithm for determining if a graph is connected requires $\Omega(|V| + |E|)$ time.
2. Show that finding the diameter of an unweighted graph requires $\Omega(|V| \cdot |E|)$ time in the worst case, even though BFS runs in $O(|V| + |E|)$.
3. Design an algorithm to find all shortest paths (not just one) between two vertices in $O(|V| + |E| + k)$ time, where k is the total size of all shortest paths.
4. Prove that the push-relabel algorithm terminates in $O(|V|^2 \cdot |E|)$ time by analyzing the total number of relabel operations.

5. For a graph with $|V|$ vertices and constant maximum degree Δ, compare the complexity of graph algorithms on adjacency list vs. adjacency matrix representations.

15.9 References

1. Cormen, T. H., Leiserson, C. E., Rivest, R. L., & Stein, C. (2022). *Introduction to Algorithms* (4th ed.).

2. Tarjan, R. E. (1983). Data structures and network algorithms. *SIAM.*

3. Goldberg, A. V., & Tarjan, R. E. (1988). A new approach to the maximum-flow problem. *Journal of the ACM.*

4. Babai, L. (2016). Graph isomorphism in quasipolynomial time. *Proceedings of STOC.*

5. Chazelle, B. (2000). A minimum spanning tree algorithm with inverse-Ackermann type complexity. *Journal of the ACM.*

Chapter 16

String Algorithm Complexity

String algorithms form the backbone of countless applications, from text editors and search engines to DNA sequence analysis and data compression. Understanding their computational complexity is crucial for designing efficient systems that process textual data. This chapter explores the fundamental string processing problems and analyzes the time and space complexity of various algorithmic solutions.

16.1 String Matching Fundamentals

16.1.1 Problem Definition and Notation

String matching, also known as pattern matching, is the problem of finding all occurrences of a pattern string P of length m within a text string T of length n, where typically $m \leq n$. We denote characters in strings using array notation: $T[i]$ represents the i-th character of text T, and $P[j]$ represents the j-th character of pattern P.

The string matching problem has several variants:

- **Exact matching**: Finding exact occurrences of P in T
- **Approximate matching**: Finding occurrences allowing up to k mismatches or edits
- **Multiple pattern matching**: Finding occurrences of multiple patterns simultaneously
- **Regular expression matching**: Finding substrings matching a regular expression

16.1.2 Complexity Metrics for String Algorithms

When analyzing string algorithms, we consider several complexity measures:

1. **Preprocessing time**: Time spent preparing data structures before the main search
2. **Searching time**: Time spent finding pattern occurrences
3. **Space complexity**: Additional memory required beyond input storage
4. **Number of character comparisons**: A fine-grained measure of algorithm efficiency

The total time complexity is often expressed as $\mathcal{O}\left(\text{preprocessing} + \text{searching}\right)$. For online algorithms that cannot preprocess the text, only searching time matters. For algorithms that preprocess the pattern, the preprocessing cost can be amortized over multiple searches.

16.1.3 Lower Bounds and Optimality

A fundamental question in string matching is: what is the minimum number of character comparisons needed to solve the problem?

Theorem 16.1.1. *Any deterministic string matching algorithm must examine at least $n - m + 1$ characters in the worst case to verify that no match exists.*

This establishes a lower bound of $\Omega\left(n\right)$ for the searching phase. However, this doesn't mean we cannot do better than $\mathcal{O}\left(nm\right)$ overall. As we'll see, clever preprocessing and efficient state machines can achieve optimal $\mathcal{O}(n)$ searching time after $\mathcal{O}\left(m\right)$ preprocessing.

16.2 Naive and Efficient Pattern Matching

16.2.1 The Naive Algorithm

The naive or brute-force algorithm checks for pattern occurrence at every position in the text:

Algorithm 20 Naive String Matcher

Require: Text $T[0 \dots n-1]$, Pattern $P[0 \dots m-1]$
Ensure: All positions where P occurs in T

```
n ← length(T)
m ← length(P)
for s = 0 to n − m do
    if P[0...m − 1] = T[s...s + m − 1] then
        print "Pattern occurs at position s"
    end if
end for
```

Time Complexity Analysis:

- **Best case:** $\mathcal{O}(n)$ when the first character of P never matches in T
- **Worst case:** $\mathcal{O}(nm)$ when we must compare all m characters at each position
- **Average case:** $\mathcal{O}(n)$ assuming random strings with alphabet size σ

The worst case occurs with inputs like $T =$ `aaa...a` and $P =$ `aaa...ab`, where we perform m comparisons at each of the $n - m + 1$ positions.

Space Complexity: $\mathcal{O}(1)$ additional space

16.2.2 The Knuth-Morris-Pratt (KMP) Algorithm

The KMP algorithm achieves optimal $\mathcal{O}(n)$ searching time by never backing up in the text. It preprocesses the pattern to compute a failure function that determines how far to shift the pattern upon mismatch.

Definition 16.2.1 (Failure Function)**.** For pattern P, the failure function $\pi[j]$ gives the length of the longest proper prefix of $P[0 \dots j]$ that is also a suffix of $P[0 \dots j]$.

Algorithm 21 Compute Prefix Function

Require: Pattern $P[0 \dots m-1]$
Ensure: Failure function $\pi[0 \dots m-1]$

$m \leftarrow \text{length}(P)$
$\pi[0] \leftarrow 0$
$k \leftarrow 0$
for $q = 1$ to $m - 1$ **do**
    while $k > 0$ and $P[k] \neq P[q]$ **do**
        $k \leftarrow \pi[k-1]$
    end while
    if $P[k] = P[q]$ **then**
        $k \leftarrow k + 1$
    end if
    $\pi[q] \leftarrow k$
end forreturn π

Complexity Analysis:

- **Preprocessing**: $\mathcal{O}(m)$ to compute the failure function
- **Searching**: $\mathcal{O}(n)$ as each character is examined at most once
- **Total time**: $\mathcal{O}(m+n)$
- **Space**: $\mathcal{O}(m)$ for the failure function array

The key insight is that the failure function encodes information about pattern self-overlap, allowing us to skip comparisons we know will fail.

16.2.3 The Boyer-Moore Algorithm

The Boyer-Moore algorithm achieves sublinear average-case performance by comparing characters from right to left and using two heuristics to skip portions of the text.

Definition 16.2.2 (Bad Character Heuristic)**.** When a mismatch occurs at $T[s+j] \neq P[j]$, we can shift the pattern so the rightmost occurrence of $T[s+j]$ in P aligns with position $s+j$.

Definition 16.2.3 (Good Suffix Heuristic)**.** When a suffix of P matches but a mismatch occurs, shift the pattern to align the next occurrence of this suffix (if it exists) or a proper prefix of P that matches a suffix of the good suffix.

Complexity Analysis:

- **Preprocessing**: $\mathcal{O}(m+\sigma)$ where σ is the alphabet size
- **Searching worst case**: $\mathcal{O}(nm)$ for pathological cases
- **Searching average case**: $\mathcal{O}(n/m)$ for random text
- **Space**: $\mathcal{O}(m+\sigma)$

The average-case $\mathcal{O}(n/m)$ behavior makes Boyer-Moore particularly effective for long patterns, as it can skip large portions of the text.

16.2.4 The Rabin-Karp Algorithm

The Rabin-Karp algorithm uses hashing to find pattern occurrences, treating strings as numbers in base-d notation where d is the alphabet size.

Definition 16.2.4 (Rolling Hash Function)**.** For a string S, define:

$$\text{hash}(S) = \sum_{i=0}^{m-1} S[i] \times d^{m-1-i} \bmod q$$

where q is a large prime.

The key insight is that we can compute the hash of $T[s+1 \ldots s+m]$ from $T[s \ldots s+m-1]$ in $\mathcal{O}(1)$ time using:

$$h(s+1) = (d \times (h(s) - T[s] \times d^{m-1}) + T[s+m]) \bmod q$$

Complexity Analysis:

- **Preprocessing**: $\mathcal{O}(m)$ to compute pattern hash
- **Expected searching time**: $\mathcal{O}(n+km)$ where k is the number of matches
- **Worst-case time**: $\mathcal{O}(nm)$ if many hash collisions occur
- **Space**: $\mathcal{O}(1)$

16.3 Suffix Trees and Arrays

16.3.1 Suffix Trees

A suffix tree for string S is a compressed trie containing all suffixes of $S\$$, where \$ is a special terminator character. Each edge is labeled with a substring of S, and each leaf corresponds to a suffix.

Theorem 16.3.1 (Suffix Tree Properties). *A suffix tree for a string of length n has:*

- $\mathcal{O}(n)$ *internal nodes and exactly* $n+1$ *leaves*
- $\mathcal{O}(n)$ *space complexity with careful implementation*
- $\mathcal{O}(n)$ *height in the worst case*

Construction Algorithms:

- **Naive construction**: $\mathcal{O}(n^2)$ by inserting suffixes one by one
- **Ukkonen's algorithm**: $\mathcal{O}(n)$ online construction using suffix links
- **McCreight's algorithm**: $\mathcal{O}(n)$ offline construction

Applications and Query Complexity:

- **Pattern matching**: $\mathcal{O}(m + \text{occ})$ where occ is the number of occurrences
- **Longest repeated substring**: $\mathcal{O}(n)$ after construction
- **Longest common substring of two strings**: $\mathcal{O}(n_1 + n_2)$
- **All-pairs suffix-prefix matching**: $\mathcal{O}(n + \text{output})$

16.3.2 Suffix Arrays

A suffix array SA for string S is an array of integers providing the starting positions of all suffixes of S in lexicographical order.

Definition 16.3.1 (Suffix Array). $SA[i] = j$ if and only if $S[j \ldots n-1]$ is the i-th smallest suffix in lexicographical order.

Construction Algorithms:

- **Naive sorting**: $\mathcal{O}\left(n^2 \log n\right)$ using standard comparison sort
- **Prefix doubling**: $\mathcal{O}\left(n \log^2 n\right)$ or $\mathcal{O}(n \log n)$ with radix sort
- **DC3 algorithm**: $\mathcal{O}(n)$ using difference cover modulo 3
- **SA-IS algorithm**: $\mathcal{O}(n)$ induced sorting approach

Space-Time Tradeoffs:

- **Basic suffix array**: $\mathcal{O}(n)$ space, $\mathcal{O}(m \log n)$ pattern search
- **With LCP array**: $\mathcal{O}(n)$ space, $\mathcal{O}(m + \log n + \text{occ})$ search
- **Enhanced with RMQ**: $\mathcal{O}(n)$ space, $\mathcal{O}(m + \text{occ})$ search

16.3.3 Compressed Suffix Structures

Modern applications often require processing massive strings, motivating space-efficient suffix structures.

Definition 16.3.2 (FM-Index)**.** The FM-Index (Ferragina-Manzini) achieves:

- **Space**: $\mathcal{O}(n \times H_0(S))$ bits where H_0 is the zero-order entropy
- **Pattern search**: $\mathcal{O}(m)$ time
- **Extracting substring**: $\mathcal{O}(l + \log^{\epsilon} n)$ for length-l substring

16.4 String Compression Algorithms

16.4.1 Lempel-Ziv Algorithms

The Lempel-Ziv family achieves compression by replacing repeated substrings with references to previous occurrences.

LZ77 (Sliding Window):

- **Compression time**: $\mathcal{O}(n)$ with suffix trees, $\mathcal{O}(n^2)$ naive
- **Decompression time**: $\mathcal{O}(n)$
- **Space**: $\mathcal{O}(\text{window size})$
- **Compression ratio**: Approaches entropy for large windows

LZ78 (Dictionary-Based):

- **Compression time**: $\mathcal{O}(n)$ with tries
- **Decompression time**: $\mathcal{O}(n)$
- **Dictionary size**: $\mathcal{O}(n/\log n)$ phrases in worst case
- **Space**: $\mathcal{O}(\text{phrases} \times \text{avg phrase length})$

16.4.2 Huffman Coding

Huffman coding assigns variable-length codes to characters based on their frequencies, achieving optimal prefix-free encoding.

Theorem 16.4.1 (Huffman Optimality)**.** *Huffman coding achieves the minimum expected code length among all prefix-free codes:*

$$L \leq H(S) + 1$$

where $H(S)$ is the entropy of the source.

Algorithm Complexity:

- **Building Huffman tree**: $\mathcal{O}(n \log n)$ where n is alphabet size
- **Encoding**: $\mathcal{O}(m)$ where m is text length
- **Decoding**: $\mathcal{O}(m)$ bit operations
- **Space**: $\mathcal{O}(n)$ for the tree

16.4.3 Burrows-Wheeler Transform (BWT)

The BWT is a reversible transformation that tends to group similar characters together, improving compressibility.

Definition 16.4.1 (Burrows-Wheeler Transform). Given string S, the BWT is the last column of the matrix formed by all cyclic rotations of S sorted lexicographically.

Transform Complexity:

- **Forward Transform**: $\mathcal{O}(n^2)$ naive, $\mathcal{O}(n)$ using suffix arrays
- **Inverse Transform**: $\mathcal{O}(n)$ using counting sort
- **Space**: $\mathcal{O}(n + \sigma)$ where σ is alphabet size

16.5 Edit Distance and Sequence Alignment

16.5.1 Edit Distance (Levenshtein Distance)

The edit distance between two strings is the minimum number of single-character insertions, deletions, and substitutions needed to transform one into the other.

Algorithm 22 Edit Distance Dynamic Programming

Require: Strings $S_1[0 \ldots m-1]$, $S_2[0 \ldots n-1]$
Ensure: Edit distance between S_1 and S_2
Create table $D[0 \ldots m][0 \ldots n]$
for $i = 0$ to m **do**
    $D[i][0] \leftarrow i$
end for
for $j = 0$ to n **do**
    $D[0][j] \leftarrow j$
end for
for $i = 1$ to m **do**
    for $j = 1$ to n **do**
        if $S_1[i-1] = S_2[j-1]$ **then**
            $D[i][j] \leftarrow D[i-1][j-1]$
        else
            $D[i][j] \leftarrow 1 + \min\{D[i-1][j], D[i][j-1], D[i-1][j-1]\}$
        end if
    end for
end forreturn $D[m][n]$

Complexity Analysis:

- **Time:** $\mathcal{O}(mn)$ for strings of length m and n
- **Space:** $\mathcal{O}(mn)$ for the full table, $\mathcal{O}(\min(m,n))$ with optimization
- **Backtrace for alignment:** $\mathcal{O}(m+n)$ additional time

16.5.2 Longest Common Subsequence (LCS)

The LCS problem finds the longest sequence that appears as a subsequence in both input strings.

Theorem 16.5.1 (LCS-Edit Distance Relationship). *For strings S_1 and S_2 of lengths m and n:*

$$ED(S_1, S_2) = m + n - 2 \times LCS(S_1, S_2)$$

when only insertions and deletions are allowed.

Dynamic Programming Complexity:

- **Time:** $\mathcal{O}(mn)$ standard DP
- **Space:** $\mathcal{O}(mn)$ for the table, $\mathcal{O}(\min(m,n))$ for length only
- **Improved algorithms:** $\mathcal{O}(mn/\log n)$ using Four Russians technique

16.5.3 Approximate String Matching

Finding all occurrences of pattern P in text T allowing up to k errors.

Dynamic Programming Approach:

- **Time**: $\mathcal{O}(mn)$ where $m = |P|$ and $n = |T|$
- **Space**: $\mathcal{O}(m)$ using sliding window

Bit-Parallel Algorithms:

- **Time**: $\mathcal{O}(\lceil km/w \rceil n)$ where w is the word size
- **Space**: $\mathcal{O}(\lceil m/w \rceil \sigma)$ for preprocessing

16.5.4 Multiple Sequence Alignment

Aligning k sequences simultaneously to identify conserved regions.

Theorem 16.5.2 (MSA Complexity). *The multiple sequence alignment problem with Sum-of-Pairs score is NP-complete for $k \geq 3$ sequences.*

Complexity Results:

- **Optimal alignment**: $\mathcal{O}(n^k)$ for k sequences of length n
- **Approximation**: 2-approximation achievable in polynomial time
- **Progressive alignment**: $\mathcal{O}(k^2 n^2)$ heuristic approach

16.6 Regular Expression Matching

16.6.1 Finite Automata Construction

Regular expressions can be converted to finite automata for efficient matching.

Thompson's Construction (RE → NFA):

- **Time**: $\mathcal{O}(m)$ where m is the RE length
- **Space**: $\mathcal{O}(m)$ states in the NFA
- **Matching time**: $\mathcal{O}(mn)$ for text of length n

Subset Construction (NFA → DFA):

- **Time**: $\mathcal{O}(2^m \times \sigma)$ worst case
- **Space**: $\mathcal{O}(2^m)$ states worst case
- **Matching time**: $\mathcal{O}(n)$ optimal for DFA

16.6.2 Regular Expression Complexity Classes

Different RE features have varying complexity implications:

Theorem 16.6.1 (Backreference Complexity). *Regular expression matching with backreferences is NP-complete.*

Basic Regular Expressions:

- **Matching**: $\mathcal{O}(mn)$ with NFA, $\mathcal{O}(n)$ with DFA
- **DFA size**: Exponential in RE size for some patterns

Extended Features:

- **Backreferences**: Makes matching NP-complete
- **Lookahead/Lookbehind**: Increases practical complexity
- **Possessive quantifiers**: Can improve average-case performance

16.6.3 Modern Regex Engine Strategies

Backtracking Engines:

- **Time complexity**: $\mathcal{O}(2^m \times n)$ worst case
- **Space**: $\mathcal{O}(m)$ for the parse tree
- **Optimization**: Memoization reduces repeated work

DFA-Based Engines:

- **Compilation time**: $\mathcal{O}(2^m)$ worst case
- **Matching time**: $\mathcal{O}(n)$ guaranteed linear
- **Space**: $\mathcal{O}(2^m)$ worst case for DFA

16.6.4 Practical Considerations

Pattern Complexity Impact:

- Nested quantifiers can cause exponential behavior
- Alternation order affects backtracking performance
- Anchoring patterns (^, $) improves efficiency

16.7 Advanced Topics and Open Problems

16.7.1 Parameterized String Matching

Finding matches where characters can be consistently renamed:

- **Time**: $\mathcal{O}(n \log \min(n, \sigma))$ optimal algorithm
- **Applications**: Code clone detection, DNA analysis

16.7.2 Order-Preserving Pattern Matching

Matching patterns based on relative order of characters:

- **Time**: $\mathcal{O}(n + m \log m)$ for pattern preprocessing
- **Applications**: Time series analysis, stock patterns

16.7.3 Streaming String Algorithms

Processing strings with limited memory:

- **Space**: $\mathcal{O}(\log n)$ for many problems
- **Approximate counting**: Frequency moments, distinct elements
- **Sketch-based approaches**: Min-hash, rolling hash

16.7.4 Open Problems

1. **Fine-grained complexity**: Can string matching be solved in $\mathcal{O}\left(n^{1-\epsilon}\right)$ time for any $\epsilon > 0$?
2. **Compressed pattern matching**: Optimal algorithms for searching in compressed text without decompression
3. **Dynamic string matching**: Maintaining pattern occurrences under text updates
4. **Quantum string matching**: Achieving proven quantum speedups for practical string problems

16.8 Chapter Summary

String algorithms represent a rich area where theoretical complexity meets practical importance. We've explored the spectrum from simple $\mathcal{O}(nm)$ naive matching to sophisticated $\mathcal{O}(n)$ linear-time algorithms, and from exact matching to approximate and regular expression matching.

Key Takeaways:

1. **Preprocessing pays off**: Investing $\mathcal{O}(m)$ or $\mathcal{O}(n)$ preprocessing time often yields optimal $\mathcal{O}(n)$ or $\mathcal{O}(m)$ searching time.
2. **Space-time tradeoffs are fundamental**: Suffix trees offer $\mathcal{O}(m)$ queries but require $\mathcal{O}(n)$ space, while compressed structures reduce space at the cost of query time.
3. **Average case often beats worst case**: Algorithms like Boyer-Moore achieve sublinear average-case behavior despite $\mathcal{O}(nm)$ worst-case complexity.
4. **Problem structure matters**: Edit distance's quadratic complexity seems unavoidable (assuming SETH), while exact matching achieves linear time.
5. **Practical considerations dominate**: Cache effects, alphabet size, and pattern characteristics often matter more than asymptotic complexity.
6. **Compression and matching are related**: Many efficient string algorithms exploit redundancy, whether for compression or pattern detection.

The complexity landscape of string algorithms continues to evolve, with applications in bioinformatics, information retrieval, and data compression driving both theoretical advances and practical improvements. Understanding these complexity bounds helps us choose appropriate algorithms and recognize when we're approaching fundamental limits.

16.9 Exercises

1. Prove that any string matching algorithm requires $\Omega(n)$ time in the worst case.
2. Implement the KMP failure function and analyze its amortized complexity using the potential method.

3. Show that the suffix array can be constructed from the suffix tree in $\mathcal{O}(n)$ time.
4. Design an algorithm to find the longest palindromic substring in $\mathcal{O}(n)$ time using suffix trees or Manacher's algorithm.
5. Prove that finding the optimal alignment of k sequences under the sum-of-pairs score is NP-hard for $k \geq 3$.
6. Analyze the expected number of character comparisons for the Rabin-Karp algorithm on random strings.
7. Show how to solve the longest common substring problem for k strings in $\mathcal{O}(kn \log n)$ time where n is the total length.
8. Implement a compressed suffix array that uses $2n + o(n)$ bits and supports pattern searches in $\mathcal{O}(m \log n)$ time.
9. Design an algorithm for approximate pattern matching allowing k errors in $\mathcal{O}\left(n\sqrt{km}\right)$ expected time.
10. Prove that regular expression matching with backreferences is NP-complete by reduction from 3SAT.

16.10 Further Reading

- Gusfield, D. (1997). *Algorithms on Strings, Trees, and Sequences: Computer Science and Computational Biology.* Cambridge University Press.
- Crochemore, M., & Rytter, W. (2002). *Jewels of Stringology: Text Algorithms.* World Scientific Publishing.
- Navarro, G., & Raffinot, M. (2002). *Flexible Pattern Matching in Strings: Practical On-line Search Algorithms for Texts and Biological Sequences.* Cambridge University Press.
- Ohlebusch, E. (2013). *Bioinformatics Algorithms: Sequence Analysis, Genome Rearrangements, and Phylogenetic Reconstruction.* Oldenbusch Verlag.
- Adjeroh, D., Bell, T., & Mukherjee, A. (2008). *The Burrows-Wheeler Transform: Data Compression, Suffix Arrays, and Pattern Matching.* Springer.

Part VI

Approximation and Heuristics

Chapter 17

Approximation Algorithms

Introduction

When faced with NP-hard optimization problems, exact solutions often require exponential time, making them impractical for large instances. Approximation algorithms offer a pragmatic compromise: they run in polynomial time while providing solutions with provable quality guarantees. This chapter explores the theory and practice of approximation algorithms, from fundamental concepts to advanced techniques and impossibility results.

17.1 When Exact Solutions Are Intractable

17.1.1 The Need for Approximation

Many real-world optimization problems are NP-hard, including the Traveling Salesman Problem (TSP), Vertex Cover, and Knapsack. For these problems, no polynomial-time exact algorithms are known, and if $\mathsf{P} \neq \mathsf{NP}$, none exist. As problem instances grow, exact algorithms become infeasible, yet practical applications demand timely solutions.

17.1.2 Trade-offs in Algorithm Design

When designing algorithms for NP-hard problems, we face three fundamental constraints:

1. **Optimality**: Finding the best possible solution
2. **Efficiency**: Running in polynomial time
3. **Generality**: Working for all possible inputs

Since we cannot simultaneously achieve all three for NP-hard problems (assuming $\mathsf{P} \neq \mathsf{NP}$), approximation algorithms sacrifice optimality while maintaining efficiency and generality.

17.1.3 Practical Motivations

Consider a delivery company optimizing routes for 1000 locations. An exact TSP solution might take centuries to compute, while a 1.5-approximation algorithm could provide a route at most 50% longer than optimal in seconds. For business operations, this trade-off is not just acceptable—it's essential.

17.1.4 Framework for Analysis

To analyze approximation algorithms, we need:

- **Cost function**: $C(S)$ denoting the objective value of solution S
- **Optimal value**: $\text{OPT} = C(S^*)$ where S^* is an optimal solution
- **Approximation guarantee**: A bound on $|C(A(I)) - \text{OPT}|$ for algorithm A on instance I

17.1.5 Types of Optimization Problems

Approximation techniques vary based on problem structure:

- **Minimization problems**: Seek solutions with $C(S) \geq \text{OPT}$
- **Maximization problems**: Seek solutions with $C(S) \leq \text{OPT}$
- **Metric problems**: Distance functions satisfy triangle inequality
- **Geometric problems**: Points in Euclidean space with special properties

17.2 Approximation Ratios and Schemes

17.2.1 Approximation Ratio Definition

Definition 17.2.1 (Approximation Ratio)**.** For a minimization problem, an algorithm A has approximation ratio α if for every instance I:

$$C(A(I)) \leq \alpha \cdot \text{OPT}(I)$$

For maximization problems:

$$C(A(I)) \geq \frac{1}{\alpha} \cdot \text{OPT}(I)$$

We call A an α-approximation algorithm. The ratio $\alpha \geq 1$ for minimization and $\alpha \leq 1$ for maximization represents the worst-case performance guarantee.

17.2.2 Absolute vs. Relative Approximation

Absolute approximation: Algorithm A guarantees $|C(A(I)) - \text{OPT}(I)| \leq k$ for constant k.

- Rare for NP-hard problems
- Example: Edge coloring can be solved within +1 of optimal

Relative approximation: Algorithm guarantees $C(A(I))/\text{OPT}(I) \leq \alpha$ (or $\geq 1/\alpha$).

- More common and practical
- Scales with problem size

17.2.3 Approximation Schemes

Definition 17.2.2 (Approximation Scheme). An *approximation scheme* is a family of algorithms $\{A_\varepsilon\}$ where for any $\varepsilon > 0$, algorithm A_ε is a $(1 + \varepsilon)$-approximation algorithm.

Types of approximation schemes:

1. **PTAS (Polynomial-Time Approximation Scheme)**
   - Running time: polynomial in n for fixed ε
   - Example: $O(n^{1/\varepsilon})$ or $O(n^{1/\varepsilon^2})$
2. **FPTAS (Fully Polynomial-Time Approximation Scheme)**
   - Running time: polynomial in both n and $1/\varepsilon$
   - Example: $O(n^3/\varepsilon)$
   - Much more desirable than PTAS
3. **EPTAS (Efficient PTAS)**
   - Running time: $f(1/\varepsilon) \cdot \text{poly}(n)$ for some function f
   - Fixed-parameter tractable in $1/\varepsilon$

17.2.4 Performance Analysis Techniques

To prove approximation ratios, common techniques include:

- **Dual fitting**: Relate primal solution to dual bound
- **Factor revealing LPs**: Optimize worst-case ratio
- **Probabilistic analysis**: Expected approximation ratio
- **Local ratio**: Decompose into subproblems

17.2.5 Example: 2-Approximation for Vertex Cover

Algorithm 23 Greedy Matching for Vertex Cover

```
Initialize C ← ∅
while E ≠ ∅ do
    Pick any edge (u, v) ∈ E
    Add both u and v to C
    Remove all edges incident to u or v from E
end whilereturn C
```

Theorem 17.2.1. *The Greedy Matching algorithm is a 2-approximation for Vertex Cover.*

Proof. Let M be the set of edges picked by the algorithm.

- M forms a matching (no two edges share a vertex)
- Any vertex cover must include at least one endpoint of each edge in M
- Therefore: $\text{OPT} \geq |M|$
- Our solution: $|C| = 2|M| \leq 2 \cdot \text{OPT}$

17.3 Greedy Approximation Algorithms

17.3.1 The Greedy Paradigm

Greedy algorithms make locally optimal choices at each step, hoping to achieve a globally good solution. While they often fail to find optimal solutions for NP-hard problems, many provide excellent approximation guarantees with simple, efficient implementations.

17.3.2 Set Cover: A Classic Example

Problem: Given universe U and collection $\mathcal{S}$ of subsets, find minimum subcollection covering U.

Algorithm 24 Greedy Set Cover

```
C ← ∅
while U is not covered do
    Select S ∈ 𝒮 maximizing |S ∩ (uncovered elements)|
    C ← C ∪ {S}
    Mark elements in S as covered
end whilereturn C
```

Theorem 17.3.1. *Greedy Set Cover achieves approximation ratio* $H(n) = 1 + \frac{1}{2} + \ldots + \frac{1}{n} \approx \ln(n)$.

Analysis sketch:

- Number uncovered elements when OPT uses k sets
- Each greedy choice covers at least $1/k$ fraction of remaining elements
- After $k \cdot H(n)$ iterations, all elements covered

17.3.3 Traveling Salesman Problem

For **Metric TSP** (distances satisfy triangle inequality):

Algorithm 25 Christofides Algorithm

```
Compute MST T of the graph
Find minimum-weight perfect matching M on odd-degree vertices of T
Combine T and M to form Eulerian graph
Find Eulerian tour
Convert to Hamiltonian tour by shortcutting return Hamiltonian tour
```

Theorem 17.3.2. *Christofides Algorithm is a* $\frac{3}{2}$*-approximation for Metric TSP.*

Analysis:

- MST weight $\leq$ OPT (TSP tour minus one edge is spanning tree)
- Matching weight $\leq$ OPT/2 (optimal TSP on odd vertices, split into two matchings)
- Total: $\leq \frac{3}{2} \cdot \text{OPT}$

17.3.4 Knapsack Problem

Greedy by Value/Weight Ratio:

Algorithm 26 Greedy 2-Approximation for 0/1 Knapsack

Sort items by value/weight ratio
Pack items greedily until capacity exceeded
Compare greedy solution with single most valuable item **return** Better of the two solutions

---

17.3.5 Submodular Function Maximization

For monotone submodular functions with cardinality constraint:

Theorem 17.3.3. *The greedy algorithm achieves approximation ratio* $(1 - 1/e) \approx 0.632$ *for maximizing a monotone submodular function subject to cardinality constraint. This ratio is optimal unless* $\mathsf{P} = \mathsf{NP}$.

17.4 Linear Programming Relaxation

17.4.1 The Relaxation Technique

Many combinatorial optimization problems can be formulated as Integer Linear Programs (ILP). Since ILP is NP-hard, we relax integrality constraints to obtain a Linear Program (LP) solvable in polynomial time.

17.4.2 Vertex Cover via LP Relaxation

Integer Linear Program:

$$\text{minimize} \quad \sum_{v \in V} x_v \tag{17.1}$$

$$\text{subject to} \quad x_u + x_v \geq 1 \quad \forall (u, v) \in E \tag{17.2}$$

$$x_v \in \{0, 1\} \quad \forall v \in V \tag{17.3}$$

LP Relaxation:

$$\text{minimize} \quad \sum_{v \in V} x_v \tag{17.4}$$

$$\text{subject to} \quad x_u + x_v \geq 1 \quad \forall (u, v) \in E \tag{17.5}$$

$$0 \leq x_v \leq 1 \quad \forall v \in V \tag{17.6}$$

17.4.3 Rounding Techniques

Algorithm 27 Deterministic Rounding for Vertex Cover

1: Solve LP relaxation to get x^*
2: $C \leftarrow \{v : x_v^* \geq 1/2\}$ **return** C

Theorem 17.4.1. *Deterministic rounding yields a 2-approximation for Vertex Cover.*

Proof.

- For each edge (u, v): $x_u^* + x_v^* \geq 1$
- Therefore, at least one of $x_u^*, x_v^* \geq 1/2$
- C is a valid vertex cover
- $|C| \leq 2 \cdot \sum_v x_v^* \leq 2 \cdot \text{OPT}_{LP} \leq 2 \cdot \text{OPT}$

17.4.4 Set Cover via LP

Primal LP:

$$\text{minimize} \quad \sum_{S \in \mathcal{S}} c_S \cdot x_S \tag{17.7}$$

$$\text{subject to} \quad \sum_{S : e \in S} x_S \geq 1 \quad \forall e \in U \tag{17.8}$$

$$x_S \geq 0 \quad \forall S \in \mathcal{S} \tag{17.9}$$

Dual LP:

$$\text{maximize} \quad \sum_{e \in U} y_e \tag{17.10}$$

$$\text{subject to} \quad \sum_{e \in S} y_e \leq c_S \quad \forall S \in \mathcal{S} \tag{17.11}$$

$$y_e \geq 0 \quad \forall e \in U \tag{17.12}$$

17.4.5 Integrality Gap

Definition 17.4.1 (Integrality Gap). The *integrality gap* is the worst-case ratio between optimal integral and fractional solutions:

$$IG = \max_I \frac{\text{OPT}_{ILP}(I)}{\text{OPT}_{LP}(I)}$$

Important results:

- Vertex Cover: $IG = 2$
- Set Cover: $IG = \Theta(\log n)$
- TSP (Held-Karp relaxation): $IG \leq 3/2$

17.5 PTAS and FPTAS

17.5.1 Polynomial-Time Approximation Schemes (PTAS)

A PTAS provides $(1+\varepsilon)$-approximation for any $\varepsilon > 0$, with running time polynomial in input size n for fixed ε.

17.5.2 Knapsack FPTAS

Algorithm 28 FPTAS for Knapsack via Scaling

Let $K = \varepsilon \cdot v_{\max}/n$ where $v_{\max}$ = maximum value
Scale values: $v_i' = \lfloor v_i/K \rfloor$
Solve scaled problem optimally using DP **return** Corresponding original solution

Theorem 17.5.1. *The scaling algorithm gives an FPTAS for Knapsack with:*

- *Running time:* $O(n^3/\varepsilon)$
- *Approximation ratio:* $(1+\varepsilon)$

Analysis:

- Scaling error per item: at most K
- Total error: at most $nK = \varepsilon \cdot v_{\max} \leq \varepsilon \cdot \mathrm{OPT}$
- Scaled problem has pseudo-polynomial complexity $O(n^2 \cdot v_{\max}/K) = O(n^3/\varepsilon)$

17.5.3 Euclidean TSP: PTAS via Decomposition

Arora's Algorithm for Euclidean TSP:

Theorem 17.5.2. *There exists a randomized PTAS for Euclidean TSP with:*

- *Running time:* $n \cdot (\log n)^{O(1/\varepsilon)}$

- *Approximation ratio:* $(1+\varepsilon)$ *with high probability*

Main ideas:

1. Randomly shifted quadtree decomposition
2. Dynamic programming on tree structure
3. Portal-based crossing restrictions

17.5.4 FPTAS Design Techniques

1. Scaling and Rounding:

- Reduce precision of input values
- Solve simplified problem exactly
- Control accumulated error

2. Interval Partitioning:

- Divide solution space into intervals
- Maintain one solution per interval
- Polynomial number of intervals via geometric growth

3. Trimming the State Space:

Algorithm 29 Trimming for Subset Sum

```
Sort partial sums
Keep only "representative" sums
if S_1 ≤ S_2 ≤ (1 + δ)S_1 then
    Discard S_2
end if
Choose δ = ε/n for (1 + ε)-approximation
```

17.5.5 Limitations and Impossibility

Theorem 17.5.3. *Unless* P = NP*:*

- *Max-3SAT, Vertex Cover, Max Clique have no PTAS*
- *Strong* NP*-hard problems have no FPTAS*

17.6 Inapproximability Results

17.6.1 The PCP Theorem and Hardness of Approximation

Theorem 17.6.1 (PCP Theorem). $\mathsf{NP} = \mathsf{PCP}(\log n, 1)$

This means every NP problem has proofs checkable by reading $O(1)$ random bits, implying many approximation problems are NP-hard.

17.6.2 Gap-Introducing Reductions

Traditional reductions preserve exact solutions. Gap-introducing reductions create a gap between YES and NO instances:

Example 17.6.1 (Gap for Max-3SAT).

- YES instances: satisfiable (OPT $= m$ clauses)
- NO instances: at most $(1 - \varepsilon)m$ clauses satisfiable
- Gap: factor of $1/(1 - \varepsilon)$
- Implies $(1 - \varepsilon)$-approximation is NP-hard

17.6.3 Unique Games Conjecture (UGC)

Conjecture 17.6.2 (Unique Games Conjecture). *For every $\varepsilon > 0$, there exists k such that $(1 - \varepsilon, \varepsilon)$-approximating Unique Games with alphabet size k is* NP*-hard.*

Implications if UGC is true:

- Vertex Cover: no $(2 - \varepsilon)$-approximation
- Max Cut: no better than Goemans-Williamson $0.878\ldots$
- Sparsest Cut: no constant-factor approximation

17.6.4 Specific Inapproximability Results

Proven Results (assuming $\mathsf{P} \neq \mathsf{NP}$):

1. **Max Clique**: No $n^{1-\varepsilon}$-approximation for any $\varepsilon > 0$
2. **Chromatic Number**: No $n^{1-\varepsilon}$-approximation for any $\varepsilon > 0$
3. **Set Cover**: No $(1 - \varepsilon) \ln n$-approximation for any $\varepsilon > 0$

4. **Max-3SAT**: No 8/7-approximation
5. **Vertex Cover**: No approximation better than 1.36

Conditional Results (assuming UGC):

1. **Vertex Cover**: No $(2 - \varepsilon)$-approximation
2. **Max Cut**: No approximation better than $\alpha_{GW} \approx 0.878$
3. **Multicut**: No constant-factor approximation

17.6.5 APX-Completeness

Definition 17.6.1. APX = problems with constant-factor approximation algorithms

APX-complete problems:

- Max-3SAT
- Vertex Cover
- Metric TSP
- Max Cut

Theorem 17.6.3. *If any APX-complete problem has PTAS, then* P = NP.

17.6.6 Lower Bound Techniques

1. Self-Improvement:

- Start with weak hardness result
- Amplify gap via problem composition
- Example: Parallel repetition for 2-Prover 1-Round games

2. Long Code and Fourier Analysis:

- Encode assignments using long code
- Analyze tests via Fourier coefficients
- Derive tight hardness results

3. Integrality Gap Constructions:

- Build instances with large LP/ILP gap
- Implies hardness for LP-based algorithms
- Often matches algorithmic results

Summary and Key Insights

When to Use Approximation Algorithms

1. **Problem is NP-hard**: No polynomial exact algorithm likely exists
2. **Solution quality matters**: Need provable guarantees
3. **Large instances**: Exact algorithms become impractical
4. **Real-time constraints**: Must produce solutions quickly
5. **Robust solutions**: Approximations often more stable

Design Principles

1. **Start simple**: Greedy algorithms often surprisingly effective
2. **Exploit structure**: Metric properties, planarity, etc.
3. **Relax carefully**: LP relaxations reveal problem structure
4. **Combine techniques**: Primal-dual + randomization
5. **Know limits**: Understand inapproximability barriers

Practical Considerations

1. **Average vs. worst case**: Approximation ratios are pessimistic
2. **Hybrid approaches**: Combine with local search, heuristics
3. **Implementation matters**: Constants hidden in big-O
4. **Problem-specific insights**: Domain knowledge improves solutions
5. **Experimental validation**: Test on real instances

Future Directions

The field of approximation algorithms continues to evolve:

- **Streaming and online algorithms**: Approximation with limited memory/information
- **Distributed approximation**: Coordinated approximation across networks

- **Learning-augmented algorithms**: Using ML predictions to improve approximations
- **Fine-grained approximation**: Parameterized by solution quality
- **Practical algorithms**: Bridging theory-practice gap

Approximation algorithms represent a triumph of algorithmic thinking: by accepting near-optimal solutions, we transform intractable problems into practical ones, enabling efficient computation at scale while maintaining mathematical rigor and performance guarantees.

Chapter 18

Heuristic Complexity Analysis

Introduction

While previous chapters have focused on exact algorithms and approximation algorithms with proven guarantees, many real-world problems are solved using heuristic approaches that lack formal performance guarantees but demonstrate excellent empirical behavior. This chapter explores the complexity analysis of heuristic algorithms, bridging the gap between theoretical rigor and practical effectiveness.

Heuristics represent a pragmatic approach to computational problem-solving, particularly for NP-hard problems where exact solutions are computationally infeasible for large instances. Understanding their complexity characteristics is crucial for algorithm selection, parameter tuning, and performance prediction in practical applications.

18.1 Analyzing Heuristic Algorithms

18.1.1 Defining Heuristics

Definition 18.1.1 (Heuristic Algorithm). A *heuristic algorithm* is a problem-solving approach that employs practical methods to find satisfactory solutions within reasonable computational bounds, without guaranteeing optimality or even feasibility in all cases.

Unlike approximation algorithms, heuristics typically lack worst-case performance guarantees. Their key characteristics include:

- **Solution Quality Variability**: Performance depends heavily on problem instance characteristics
- **Empirical Justification**: Effectiveness demonstrated through experimental validation rather than formal proofs
- **Problem-Specific Design**: Often incorporate domain knowledge and problem structure
- **Trade-off Orientation**: Balance solution quality against computational resources

18.1.2 Complexity Metrics for Heuristics

Traditional worst-case analysis often fails to capture heuristic performance accurately. We introduce alternative metrics:

Definition 18.1.2 (Time-to-Target Analysis). The time complexity to reach a solution of specified quality q is defined as:

$$T(n, q) = \text{expected time to find solution } s \text{ where } f(s) \leq q \cdot \text{OPT}$$

Definition 18.1.3 (Solution Quality Distribution). For a fixed computational budget B:

$$\Pr\left[f(s) \leq \alpha \cdot \text{OPT} \mid \text{time} \leq B\right]$$

Definition 18.1.4 (Empirical Complexity). Average-case behavior over benchmark instance distributions:

$$\mathbb{E}\left[T(I)\right] \text{ over instances } I \in \mathcal{D}$$

18.1.3 Analysis Framework

We propose a three-step framework for analyzing heuristic algorithms:

1. **Instance Characterization**
    - Identify problem features affecting heuristic performance
    - Define instance difficulty metrics
    - Establish benchmark sets representing practical scenarios
2. **Performance Profiling**
    - Measure solution quality progression over time
    - Analyze convergence behavior

- Identify performance phases (initial improvement, plateau, refinement)

3. **Complexity Bounds**

- Derive expected-case bounds when possible
- Establish empirical growth rates
- Analyze parameter sensitivity

18.1.4 Case Study: Greedy Heuristics

Consider the greedy heuristic for the Set Cover problem:

Algorithm 30 Greedy Set Cover

Require: Universe U, collection of sets $\mathcal{S}$
Ensure: Cover $C \subseteq \mathcal{S}$

```
C ← ∅                                   ▷ Selected sets
while U ≠ ∅ do
    Select S ∈ 𝒮 maximizing |S ∩ U|/cost(S)
    C ← C ∪ {S}
    U ← U \ S
end whilereturn C
```

Theorem 18.1.1. *The greedy set cover heuristic has:*

- *Time Complexity:* $\mathcal{O}(mn)$ *where* $m = |\mathcal{S}|$ *and* $n = |U|$
- *Solution Quality: Approximation ratio of* $\ln(n) + 1$
- *Expected Performance: Often within* 1.2–1.5× *optimal on practical instances*

18.2 Local Search and Metaheuristics

18.2.1 Local Search Fundamentals

Local search algorithms explore solution spaces through iterative neighborhood exploration:

Algorithm 31 Generic Local Search

Require: Initial solution s_0
Ensure: Locally optimal solution s^*

$s \leftarrow s_0$
while not termination condition **do**
    $N(s) \leftarrow \textsc{GenerateNeighborhood}(s)$
    $s' \leftarrow \textsc{SelectNeighbor}(N(s))$
    if $\textsc{Accept}(s', s)$ **then**
        $s \leftarrow s'$
    end if
end whilereturn s

Proposition 18.2.1 (Local Search Complexity). *The complexity of local search is determined by:*

- ***Neighborhood Size:*** *$|N(s)|$ determines per-iteration complexity*
- ***Iteration Count:*** *Depends on landscape characteristics and acceptance criteria*
- ***Overall Complexity:*** *$\mathcal{O}\left(iterations \times neighborhood\ evaluation\right)$*

18.2.2 Neighborhood Structures and Complexity

k-opt Neighborhoods (TSP)

- 2-opt: $\mathcal{O}(n^2)$ neighborhood size
- 3-opt: $\mathcal{O}(n^3)$ neighborhood size
- Variable k-opt: $\mathcal{O}(n^k)$ worst-case

Hamming Neighborhoods (Binary Problems)

- 1-flip: $\mathcal{O}(n)$ neighbors
- k-flip: $\mathcal{O}(n^k)$ neighbors
- Variable-depth: Adaptive complexity

18.2.3 Metaheuristic Frameworks

Tabu Search Complexity

$$\text{Time per iteration} = \mathcal{O}\left(()\, |N(s)| + \text{tabu list management}\right) \tag{18.1}$$

$$\text{Space complexity} = \mathcal{O}\left(()\, \text{tabu tenure} \times \text{attributes per move}\right) \tag{18.2}$$

Key factors:

- Tabu tenure affects both solution quality and memory requirements
- Aspiration criteria add $\mathcal{O}(1)$ to $\mathcal{O}(n)$ overhead per iteration
- Long-term memory structures increase space complexity

Variable Neighborhood Search (VNS)

Theorem 18.2.2 (VNS Complexity). *Given k neighborhoods $N_1, N_2, \ldots, N_k$:*

$$Time = \sum_{i=1}^{k} (shaking\_time(N_i) + local\_search\_time(N_i)) \tag{18.3}$$

$$Typical = \mathcal{O}\left(()\, k \times n^2 \times local\ iterations\right) \tag{18.4}$$

18.2.4 Convergence Analysis

Proposition 18.2.3 (First Improvement vs. Best Improvement).

- *First Improvement: $\mathcal{O}\left(expected\ neighbors\ examined\right)$ per iteration*
- *Best Improvement: $\mathcal{O}\left(|N(s)|\right)$ per iteration*
- *Trade-off: More iterations vs. better moves*

Theorem 18.2.4 (Expected Iterations to Local Optimum). *For smooth landscapes:*

$$\mathbb{E}[iterations] = \mathcal{O}\left(n \cdot \log\left(\frac{initial\ gap}{final\ gap}\right)\right)$$

For rugged landscapes:

$$\mathbb{E}\left[iterations\right] = \mathcal{O}\left(()\, n^{\alpha}\right)$$

where α depends on landscape correlation.

18.3 Genetic Algorithms and Complexity

18.3.1 GA Components and Their Complexity

Algorithm 32 Basic Genetic Algorithm

Require: Population size p, generations g
Ensure: Best solution found

```
P ← InitializePopulation(p)                          ▷ O(p × n)
for i = 1 to g do
    P' ← ∅
    for j = 1 to p do
        parents ← Selection(P)                       ▷ O(tournament size)
        offspring ← Crossover(parents)               ▷ O(n)
        offspring ← Mutation(offspring)              ▷ O(n × p_m)
        P' ← P' ∪ {offspring}
    end for
    P ← P'
end forreturn best(P)
```

Theorem 18.3.1 (GA Time Complexity). *The overall time complexity of a genetic algorithm is:*

$$\mathcal{O}\left(()\, g \times p \times (f(n) + n)\right)$$

where g is the number of generations, p is the population size, $f(n)$ is the fitness evaluation complexity, and n is the problem size.

18.3.2 Selection Mechanisms

Method	**Setup**	**Per Selection**	**Properties**
Tournament	$\mathcal{O}(1)$	$\mathcal{O}(k)$	No sorting required
Roulette Wheel	$\mathcal{O}(p)$	$\mathcal{O}(\log p)$	Requires fitness scaling
Rank Selection	$\mathcal{O}(p \log p)$	$\mathcal{O}(1)$	Uniform pressure

Table 18.1: Complexity of Selection Mechanisms

18.3.3 Crossover and Mutation Analysis

Crossover Complexity by Type

- Single-point: $\mathcal{O}(n)$

- Multi-point: $\mathcal{O}(n+k)$ for k crossover points
- Uniform: $\mathcal{O}(n)$
- Order-based (TSP): $\mathcal{O}(n^2)$ worst-case
- Edge recombination: $\mathcal{O}(n^2)$

Mutation Rates and Expected Changes

Proposition 18.3.2. *Given mutation probability p_m per gene:*

$$\mathbb{E}[mutations\ per\ individual] = n \times p_m \tag{18.5}$$

$$Time\ complexity = \mathcal{O}(()\, n \times p_m) \tag{18.6}$$

$$Typically:\ p_m = 1/n \Rightarrow \mathcal{O}(()\, 1)\ expected\ mutations \tag{18.7}$$

18.3.4 Population Dynamics and Convergence

Theorem 18.3.3 (Schema Theorem)**.** *The growth rate of good schemata H follows:*

$$m(H, t+1) \geq m(H, t) \times \frac{f(H)}{\bar{f}} \times p_{survival}$$

where $m(H, t)$ is the number of instances of schema H at time t, $f(H)$ is the average fitness of H, and $\bar{f}$ is the population average fitness.

Corollary 18.3.4 (Building Block Hypothesis)**.** *Time to assemble k building blocks:*

$$T = \mathcal{O}(()\, p \times \log k \times average\ BB\ discovery\ time)$$

18.3.5 Parallel GA Complexity

Proposition 18.3.5 (Island Model Complexity)**.**

$$Time = \mathcal{O}(()\, g \times p_{island} \times operators + migration\ overhead) \tag{18.8}$$

$$Communication = \mathcal{O}(()\, migration\ frequency \times migrants \times islands) \tag{18.9}$$

$$Speedup \approx linear\ for\ low\ migration\ rates \tag{18.10}$$

18.4 Simulated Annealing Analysis

18.4.1 Basic SA Algorithm Complexity

Algorithm 33 Simulated Annealing

Require: Initial solution s_0, initial temperature T_0
Ensure: Best solution found

$s \leftarrow s_0$
$T \leftarrow T_0$
while $T > T_{\text{final}}$ **do**
  for $i = 1$ to iterations_per_temp **do**
    $s' \leftarrow \text{RandomNeighbor}(s)$ ▷ $\mathcal{O}$ (neighbor generation)
    $\Delta \leftarrow f(s') - f(s)$ ▷ $\mathcal{O}$ (evaluation)
    if $\Delta < 0$ or random() $< \exp(-\Delta/T)$ **then**
      $s \leftarrow s'$
    end if
  end for
  $T \leftarrow \text{CoolingSchedule}(T)$
end whilereturn s

Theorem 18.4.1 (SA Time Complexity).

$$\mathcal{O}\left(()\ \textit{temperature levels} \times \textit{iterations per temp} \times (\textit{neighbor} + \textit{evaluation})\right)$$

18.4.2 Cooling Schedules and Convergence

Definition 18.4.1 (Geometric Cooling).

$$T(t) = T_0 \times \alpha^t, \quad \text{where } 0.8 \leq \alpha \leq 0.99$$

Temperature levels: $\mathcal{O}(\log(T_0/T_f))$

Theorem 18.4.2 (Logarithmic Cooling). *The cooling schedule*

$$T(t) = \frac{T_0}{\log(1+t)}$$

guarantees convergence to the global optimum but requires $\mathcal{O}(\exp(n))$ *time for convergence.*

18.4.3 Markov Chain Analysis

Theorem 18.4.3 (Stationary Distribution). *At temperature T, the probability of state s in the stationary distribution is:*

$$\pi(s) = \frac{\exp(-f(s)/T)}{Z(T)}$$

where $Z(T) = \sum_{s' \in S} \exp(-f(s')/T)$ is the partition function.

Proposition 18.4.4 (Mixing Time). *Time to reach near-stationary distribution:*

$$\tau_{mix} = \mathcal{O}\left(()\, n^2 \times \exp(\textit{barrier height}/T)\right)$$

Theorem 18.4.5 (Expected Hitting Time). *Time to reach optimal solution:*

$$\mathbb{E}\left[T_{hit}\right] = \mathcal{O}\left(()\, |S| \times \exp(\max\ \textit{barrier}/T)\right)$$

18.4.4 Finite-Time Analysis

Theorem 18.4.6 (Probability of Finding Optimal). *After t iterations at appropriate temperature:*

$$\Pr\left[\textit{finding optimal}\right] \geq 1 - \exp(-t/\tau)$$

where τ depends on problem structure.

18.5 Machine Learning and Complexity

18.5.1 Learning-Enhanced Heuristics

Definition 18.5.1 (Supervised Learning for Heuristic Guidance).

$$\text{Training complexity} = \mathcal{O}\left(()\, \text{training samples} \times \text{model complexity}\right) \tag{18.11}$$

$$\text{Inference per decision} = \mathcal{O}\left(()\, \text{model inference}\right) \tag{18.12}$$

$$\text{Total} = \mathcal{O}\left(()\, \text{preprocessing} + \text{iterations} \times \text{inference overhead}\right) \tag{18.13}$$

Example 18.5.1 (Learned Branching in Branch-and-Bound).

- Feature extraction: $\mathcal{O}(\text{problem features})$
- Model prediction: $\mathcal{O}(\text{model size})$
- Overhead per node: $\mathcal{O}(\text{features} + \text{prediction})$
- Typical speedup: 2–10× despite overhead

18.5.2 Reinforcement Learning in Optimization

Proposition 18.5.1 (Policy Gradient Methods).

$$\text{Per episode} = \mathcal{O}\left(()\ \text{episode length} \times \text{action space} \times \text{policy evaluation}\right) \tag{18.14}$$

$$\text{Convergence} = \mathcal{O}\left(()\ \text{episodes to convergence} \times \text{episode complexity}\right) \tag{18.15}$$

Definition 18.5.2 (Q-Learning for Combinatorial Optimization).

- State space: Often exponential, requiring approximation
- Update complexity: $\mathcal{O}(1)$ per step with function approximation
- Convergence: Depends on exploration strategy and approximation quality

18.5.3 Neural Heuristics Complexity

Theorem 18.5.2 (Graph Neural Networks for CO).

$$\text{Forward pass} = \mathcal{O}\left(()\ \text{layers} \times \text{edges} \times \text{hidden\_dim}^2\right) \tag{18.16}$$

$$\text{Training} = \mathcal{O}\left(()\ \text{epochs} \times \text{graphs} \times \text{forward pass}\right) \tag{18.17}$$

$$\text{Inference} = \mathcal{O}\left(()\ \text{forward pass}\right) \tag{18.18}$$

Proposition 18.5.3 (Attention Mechanisms).

$$\text{Self-attention} = \mathcal{O}\left(()\ n^2 \times d\right) \quad \text{where } n = \text{sequence length}, d = \text{dimension} \tag{18.19}$$

$$\text{Typical for TSP} = \mathcal{O}\left(()\ n^2 \times \text{hidden\_dim}\right) \tag{18.20}$$

$$\text{Trade-off}: \text{Better solutions vs. quadratic scaling} \tag{18.21}$$

18.5.4 Learning Complexity Trade-offs

Definition 18.5.3 (Amortized Analysis).

$$\text{Total cost} = \text{Training cost} + n_{\text{instances}} \times \text{Inference cost} \tag{18.22}$$

$$\text{Break-even} = \frac{\text{Training cost}}{(\text{Original} - \text{Enhanced}) \text{ per instance}} \tag{18.23}$$

18.5.5 Hybrid Approaches

Theorem 18.5.4 (Learn to Search). *Combining exact methods with learned guidance:*

$$\textit{Time} = \mathcal{O}\left(()\ \textit{search tree size} \times (\textit{node evaluation} + \textit{learned heuristic})\right) \tag{18.24}$$

$$\textit{Reduction}: \textit{Learned pruning can reduce tree size exponentially} \tag{18.25}$$

$$\textit{Net complexity}: \textit{Often}\ \mathcal{O}\left(()\, n^k\right)\ \textit{reduced to}\ \mathcal{O}\left(()\, n^{k-1}\right)\ \textit{or better} \tag{18.26}$$

18.6 Practical Considerations and Guidelines

18.6.1 Choosing Analysis Methods

Analysis Type	When to Use
Worst-case	Safety-critical applications, guaranteed performance needs
Average-case	Large-scale repeated solving, statistical guarantees sufficient
Empirical	Complex real-world problems, benchmark-driven development
Smoothed	Understanding typical vs. pathological behavior

Table 18.2: Analysis Method Selection Guide

18.6.2 Implementation Impact on Complexity

Data Structure Choices

- Priority queues for best-first search: $\mathcal{O}(\log n)$ vs. $\mathcal{O}(n)$
- Hash tables for tabu lists: $\mathcal{O}(1)$ expected vs. $\mathcal{O}(n)$ list search
- Incremental evaluation: $\mathcal{O}(1)$ vs. $\mathcal{O}(n)$ full re-evaluation

Parallelization Opportunities

- Population-based: Embarrassingly parallel fitness evaluation
- Local search: Parallel neighborhood evaluation
- Tree search: Parallel branch exploration

18.6.3 Parameter Tuning Complexity

Definition 18.6.1 (Grid Search).

$$\mathcal{O}\left(\prod_{i=1}^{k} |\Theta_i| \cdot T_{\text{eval}}\right)$$

Definition 18.6.2 (Automated Tuning).

- Bayesian optimization: $\mathcal{O}$ (iterations × acquisition optimization)
- Racing algorithms: $\mathcal{O}$ (candidates × statistical tests)
- Landscape analysis: $\mathcal{O}$ (feature extraction × correlation analysis)

Summary

Heuristic complexity analysis requires a multifaceted approach combining theoretical insights with empirical validation. Key takeaways include:

1. **Traditional complexity metrics often inadequate** – Need problem-specific measures
2. **Landscape characteristics drive performance** – Understanding problem structure essential
3. **Hybrid approaches often most effective** – Combining multiple strategies
4. **Learning can transform complexity** – ML-enhanced heuristics change traditional trade-offs
5. **Implementation details matter** – Constant factors and data structures significantly impact practice

The field continues to evolve with advances in machine learning, parallel computing, and our understanding of problem structure. Successful practitioners must balance theoretical understanding with empirical experimentation, always keeping in mind that heuristic effectiveness is ultimately measured by real-world performance rather than worst-case guarantees.

Exercises

1. **Local Search Analysis**: For a TSP instance with n cities, derive the expected number of 2-opt improvements needed to reach a local optimum from a random initial solution.

2. **GA Population Sizing**: Determine the minimum population size needed to ensure with probability 0.95 that at least one copy of the optimal solution's building blocks appears in the initial random population.

3. **SA Temperature Setting**: Given a problem with solution values in range $[0, 1000]$ and desired initial acceptance probability of 0.8 for uphill moves of size 100, calculate the appropriate initial temperature.

4. **Metaheuristic Comparison**: Design an experiment to fairly compare tabu search, simulated annealing, and genetic algorithms on the quadratic assignment problem.

5. **Learning Overhead**: Calculate the break-even point for using a neural network heuristic that takes 1 hour to train but reduces average instance solving time from 100ms to 40ms.

Further Reading

- Hoos, H. H., & Stützle, T. (2004). *Stochastic Local Search: Foundations and Applications.* Morgan Kaufmann.

- Talbi, E. G. (2009). *Metaheuristics: From Design to Implementation.* John Wiley & Sons.

- Bengio, Y., Lodi, A., & Prouvost, A. (2021). Machine learning for combinatorial optimization: A methodological tour d'horizon. *European Journal of Operational Research*, 290(2), 405–421.

- Wolpert, D. H., & Macready, W. G. (1997). No free lunch theorems for optimization. *IEEE Transactions on Evolutionary Computation*, 1(1), 67–82.

- Burke, E. K., et al. (2013). Hyper-heuristics: A survey of the state of the art. *Journal of the Operational Research Society*, 64(12), 1695–1724.

Part VII

Practical Considerations

Chapter 19

Implementation and Constant Factors

"In theory, theory and practice are the same. In practice, they are not."

— Often attributed to Yogi Berra

Chapter Overview

Throughout this book, we have focused on asymptotic analysis as our primary tool for understanding algorithm efficiency. We have learned to think in terms of $\mathcal{O}$, Θ, and Ω notations, abstracting away constant factors and lower-order terms. This theoretical framework has served us well in understanding the fundamental scalability of algorithms. However, when we transition from the classroom to the server room, from the textbook to the production codebase, we encounter a different reality—one where a theoretically inferior $\mathcal{O}(n^2)$ algorithm might outperform an $\mathcal{O}(n \log n)$ alternative for all practical input sizes, where cache misses can dominate computation time, and where compiler optimizations can transform our carefully analyzed code beyond recognition.

This chapter bridges the gap between theoretical complexity analysis and practical performance engineering. We will explore why algorithms with identical asymptotic complexity can have vastly different real-world performance, how modern computer architectures influence actual runtime, and when it makes sense to choose a theoretically suboptimal algorithm for practical reasons.

19.1 Bridging Theory and Practice

19.1.1 The Gap Between Asymptotic Analysis and Reality

Asymptotic analysis provides a powerful lens for understanding algorithm behavior as input size approaches infinity. However, several factors create a gap between this theoretical understanding and practical performance:

1. **Finite Input Sizes**: In practice, we never deal with infinite inputs. Most real-world problems have bounded input sizes where asymptotic behavior may never dominate.
2. **Hidden Constants**: The constants hidden by Big O notation can vary by orders of magnitude between algorithms with the same asymptotic complexity.
3. **Hardware Architecture**: Modern computers are not random-access machines with uniform memory access times—they have complex memory hierarchies, instruction pipelines, and parallelism at multiple levels.
4. **Implementation Details**: The same algorithm can have dramatically different performance depending on how it's implemented, what data structures are used, and how memory is managed.

19.1.2 A Motivating Example: Matrix Multiplication

Consider the problem of matrix multiplication. The naive algorithm has $\mathcal{O}(n^3)$ complexity:

```
def naive_multiply(A, B):
    n = len(A)
    C = [[0] * n for _ in range(n)]
    for i in range(n):
        for j in range(n):
            for k in range(n):
                C[i][j] += A[i][k] * B[k][j]
    return C
```

Listing 19.1: Naive matrix multiplication

Strassen's algorithm achieves $\mathcal{O}\left(n^{2.807}\right)$ complexity, a theoretical improvement. However, for matrices smaller than approximately 512×512, the naive algorithm often performs better due to:

- Lower constant factors
- Better cache locality

- Simpler control flow allowing better compiler optimization
- No recursive overhead

Principle 19.1.1. Asymptotic superiority does not guarantee practical superiority for finite inputs.

19.1.3 The Role of Empirical Analysis

While theoretical analysis gives us scalability insights, empirical analysis reveals actual performance characteristics:

```
import time
import numpy as np

def benchmark_algorithm(algorithm, input_sizes):
    results = []
    for n in input_sizes:
        input_data = generate_input(n)
        start = time.perf_counter()
        algorithm(input_data)
        end = time.perf_counter()
        results.append((n, end - start))
    return results
```

Listing 19.2: Empirical benchmarking framework

Empirical analysis complements theoretical analysis by:

- Revealing the actual constants hidden by asymptotic notation
- Identifying the crossover points where one algorithm becomes superior to another
- Exposing architecture-specific performance characteristics
- Validating theoretical predictions

19.2 Hidden Constants in Big O Analysis

19.2.1 The Reality of Constant Factors

When we say an algorithm is $\mathcal{O}(n \log n)$, we're really saying its runtime is bounded by $c \cdot n \cdot \log(n)$ for some constant c and sufficiently large n. The constant c can make an enormous practical difference:

Example 19.2.1 (Two $\mathcal{O}(n \log n)$ Sorting Algorithms)**.**

- Algorithm A: Runtime $\approx 2n \log_2(n)$ microseconds

- Algorithm B: Runtime $\approx 100n\log_2(n)$ microseconds

For $n = 1,000,000$:

- Algorithm A: ~ 40 seconds
- Algorithm B: ~ 2000 seconds (33 minutes!)

Both are $\mathcal{O}(n \log n)$, but Algorithm B is $50\times$ slower in practice.

19.2.2 Sources of Constant Factor Variations

Several factors contribute to differences in constants:

1. **Instruction Count**: Different algorithms require different numbers of primitive operations per iteration.

```
// Lower constant: single comparison per iteration
for (int i = 0; i < n; i++) {
    if (arr[i] > max) max = arr[i];
}

// Higher constant: multiple operations per iteration
for (int i = 0; i < n; i++) {
    temp = arr[i] * 2 + 1;
    if ((temp & mask) == pattern) {
        result ^= temp;
    }
}
```

Listing 19.3: Different instruction counts

2. **Memory Access Patterns**: Random memory access is more expensive than sequential access.

3. **Branch Prediction**: Algorithms with predictable branches run faster than those with random branches.

4. **Function Call Overhead**: Recursive algorithms may have higher constants due to function call overhead.

19.2.3 Measuring and Comparing Constants

To meaningfully compare algorithms with the same asymptotic complexity, we need to measure their actual constants:

```python
def measure_constant_factor(algorithm, theoretical_complexity):
    """
    Estimates the constant factor for an algorithm
    given its theoretical complexity function.
    """
    measurements = []
    for n in [1000, 2000, 4000, 8000, 16000]:
        runtime = benchmark(algorithm, n)
        theoretical = theoretical_complexity(n)
        constant = runtime / theoretical
        measurements.append(constant)

    # Return median to reduce noise
    return statistics.median(measurements)
```

Listing 19.4: Measuring constant factors

19.2.4 Case Study: Quicksort vs. Heapsort

Both Quicksort and Heapsort have $\mathcal{O}(n \log n)$ average-case complexity, but their constants differ significantly:

Table 19.1: Comparison of Quicksort and Heapsort characteristics

Characteristic	Quicksort	Heapsort
Average comparisons	$\sim 1.39n \log_2(n)$	$\sim 2n \log_2(n)$
Cache locality	Excellent	Poor
Branch prediction	Good on average	Less predictable
Memory overhead	$\mathcal{O}(\log n)$ stack	$\mathcal{O}(1)$
Worst-case complexity	$\mathcal{O}(n^2)$	$\mathcal{O}(n \log n)$

Result: Quicksort is typically 2–3× faster than Heapsort in practice, despite having worse worst-case complexity.

19.3 Cache Effects and Memory Hierarchy

19.3.1 Understanding Modern Memory Hierarchy

Modern computers have a complex memory hierarchy:

Table 19.2: Memory hierarchy characteristics

Level	Access Time	Latency	Typical Size
CPU Registers	$\sim$ 1 cycle	$\sim$ 0.3 ns	$\sim$ 1 KB
L1 Cache	$\sim$ 4 cycles	$\sim$ 1 ns	$\sim$ 32 KB
L2 Cache	$\sim$ 10 cycles	$\sim$ 3 ns	$\sim$ 256 KB
L3 Cache	$\sim$ 40 cycles	$\sim$ 10 ns	$\sim$ 8 MB
Main Memory	$\sim$ 100 cycles	$\sim$ 30 ns	$\sim$ 16 GB
SSD	$\sim$ 10,000 cycles	$\sim$ 3 ţs	$\sim$ 1 TB
HDD	$\sim 10^7$ cycles	$\sim$ 3 ms	$\sim$ 10 TB

The performance difference between cache hit and cache miss can be 100× or more!

19.3.2 Cache-Friendly Algorithm Design

Algorithms that exhibit good spatial and temporal locality perform much better:

Spatial Locality: Accessing memory locations near recently accessed locations.

```
// Good spatial locality: sequential access
for (int i = 0; i < n; i++) {
    sum += array[i];
}

// Poor spatial locality: strided access
for (int i = 0; i < n; i++) {
    sum += array[i * stride];
}
```

Listing 19.5: Spatial locality comparison

Temporal Locality: Reusing recently accessed data before it's evicted from cache.

```
// Good temporal locality: reuse data while in cache
for (int i = 0; i < n; i++) {
    for (int j = 0; j < n; j++) {
        sum += A[i][j];  // Access A row-wise
    }
}

// Poor temporal locality: data evicted before reuse
for (int j = 0; j < n; j++) {
    for (int i = 0; i < n; i++) {
        sum += A[i][j];  // Access A column-wise
```

```
    }
}
```

Listing 19.6: Temporal locality comparison

19.3.3 Cache Complexity Analysis

Traditional complexity analysis assumes uniform memory access cost. Cache-aware complexity analysis accounts for memory hierarchy:

Definition 19.3.1 (Cache Complexity Model). -

- B = cache line size (typically 64 bytes)
- M = cache size
- Memory access cost: 1 if in cache, 100 if cache miss

Example 19.3.1 (Matrix Transposition). **Naive algorithm:**

```
for (int i = 0; i < n; i++)
    for (int j = 0; j < n; j++)
        B[j][i] = A[i][j];
```

Cache complexity: $\mathcal{O}(n^2)$ cache misses for large n

Cache-oblivious algorithm (divide-and-conquer):

```
void transpose_recursive(A, B, r0, r1, c0, c1) {
    if (r1 - r0 <= THRESHOLD && c1 - c0 <= THRESHOLD) {
        // Base case: transpose small block
        transpose_block(A, B, r0, r1, c0, c1);
    } else {
        // Divide into quadrants
        int rm = (r0 + r1) / 2;
        int cm = (c0 + c1) / 2;
        transpose_recursive(A, B, r0, rm, c0, cm);
        transpose_recursive(A, B, r0, rm, cm, c1);
        transpose_recursive(A, B, rm, r1, c0, cm);
        transpose_recursive(A, B, rm, r1, cm, c1);
    }
}
```

Cache complexity: $\mathcal{O}\left(n^2/B\right)$ cache misses (optimal)

19.3.4 Real-World Impact: Binary Search vs. Linear Search

Despite binary search's $\mathcal{O}(\log n)$ complexity versus linear search's $\mathcal{O}(n)$, for small arrays (< 100 elements), linear search often wins due to:

- Better cache locality

- Simpler control flow
- No branch misprediction penalty
- Prefetcher effectiveness

Table 19.3: Binary search vs. linear search performance

Array Size	Linear Search	Binary Search
64 integers	15 ns	45 ns
1024 integers	250 ns	120 ns

The crossover point depends on element size, comparison cost, and processor architecture.

19.4 Compiler Optimizations Impact

19.4.1 How Compilers Transform Code

Modern compilers apply sophisticated optimizations that can dramatically change performance characteristics:

1. **Constant Folding and Propagation**

```
// Original code
int x = 5 * 20;
int y = x / 10;

// After optimization
int y = 10;  // Computed at compile time
```

2. **Loop Unrolling**

```
// Original loop
for (int i = 0; i < n; i++) {
    sum += arr[i];
}

// After unrolling (by factor of 4)
int i;
for (i = 0; i < n - 3; i += 4) {
    sum += arr[i] + arr[i+1] + arr[i+2] + arr[i+3];
}
for (; i < n; i++) {
    sum += arr[i];
}
```

3. **Vectorization (SIMD)**

```
// Original scalar code
for (int i = 0; i < n; i++) {
    c[i] = a[i] + b[i];
}

// After vectorization (using AVX)
for (int i = 0; i < n; i += 8) {
    __m256 va = _mm256_load_ps(&a[i]);
    __m256 vb = _mm256_load_ps(&b[i]);
    __m256 vc = _mm256_add_ps(va, vb);
    _mm256_store_ps(&c[i], vc);
}
```

19.4.2 Optimization Levels and Their Effects

Different optimization levels can change performance by orders of magnitude:

Table 19.4: Effect of optimization levels on matrix multiplication (100×100)

Flag	Runtime	Speedup
-O0	45.2 ms	1.0×
-O1	12.3 ms	3.7×
-O2	4.8 ms	9.4×
-O3	2.1 ms	21.5×

19.4.3 Writing Optimization-Friendly Code

Certain coding patterns enable better compiler optimization:

1. **Const Correctness**

```
// Helps compiler optimize
void process(const int* restrict a, int* restrict b, int n) {
    for (int i = 0; i < n; i++) {
        b[i] = a[i] * 2;  // Compiler knows a and b don't alias
    }
}
```

2. **Loop-Invariant Code Motion**

```
// Before: computation inside loop
for (int i = 0; i < n; i++) {
    result[i] = data[i] * (x * y + z);  // Redundant computation
}

// After: move invariant outside
```

```
int factor = x * y + z;
for (int i = 0; i < n; i++) {
    result[i] = data[i] * factor;
}
```

3. Avoiding Function Pointers in Hot Paths

```
// Indirect call prevents inlining
for (int i = 0; i < n; i++) {
    result[i] = (*operation)(data[i]);  // Can't inline
}

// Template allows inlining
template<typename Op>
void process(Op operation) {
    for (int i = 0; i < n; i++) {
        result[i] = operation(data[i]);  // Can inline
    }
}
```

19.4.4 Profile-Guided Optimization (PGO)

PGO uses runtime profiling to optimize for actual usage patterns:

```
# Step 1: Compile with profiling
gcc -fprofile-generate program.c -o program

# Step 2: Run with representative workload
./program < typical_input.txt

# Step 3: Recompile with profile data
gcc -fprofile-use program.c -o program_optimized

# Results: Often 10-30% additional speedup
```

19.5 Profiling and Empirical Analysis

19.5.1 The Profiling Workflow

Effective performance optimization follows a systematic workflow:

1. **Measure**: Profile to identify bottlenecks
2. **Analyze**: Understand why the bottleneck exists
3. **Optimize**: Apply targeted improvements
4. **Verify**: Confirm improvements with benchmarks

19.5.2 Types of Profiling

1. CPU Profiling

```
# Using perf on Linux
perf record ./program
perf report

# Top functions by CPU time:
45.23%  program  [.] matrix_multiply
22.17%  program  [.] vector_dot_product
15.89%  program  [.] transpose
```

2. Memory Profiling

```
# Using valgrind's cachegrind
valgrind --tool=cachegrind ./program

# Cache miss analysis:
L1 misses:      1,234,567 (0.5%)
L2 misses:        456,789 (15.2%)
L3 misses:         12,345 (45.6%)
```

3. Micro-benchmarking

```
#include <benchmark/benchmark.h>

static void BM_StringCompare(benchmark::State& state) {
    std::string s1 = "hello";
    std::string s2 = "world";
    for (auto _ : state) {
        benchmark::DoNotOptimize(s1.compare(s2));
    }
}
BENCHMARK(BM_StringCompare);
```

19.5.3 Statistical Rigor in Benchmarking

Reliable benchmarks require statistical analysis:

```
def benchmark_with_statistics(algorithm, input, runs=100):
    times = []
    for _ in range(runs):
        start = time.perf_counter()
        algorithm(input)
        end = time.perf_counter()
        times.append(end - start)

    return {
        'mean': statistics.mean(times),
        'median': statistics.median(times),
```

```
        'stdev': statistics.stdev(times),
        'min': min(times),
        'max': max(times),
        'percentile_95': np.percentile(times, 95),
        'confidence_interval': calculate_ci(times, 0.95)
    }
```

Listing 19.7: Statistical benchmarking

19.5.4 Common Profiling Pitfalls

1. **Benchmarking Debug Builds**: Always profile optimized builds
2. **Ignoring Warm-up**: JIT-compiled languages need warm-up runs
3. **Unrealistic Inputs**: Profile with production-like data
4. **Measurement Overhead**: Ensure profiling doesn't distort results
5. **Environmental Noise**: Control for background processes, frequency scaling

19.5.5 Case Study: Optimizing a JSON Parser

Initial profiling of a JSON parser revealed:

Table 19.5: JSON parser profiling results

Function	Time %	Cumulative %
`parse_value()`	35.2%	35.2%
`allocate_node()`	28.7%	63.9%
`parse_string()`	15.3%	79.2%
`skip_whitespace()`	8.9%	88.1%

Optimization strategy:

1. **Memory pooling** for `allocate_node()`: 28.7% → 5.2%
2. **SIMD string parsing**: 15.3% → 4.1%
3. **Lookup table for whitespace**: 8.9% → 2.3%

Result: 3.8× overall speedup without changing algorithmic complexity.

19.6 When to Ignore Asymptotic Complexity

19.6.1 Small Input Sizes

For small inputs, asymptotically inferior algorithms often win:

```
# Insertion sort (O(n^2)) vs Quicksort (O(n log n))
# Crossover point: ~47 elements on typical systems

def hybrid_sort(arr):
    if len(arr) < 47:
        return insertion_sort(arr)  # O(n^2) but faster
    else:
        return quicksort(arr)       # O(n log n)
```

Listing 19.8: Hybrid sorting strategy

19.6.2 Real-Time Constraints

In real-time systems, worst-case behavior matters more than average case:

```
// Heapsort: O(n log n) worst-case, predictable
// Better for real-time despite slower average case
void real_time_sort(int* data, int n) {
    heapsort(data, n);  // Predictable timing
    // NOT quicksort - O(n^2) worst case could miss deadline
}
```

Listing 19.9: Real-time sorting choice

19.6.3 Memory Constraints

Space complexity can override time complexity considerations:

```
# In-place algorithm (O(n^2) time, O(1) space)
def bubble_sort_in_place(arr):
    for i in range(len(arr)):
        for j in range(len(arr) - 1):
            if arr[j] > arr[j + 1]:
                arr[j], arr[j + 1] = arr[j + 1], arr[j]

# Merge sort (O(n log n) time, O(n) space)
# May be impossible with limited memory
```

Listing 19.10: Space-time tradeoff

19.6.4 Development Time and Maintainability

Simple algorithms reduce bugs and development time:

```python
# Simple O(n^2) solution: 5 lines, obvious correctness
def find_pair_with_sum(arr, target):
    for i in range(len(arr)):
        for j in range(i + 1, len(arr)):
            if arr[i] + arr[j] == target:
                return (i, j)
    return None

# Optimal O(n) solution: 15 lines, more complex
def find_pair_with_sum_optimal(arr, target):
    seen = {}
    for i, num in enumerate(arr):
        complement = target - num
        if complement in seen:
            return (seen[complement], i)
        seen[num] = i
    return None
```

Listing 19.11: Simplicity vs. optimality

For rarely-used code with small inputs, the simple solution may be preferable.

19.6.5 Platform-Specific Optimizations

Hardware acceleration can override algorithmic complexity:

```c
// CPU: O(n^2) matrix-vector multiply
void cpu_matvec(float* y, float* A, float* x, int n) {
    for (int i = 0; i < n; i++) {
        y[i] = 0;
        for (int j = 0; j < n; j++) {
            y[i] += A[i*n + j] * x[j];
        }
    }
}

// GPU: Same O(n^2) complexity, but 100x faster for large n
__global__ void gpu_matvec(float* y, float* A, float* x, int n)
    {
    int i = blockIdx.x * blockDim.x + threadIdx.x;
    if (i < n) {
        float sum = 0;
        for (int j = 0; j < n; j++) {
            sum += A[i*n + j] * x[j];
        }
        y[i] = sum;
```

```
    }
}
```

Listing 19.12: CPU vs. GPU implementation

19.6.6 The Practicality Threshold

Define a "practicality threshold" for your application:

```
def choose_algorithm(n, time_budget_ms):
    # Empirically measured runtimes
    simple_runtime_ms = 0.001 * n * n       # O(n^2)
    complex_runtime_ms = 0.1 * n * log(n)   # O(n log n)

    # Choose based on actual runtime, not complexity
    if simple_runtime_ms < time_budget_ms and \
       simple_runtime_ms < complex_runtime_ms:
        return "simple"
    else:
        return "complex"

# For n=100, time_budget=20ms:
# simple: 10ms (wins despite O(n^2))
# complex: 66ms
```

Listing 19.13: Algorithm selection based on practical constraints

19.7 Summary and Best Practices

19.7.1 Key Takeaways

1. **Asymptotic complexity is a guide, not a guarantee** of real-world performance. Always validate with empirical measurements.

2. **Constants matter** when comparing algorithms with the same complexity. A 10× difference in constants can determine the practical winner.

3. **Cache effects dominate** modern performance. An algorithm with good locality can outperform an asymptotically superior algorithm with poor locality.

4. **Compiler optimizations** can change performance characteristics dramatically. Write optimization-friendly code and use appropriate compiler flags.

5. **Profile before optimizing**. Intuition about bottlenecks is often wrong; measurement reveals truth.

6. **Choose algorithms based on actual constraints**: input size, memory limits, real-time requirements, and development resources.

19.7.2 Best Practices for Performance Engineering

1. **Start with correctness**, then optimize. A fast wrong answer is useless.

2. **Establish performance requirements** early. Define what "fast enough" means for your application.

3. **Measure continuously**. Set up automated benchmarks to catch performance regressions.

4. **Optimize the common case**. Focus on the hot path that executes most frequently.

5. **Consider the whole system**. Sometimes the bottleneck is I/O, network, or database—not your algorithm.

6. **Document performance decisions**. Explain why you chose a theoretically suboptimal algorithm.

7. **Know your platform**. Understand your target hardware, compiler, and runtime environment.

19.7.3 The Art of Balance

Performance engineering is ultimately about balance:

- Balance between theoretical elegance and practical efficiency
- Balance between optimization effort and maintainability
- Balance between average-case and worst-case performance
- Balance between CPU, memory, and development time

The skilled practitioner knows when to apply theoretical knowledge and when to trust empirical evidence, when to optimize and when to accept "good enough," when to follow asymptotic analysis and when to ignore it in favor of practical considerations.

19.8 Exercises

1. **Constant Factor Analysis**: Implement three different $\mathcal{O}(n \log n)$ sorting algorithms and empirically measure their constant factors. Plot runtime vs. n and extract the constants.

2. **Cache Effect Demonstration**: Write two programs that sum a 2D array—one row-major, one column-major. Measure and explain the performance difference for various array sizes.

3. **Compiler Optimization Study**: Implement matrix multiplication and compile with different optimization levels. Use profiling tools to identify which optimizations the compiler applied.

4. **Crossover Point Finding**: Implement insertion sort and quicksort. Empirically determine the input size where quicksort becomes faster than insertion sort on your system.

5. **Real-World Profiling**: Take an existing program you've written, profile it, identify the top bottleneck, optimize it, and measure the improvement.

6. **Architecture-Specific Optimization**: Implement a simple operation (like array sum) in three ways: naive, cache-optimized, and SIMD-vectorized. Compare their performance.

7. **Statistical Benchmarking**: Create a benchmarking framework that reports not just mean runtime but also variance, percentiles, and confidence intervals.

8. **Memory vs. Time Trade-off**: Implement an algorithm with multiple space-time trade-off options (like dynamic programming with and without memoization). Determine when each is preferable.

19.9 Further Reading

- Bentley, J. *Programming Pearls* – Classic examples of practical algorithm engineering
- Agner Fog's Optimization Manuals – Comprehensive guides to low-level optimization
- "What Every Programmer Should Know About Memory" by Ulrich Drepper

- Intel VTune Profiler Documentation – Professional profiling techniques
- Google Benchmark Library – Framework for microbenchmarking
- Bryant, R. and O'Hallaron, D. *Computer Systems: A Programmer's Perspective*

Chapter 20

Parallel and Distributed Complexity

Introduction

As we reach the physical limits of single-processor performance improvements, parallel and distributed computing have become essential paradigms for solving computationally intensive problems. This chapter explores the complexity analysis of algorithms designed for multiple processors working together, whether in tightly-coupled parallel systems or loosely-coupled distributed networks. We'll examine how traditional complexity measures adapt to these new computational models and introduce new metrics specific to parallel and distributed environments.

20.1 Models of Parallel Computation

20.1.1 The PRAM Model

The Parallel Random Access Machine (PRAM) model serves as the theoretical foundation for parallel algorithm analysis. In this idealized model, we assume:

- **P processors** operating synchronously
- **Shared memory** accessible by all processors
- **Unit-time operations** for basic computations and memory access

PRAM Variants

The PRAM model comes in several flavors based on how concurrent memory access is handled:

1. **EREW (Exclusive Read, Exclusive Write)**: No two processors can simultaneously access the same memory location
2. **CREW (Concurrent Read, Exclusive Write)**: Multiple processors can read the same location simultaneously, but only one can write
3. **CRCW (Concurrent Read, Concurrent Write)**: Multiple processors can both read and write simultaneously
   - *Common CRCW*: Concurrent writes must write the same value
   - *Arbitrary CRCW*: An arbitrary processor succeeds in writing
   - *Priority CRCW*: The processor with the lowest index succeeds

Algorithm 34 CRCW Maximum Finding

```
procedure CRCW-Maximum(A[1..n])
    Input: Array A with n elements, n^2 processors P[i, j]
    Output: Maximum element
    for all P[i, j] where 1 ≤ i, j ≤ n in parallel do
        if A[i] < A[j] then
            M[i] ← 0
        else
            M[i] ← 1
        end if
    end for
    for all P[i, 1] where 1 ≤ i ≤ n in parallel do
        if M[i] = 1 then
            max ← A[i]
        end if
    end for
    return max
end procedure
```

Time Complexity: $\mathcal{O}(1)$ with n^2 processors

20.1.2 Network Models

Real parallel systems have processors connected through specific network topologies:

Common Topologies

- **Linear Array**: Processors in a line, each connected to neighbors
- **Mesh**: 2D or 3D grid of processors
- **Hypercube**: n-dimensional cube with 2^n processors
- **Tree**: Hierarchical connection pattern
- **Complete Graph**: Every processor connected to every other

Complexity Implications

Network topology affects:

- **Diameter**: Maximum distance between any two processors
- **Bisection Width**: Minimum number of edges to cut network in half
- **Degree**: Maximum connections per processor

20.1.3 The BSP Model

The Bulk Synchronous Parallel (BSP) model provides a more realistic abstraction:

BSP Components

1. **Computation supersteps**: Processors compute on local data
2. **Communication phase**: Processors exchange messages
3. **Barrier synchronization**: All processors wait for completion

BSP Cost Model

$$\text{Total Time} = \max_i(W_i) + h \cdot g + L \tag{20.1}$$

where:

$$W_i = \text{computation time for processor } i \tag{20.2}$$
$$h = \text{maximum messages sent/received by any processor} \tag{20.3}$$
$$g = \text{bandwidth inefficiency parameter} \tag{20.4}$$
$$L = \text{latency (synchronization cost)} \tag{20.5}$$

20.1.4 The LogP Model

LogP captures more network characteristics:

- **L**: Latency (time for message transmission)
- **o**: Overhead (time processor is busy sending/receiving)
- **g**: Gap (minimum time between consecutive messages)
- **P**: Number of processors

LogP Cost Analysis

For sending k messages:

$$\text{Time} = L + (k-1) \cdot \max(g, o) + o \tag{20.6}$$

20.2 Work and Depth in Parallel Algorithms

20.2.1 Fundamental Metrics

Definition 20.2.1 (Work). **Work (W)**: Total number of operations performed by all processors

- Represents the sequential complexity
- Lower bound: $W \geq$ best sequential algorithm time

Definition 20.2.2 (Depth). **Depth (D)**: Length of the longest chain of dependencies

- Also called span or critical path length
- Represents inherent sequential bottleneck

Definition 20.2.3 (Parallelism). **Parallelism**: $P = W/D$

- Maximum useful parallelism
- Indicates scalability potential

20.2.2 Brent's Theorem

Theorem 20.2.1 (Brent's Theorem). *An algorithm with work W and depth D can be executed on p processors in time:*

$$T_p \leq \frac{W}{p} + D \tag{20.7}$$

Implications:

- When $p = 1$: $T_1 = W$ (sequential execution)
- When $p = \infty$: $T_\infty = D$ (unlimited parallelism)
- Optimal when $T_p = O(W/p + D)$

20.2.3 Work-Efficient Algorithms

Definition 20.2.4 (Work-Efficiency). An algorithm is **work-efficient** if:

$$W(n) = O(T_{\text{seq}}(n)) \tag{20.8}$$

where T_{seq} is the best sequential algorithm's time complexity.

Algorithm 35 Work-Efficient Parallel Prefix Sum

```
procedure Work-Efficient-Prefix-Sum(A[1..n])
    Phase 1: Up-sweep (reduction)
    for d = 0 to log n − 1 do
        for all k = 0 to n/2^(d+1) − 1 in parallel do
            A[2^(d+1) · (k+1) − 1] ← A[2^(d+1) · (k+1) − 1] + A[2^(d+1) · k + 2^d − 1]
        end for
    end for

    Phase 2: Down-sweep
    A[n] ← 0
    for d = log n − 1 downto 0 do
        for all k = 0 to n/2^(d+1) − 1 in parallel do
            t ← A[2^(d+1) · k + 2^d − 1]
            A[2^(d+1) · k + 2^d − 1] ← A[2^(d+1) · (k+1) − 1]
            A[2^(d+1) · (k+1) − 1] ← A[2^(d+1) · (k+1) − 1] + t
        end for
    end for
end procedure
```

$$\text{Work: } O(n) \tag{20.9}$$

$$\text{Depth: } O(\log n) \tag{20.10}$$

$$\text{Parallelism: } O(n/\log n) \tag{20.11}$$

20.2.4 Speedup and Efficiency

Definition 20.2.5 (Speedup). **Speedup**: $S(p) = T_1/T_p$

- Linear speedup: $S(p) = p$ (ideal)
- Sublinear: $S(p) < p$ (typical)
- Superlinear: $S(p) > p$ (rare, usually due to cache effects)

Definition 20.2.6 (Efficiency). **Efficiency**: $E(p) = S(p)/p = T_1/(p \cdot T_p)$

- Measures processor utilization
- $E(p) = 1$ for perfect scaling

Theorem 20.2.2 (Amdahl's Law). *For fraction f of sequential work:*

$$S(p) \leq \frac{1}{f + \frac{1-f}{p}} \tag{20.12}$$

As $p \to \infty$: $S(\infty) \leq 1/f$

20.3 Communication Complexity

20.3.1 Communication Models

Message Passing Model

- Processors have local memory
- Communication via explicit messages
- Cost = (message count) × (message size)

Shared Memory Model

- Communication through shared variables
- Cost = memory contention and coherence overhead

20.3.2 Lower Bounds on Communication

Theorem 20.3.1 (Communication-Computation Tradeoff). *For many problems, there's a fundamental limit:*

$$\textit{Communication} \geq \Omega\left(\frac{W}{M^{1/2}}\right) \tag{20.13}$$

where M is local memory size per processor.

Example: Matrix Multiplication

For $n \times n$ matrices on p processors:

- Computation per processor: $O(n^3/p)$
- Communication lower bound: $\Omega(n^2/\sqrt{p})$

20.3.3 Communication-Avoiding Algorithms

Strategy: Minimize communication even at the cost of redundant computation.

Algorithm 36 2.5D Matrix Multiplication

procedure 2.5D-MATMUL(A, B, C, c)
▷ c = memory scaling factor, $1 \le c \le p^{1/3}$
  Replicate input matrices c times
  Perform $1/c$ of the computation per replica
  Reduce partial results
end procedure

$$\text{Communication:} \quad O(n^2/\sqrt{c \cdot p}) \tag{20.14}$$

$$\text{Memory per processor:} \quad O(c \cdot n^2/p) \tag{20.15}$$

20.3.4 Collective Communication Patterns

Operation	**Description**	**Time Complexity**
Broadcast	One-to-all	$O(\log p)$
Reduce	All-to-one with operation	$O(\log p)$
All-reduce	Reduce + broadcast result	$O(\log p)$
Gather	All-to-one concatenation	$O(p)$
Scatter	One-to-all distribution	$O(p)$
All-to-all	Complete exchange	$O(p)$

Table 20.1: Common collective communication operations and their complexities

20.4 Distributed Algorithm Complexity

20.4.1 The LOCAL and CONGEST Models

LOCAL Model

- Synchronous rounds
- Unlimited message size
- Complexity = number of rounds

CONGEST Model

- $O(\log n)$ bit messages
- More realistic for networks
- Complexity = rounds × message complexity

20.4.2 Distributed Complexity Classes

Key Classes:

- $O(1)$: Constant-time (local decisions)
- $O(\log^* n)$: Iterated logarithm (coloring sparse graphs)
- $O(\log n)$: Logarithmic (many tree algorithms)
- $O(D)$: Diameter-based (D = network diameter)
- $O(n)$: Linear (global coordination required)

20.4.3 Consensus and Agreement

Byzantine Generals Problem

- n processors, f faulty
- Requirement: $f < n/3$ for Byzantine faults
- Message complexity: $O(n^2)$
- Round complexity: $O(f + 1)$

Paxos Algorithm Complexity

$$\text{Phase 1a:} \quad \text{Leader} \to \text{Acceptors} : O(n) \text{ messages} \tag{20.16}$$

$$\text{Phase 1b:} \quad \text{Acceptors} \to \text{Leader} : O(n) \text{ messages} \tag{20.17}$$

$$\text{Phase 2a:} \quad \text{Leader} \to \text{Acceptors} : O(n) \text{ messages} \tag{20.18}$$

$$\text{Phase 2b:} \quad \text{Acceptors} \to \text{Learners} : O(n^2) \text{ messages} \tag{20.19}$$

$$\text{Total:} \quad O(n^2) \text{ messages per consensus} \tag{20.20}$$

20.4.4 Distributed Graph Algorithms

Minimum Spanning Tree (GHS Algorithm)

$$\text{Phases:} \quad O(\log n) \tag{20.21}$$

$$\text{Messages per phase:} \quad O(n \log n) \tag{20.22}$$

$$\text{Total message complexity:} \quad O(n \log^2 n) \tag{20.23}$$

$$\text{Time complexity:} \quad O(n \log n) \tag{20.24}$$

Shortest Paths (Bellman-Ford Distributed)

Algorithm 37 Distributed Bellman-Ford

Rounds: $O(D)$ where D = diameter
Messages per round: $O(m)$ where m = edges
Total complexity: $O(D \cdot m)$ messages

20.5 MapReduce and Big Data Algorithms

20.5.1 The MapReduce Model

Computational Phases:

1. **Map**: Transform input (key, value) pairs
2. **Shuffle**: Group by key (automatic)
3. **Reduce**: Aggregate values per key

Complexity Metrics:

- **Number of rounds**: Sequential MapReduce jobs
- **Communication cost**: Total data shuffled
- **Computation cost**: Total work across all mappers/reducers

20.5.2 Complexity Analysis Framework

Key Parameters:

- N: Input size
- M: Number of machines
- μ: Memory per machine
- Constraint: $M \cdot \mu = O(N^{1+\epsilon})$ for small ϵ

Optimal Algorithms:

- Minimize rounds while respecting memory constraints
- Tradeoff: rounds vs. communication vs. replication

20.5.3 Algorithm Design Patterns

Example 20.5.1 (TeraSort Complexity).

```
Phase 1: Sampling
  Map: O(N/M) per mapper
  Reduce: O(M log M) for pivot selection

Phase 2: Partitioning
  Map: O(N/M log M) per mapper (binary search)
  Shuffle: O(N) total
  Reduce: O(N/M log(N/M)) per reducer

Total rounds: 2
Communication: O(N)
Computation: O(N log N / M)
```

20.5.4 Graph Algorithms in MapReduce

Algorithm 38 PageRank Implementation in MapReduce

for each iteration **do**
    Map phase:
    for each page p with rank r and links L **do**
        emit $(p, 0)$ for structure
        for each link l in L **do**
            emit $(l, r/|L|)$
        end for
    end for

    Reduce phase:
    for each page p with values V **do**
        $\text{new\_rank} = 0.15 + 0.85 \times \sum(V)$
        emit $(p, \text{new\_rank})$
    end for
end for

$$\text{Iterations: } O(\log n) \text{ for convergence} \tag{20.25}$$

$$\text{Communication per iteration: } O(\text{edges}) \tag{20.26}$$

$$\text{Total complexity: } O(\text{edges} \times \log n) \tag{20.27}$$

20.5.5 Limitations and Lower Bounds

Theorem 20.5.1 (MRC Class). *Problems solvable in:*

- $O(polylog(N))$ *rounds*
- $O(N^{1-\epsilon})$ *memory per machine*
- $O(N^{1-\epsilon})$ *machines*

Hard Problems for MapReduce:

- Graph connectivity: Requires $\Omega(\log n)$ rounds
- Shortest paths: $\Omega(D)$ rounds for diameter D
- Strongly connected components: Not in MRC^0

20.6 GPU Computing Considerations

20.6.1 GPU Architecture and Execution Model

Key Characteristics:

- **SIMT Execution**: Single Instruction, Multiple Threads
- **Warps**: Groups of 32 threads executing in lockstep
- **Memory Hierarchy**:
  - Global memory: High latency (400-800 cycles)
  - Shared memory: Low latency (few cycles)
  - Registers: Immediate access

Thread Organization:

```
Grid
 Block (0,0)  Block (0,1)  ...
      Warp 0 (32 threads)
      Warp 1 (32 threads)
      ...
 ...
```

20.6.2 Complexity Metrics for GPU

Work Complexity: Total operations across all threads

$$W_{\text{GPU}} = \text{threads\_per\_block} \times \text{blocks} \times \text{operations\_per\_thread} \tag{20.28}$$

Step Complexity: Parallel execution steps

$$S_{\text{GPU}} = \text{kernel\_launches} \times \text{max\_iterations\_per\_kernel} \tag{20.29}$$

Memory Complexity:

- **Coalesced accesses**: $O(1)$ per warp
- **Uncoalesced accesses**: $O(32)$ per warp
- **Bank conflicts**: Adds serialization overhead

20.6.3 Divergence and Efficiency

Branch Divergence Cost:
When threads in a warp take different branches:

$$\text{Time} = \text{Time(then-branch)} + \text{Time(else-branch)} \tag{20.30}$$

$$\text{Efficiency} = \text{Active\_threads}/32 \tag{20.31}$$

```
__global__ void reduce(float* data, float* result, int n) {
    extern __shared__ float sdata[];
    int tid = threadIdx.x;
    int i = blockIdx.x * blockDim.x + threadIdx.x;

    // Load to shared memory
    sdata[tid] = (i < n) ? data[i] : 0;
    __syncthreads();

    // Reduction in shared memory
    for (int s = blockDim.x/2; s > 0; s >>= 1) {
        if (tid < s) {
            sdata[tid] += sdata[tid + s];
        }
        __syncthreads();
    }

    if (tid == 0) result[blockIdx.x] = sdata[0];
}
```

Listing 20.1: Parallel Reduction on GPU

$$\text{Work:} \quad O(n) \tag{20.32}$$

$$\text{Step complexity:} \quad O(\log n) \tag{20.33}$$

$$\text{Memory accesses:} \quad O(n) \text{ coalesced reads} \tag{20.34}$$

20.6.4 Occupancy and Performance

Occupancy: Ratio of active warps to maximum warps

$$\text{Occupancy} = \frac{\text{Active\_warps}}{\text{Max\_warps\_per\_SM}} \tag{20.35}$$

Factors Limiting Occupancy:

- Register usage per thread
- Shared memory per block
- Thread block size

Optimization Strategy:

$$\text{threads\_per\_block} = \min \left\{ \begin{array}{l} \text{max\_threads\_per\_block} \\ \text{max\_registers/registers\_per\_thread} \\ \text{max\_shared\_memory/shared\_memory\_per\_block} \end{array} \right\} \tag{20.36}$$

20.6.5 GPU-Specific Algorithm Design

```
__global__ void matmul(float* A, float* B, float* C, int n) {
    __shared__ float As[TILE_SIZE][TILE_SIZE];
    __shared__ float Bs[TILE_SIZE][TILE_SIZE];

    int row = blockIdx.y * TILE_SIZE + threadIdx.y;
    int col = blockIdx.x * TILE_SIZE + threadIdx.x;
    float sum = 0.0;

    for (int t = 0; t < n/TILE_SIZE; t++) {
        // Collaborative loading to shared memory
        As[threadIdx.y][threadIdx.x] =
            A[row*n + t*TILE_SIZE + threadIdx.x];
        Bs[threadIdx.y][threadIdx.x] =
            B[(t*TILE_SIZE + threadIdx.y)*n + col];
        __syncthreads();

        // Compute partial product
        for (int k = 0; k < TILE_SIZE; k++) {
            sum += As[threadIdx.y][k] * Bs[k][threadIdx.x];
        }
        __syncthreads();
    }

    C[row*n + col] = sum;
}
```

Listing 20.2: Tiled Matrix Multiplication on GPU

$$\text{Global memory accesses: } O(n^3/\text{TILE\_SIZE}) \quad (20.37)$$

$$\text{Computation: } O(n^3) \quad (20.38)$$

$$\text{Speedup factor: } \text{TILE\_SIZE} \quad (20.39)$$

20.6.6 Comparison with CPU Parallelism

Aspect	**CPU Parallelism**	**GPU Parallelism**
Threads	10s-100s	1000s-10000s
Thread overhead	High	Low
Branch efficiency	Good	Poor (divergence)
Memory latency hiding	Cache	Thread switching
Best for	Complex, irregular	Simple, regular
Communication	Efficient	Limited

Table 20.2: CPU vs GPU parallelism characteristics

Summary

Parallel and distributed complexity analysis extends traditional complexity theory to multi-processor systems. Key insights include:

1. **Work-Depth Framework**: Provides fundamental limits on parallelization
2. **Communication Complexity**: Often dominates in distributed systems
3. **Architecture-Specific Models**: PRAM for theory, BSP/LogP for practice
4. **MapReduce Paradigm**: Enables massive scale with simple programming model
5. **GPU Computing**: Requires careful attention to memory access patterns and divergence

The choice of parallel algorithm and architecture depends critically on:

- Problem structure (regular vs. irregular)
- Data size and locality
- Communication requirements

- Available hardware resources

As we move toward exascale computing and beyond, understanding these complexity measures becomes essential for designing efficient algorithms that can harness the power of modern parallel and distributed systems.

Exercises

1. **PRAM Analysis**: Design a CREW PRAM algorithm for finding the second largest element in an array of n elements. Analyze its time complexity with p processors.
2. **Work-Efficiency**: Prove that the parallel prefix sum algorithm presented is work-efficient by showing $W(n) = O(n)$.
3. **Communication Lower Bound**: Derive the communication lower bound for parallel sorting of n elements distributed across p processors.
4. **MapReduce Design**: Design a MapReduce algorithm for finding all triangles in a graph. Analyze the number of rounds and communication complexity.
5. **GPU Optimization**: Given a naive GPU matrix transpose with uncoalesced memory accesses, redesign it to achieve coalesced accesses and analyze the performance improvement.
6. **Amdahl's Law Application**: If 90% of an algorithm can be parallelized, what is the maximum theoretical speedup with 100 processors? With infinite processors?
7. **Distributed MST**: Trace through the GHS algorithm for finding MST on a small example graph and count the total messages exchanged.
8. **BSP Cost Model**: Analyze the BSP cost of parallel merge sort with n elements and p processors.

Further Reading

- Jájá, J. (1992). *An Introduction to Parallel Algorithms*
- Grama, A., Gupta, A., Karypis, G., & Kumar, V. (2003). *Introduction to Parallel Computing*
- Lynch, N. (1996). *Distributed Algorithms*

- Karloff, H., Suri, S., & Vassilvitskii, S. (2010). "A Model of Computation for MapReduce"
- Kirk, D., & Hwu, W. (2016). *Programming Massively Parallel Processors*

Chapter 21

Modern Complexity Challenges

The landscape of algorithmic complexity has evolved dramatically with the advent of new computing paradigms and unprecedented data scales. This chapter explores contemporary challenges that extend beyond traditional complexity analysis, examining how modern computing environments demand new theoretical frameworks and analytical techniques.

21.1 Big Data and Streaming Algorithms

21.1.1 The Big Data Paradigm Shift

The explosion of data in the digital age has fundamentally challenged our traditional notions of algorithmic complexity. When datasets exceed the capacity of main memory—or even distributed storage systems—classical algorithms that assume random access to data become impractical. This section examines how complexity analysis adapts to scenarios where data volume, velocity, and variety present unique challenges.

In the big data context, we must reconsider fundamental assumptions. The traditional RAM model, which assumes $\mathcal{O}(1)$ access to any memory location, breaks down when data resides on distributed systems or arrives as continuous streams. Instead, we focus on metrics such as the number of passes over the data, communication complexity between nodes, and the trade-offs between accuracy and resource consumption.

21.1.2 Streaming Algorithm Fundamentals

Streaming algorithms process data sequentially in one or few passes, using sublinear space relative to the input size. The complexity analysis of these algorithms introduces new parameters:

- **Space complexity** $S(n)$: Typically required to be $\mathcal{O}(\text{polylog } n)$ or $\mathcal{O}(n^\epsilon)$ for $\epsilon < 1$
- **Update time**: The time to process each arriving element
- **Query time**: The time to answer queries about the stream
- **Number of passes**: How many times we can afford to read the data

Consider the classic problem of finding frequent items in a stream. The Count-Min Sketch algorithm maintains approximate frequency counts using $\mathcal{O}\left(\epsilon^{-1} \log \delta^{-1}\right)$ space to achieve ϵ-approximation with probability $1-\delta$. This represents a fundamental trade-off: we sacrifice exactness for feasibility.

Definition 21.1.1 (Count-Min Sketch)**.** A Count-Min Sketch is a probabilistic data structure that serves as a frequency table of events in a stream of data. It uses hash functions $h_1, \ldots, h_d$ mapping items to $\{1, \ldots, w\}$ and maintains a $d \times w$ array of counters.

21.1.3 Complexity in the MapReduce Model

The MapReduce paradigm introduces its own complexity measures:

1. **Number of rounds**: The depth of the computation DAG
2. **Total communication**: The sum of all data transferred between rounds
3. **Load balancing**: The maximum work assigned to any single processor

An algorithm's efficiency in MapReduce often depends on minimizing rounds while keeping communication subquadratic in the input size. For instance, computing connected components can be done in $\mathcal{O}(\log n)$ rounds with $\mathcal{O}(n \log n)$ total communication, but achieving fewer rounds often requires super-linear communication.

Theorem 21.1.1 (MapReduce Connected Components)**.** *There exists a MapReduce algorithm that computes connected components of a graph $G = (V, E)$ in $\mathcal{O}(\log |V|)$ rounds with total communication $\mathcal{O}((|V| + |E|) \log |V|)$.*

21.1.4 Sublinear Time Algorithms

For massive datasets, even linear time can be prohibitive. Sublinear algorithms make decisions by examining only a small portion of the input. The complexity analysis here involves:

- **Query complexity**: Number of queries to the input
- **Sample complexity**: Size of the sample needed for desired accuracy
- **Approximation guarantees**: The quality of the approximate solution

Property testing exemplifies this approach: determining whether a graph is bipartite or ϵ-far from bipartite can be done in $\mathcal{O}\left(\sqrt{n}/\epsilon^{3/2}\right)$ queries, independent of the number of edges.

21.2 Online Algorithms and Competitive Analysis

21.2.1 The Online Computing Model

Online algorithms must make irrevocable decisions without knowledge of future inputs. Traditional worst-case analysis often yields overly pessimistic bounds for such algorithms, leading to the development of competitive analysis as a more nuanced framework.

Definition 21.2.1 (Competitive Ratio). An online algorithm $\mathcal{A}$ is *c-competitive* if for all input sequences σ:

$$\text{cost}_{\mathcal{A}}(\sigma) \leq c \cdot \text{cost}_{\text{OPT}}(\sigma) + \alpha$$

where $\text{OPT}(\sigma)$ is the cost of the optimal offline algorithm that knows the entire input sequence in advance, and α is a constant independent of the input.

21.2.2 Classic Problems and Bounds

The paging problem illustrates fundamental concepts in competitive analysis. Any deterministic online paging algorithm is at least k-competitive (where k is the cache size), while randomized algorithms can achieve $\mathcal{O}(\log k)$ competitiveness. This gap between deterministic and randomized algorithms is characteristic of many online problems.

Theorem 21.2.1 (Paging Lower Bound). *Any deterministic online paging algorithm has competitive ratio at least k, where k is the size of the cache.*

The online bipartite matching problem demonstrates how competitive ratios can be surprisingly good despite uncertainty. The celebrated Ranking algorithm achieves $(1 - 1/e)$-competitiveness, and this bound is tight for the adversarial model.

21.2.3 Beyond Worst-Case: Refined Models

Pure competitive analysis sometimes yields overly conservative bounds. Several refinements provide more realistic analyses:

Resource Augmentation Comparing an online algorithm with more resources against an optimal offline algorithm with fewer resources. For example, an online algorithm with $(1 + \epsilon)$ times the speed might compete against an offline algorithm.

Smoothed Competitive Analysis Combining competitive analysis with smoothed analysis by adding small random perturbations to worst-case inputs.

Advice Complexity Quantifying how many bits of future information are needed to achieve certain competitive ratios. This creates a trade-off curve between advice and competitiveness.

Definition 21.2.2 (Advice Complexity)**.** An online algorithm with advice reads $b(n)$ bits of advice about the future. The advice complexity is the minimum $b(n)$ required to achieve a given competitive ratio.

21.2.4 Machine Learning-Augmented Algorithms

Recent work incorporates machine learning predictions into online algorithms. The complexity analysis now includes:

- **Consistency**: Performance when predictions are perfect
- **Robustness**: Worst-case performance regardless of prediction quality
- **Smoothness**: Graceful degradation as prediction error increases

These algorithms often achieve the best of both worlds: near-optimal performance with good predictions while maintaining reasonable worst-case guarantees.

21.3 Cache-Oblivious Algorithms

21.3.1 The Cache-Oblivious Model

Cache-oblivious algorithms achieve optimal cache performance without knowing cache parameters (size or line length). This elegant model simplifies algorithm design while maintaining efficiency across the memory hierarchy. The complexity analysis focuses on the number of cache misses, assuming an ideal cache replacement policy.

Definition 21.3.1 (Cache-Oblivious Model). In the cache-oblivious model, the algorithm is designed for a simple RAM model, but analyzed in a two-level memory model with:

- Cache of size M
- Cache lines of size B
- Optimal offline cache replacement

The algorithm does not know M or B.

The fundamental insight is that algorithms optimal for an unknown two-level hierarchy are often optimal for any multi-level hierarchy. This universality makes cache-oblivious algorithms particularly valuable in practice.

21.3.2 Analyzing Cache Complexity

Cache complexity analysis introduces the concept of cache misses $\mathcal{M}(n, B, M)$ where:

- n is the problem size
- B is the block size (cache line size)
- M is the cache size

For scanning n elements, the number of cache misses is $\Theta(n/B)$. For matrix multiplication, naive algorithms incur $\Theta\left(n^3/B\right)$ misses, while cache-oblivious algorithms achieve $\mathcal{O}\left(n^3/(B\sqrt{M})\right)$ misses—matching the cache-aware bound.

Theorem 21.3.1 (Cache-Oblivious Matrix Multiplication). *There exists a cache-oblivious algorithm for multiplying two $n \times n$ matrices that incurs*

$$\mathcal{M}(n, B, M) = \mathcal{O}\left(\frac{n^3}{B\sqrt{M}}\right)$$

cache misses, which is optimal.

21.3.3 Recursive Divide-and-Conquer

Many cache-oblivious algorithms employ recursive divide-and-conquer strategies. The van Emde Boas layout for binary search trees exemplifies this approach, achieving $\mathcal{O}(\log_B n)$ cache misses per search—optimal among comparison-based searches.

Algorithm 39 Cache-Oblivious Binary Search (van Emde Boas Layout)

Recursively layout tree of height h:
if $h \leq 1$ **then**
    Layout nodes directly
else
    Let $h' = \lfloor h/2 \rfloor$
    Layout top tree of height h'
    Recursively layout each bottom tree of height $h - h' - 1$
end if

The cache-oblivious FFT algorithm recursively decomposes the problem until it fits in cache, achieving $\mathcal{O}((n/B)\log_M n)$ cache misses. This matches the optimal cache-aware bound while remaining oblivious to cache parameters.

21.3.4 Limitations and Lower Bounds

Not all problems admit efficient cache-oblivious solutions. Permutation operations often require knowledge of cache parameters for optimality. The lower bound for cache-oblivious sorting is $\Omega\left((n/B)\log_{M/B}(n/B)\right)$, which cache-oblivious algorithms can match using techniques like funnel sort.

Theorem 21.3.2 (Cache-Oblivious Sorting Lower Bound). *Any cache-oblivious comparison-based sorting algorithm must incur*

$$\mathcal{M}(n, B, M) = \Omega\left(\frac{n}{B}\log_{M/B}\frac{n}{B}\right)$$

cache misses in the worst case.

21.4 Energy-Efficient Computing

21.4.1 Energy as a Complexity Measure

As computing becomes increasingly mobile and data centers consume massive amounts of power, energy efficiency has emerged as a critical complexity measure alongside time and space. Energy-aware complexity analysis considers:

- **Dynamic energy**: Proportional to the number of operations
- **Static energy**: Related to execution time and active components
- **Communication energy**: Often dominant in distributed systems

The energy complexity of an algorithm often differs significantly from its time complexity, creating new optimization opportunities.

21.4.2 Voltage and Frequency Scaling

Dynamic voltage and frequency scaling (DVFS) allows trading performance for energy efficiency. The power consumption typically scales as $P \propto V^2 f$, where V is voltage and f is frequency. Since frequency is roughly proportional to voltage, we get $P \propto f^3$.

This cubic relationship implies that running a processor at half speed consumes one-eighth the power. For a task that's not time-critical, doubling the execution time can reduce energy consumption by 75%. The complexity analysis must now consider:

- **Energy-delay product**: $E \times T$
- **Energy-delay-squared product**: $E \times T^2$

These metrics capture the trade-off between energy and performance.

Proposition 21.4.1 (DVFS Energy-Time Trade-off). *Under the cubic power model $P = f^3$, executing a task at frequency $f' = \alpha f$ (where $0 < \alpha \leq 1$) results in:*

- *Execution time: $T' = T/\alpha$*
- *Energy consumption: $E' = \alpha^2 E$*
- *Energy-delay product: $EDP' = \alpha \cdot EDP$*

21.4.3 Algorithm Design for Energy Efficiency

Energy-efficient algorithms often exhibit different characteristics than time-optimal algorithms:

Locality of Reference Algorithms that minimize data movement save significant energy, as moving data often costs more energy than computation.

Approximation for Energy Approximate algorithms can provide substantial energy savings. For instance, approximate matrix multiplication using sampling can reduce energy consumption by orders of magnitude while maintaining acceptable accuracy.

Race-to-idle vs. Slow-and-steady The optimal strategy depends on the workload characteristics and hardware capabilities. Complexity analysis must model both dynamic and static power consumption to determine the best approach.

21.4.4 Green Computing Complexity Classes

Emerging theoretical frameworks define complexity classes based on energy consumption:

- $\mathbf{E}[f(n)]$: Problems solvable with $\mathcal{O}(f(n))$ energy
- **Energy-efficient reductions**: Transformations that preserve energy bounds
- **Energy-complete problems**: The most energy-demanding problems in a class

These theoretical developments parallel the evolution of traditional complexity theory but with energy as the primary resource.

21.5 Quantum Algorithm Complexity

21.5.1 Quantum Computational Model

Quantum algorithms operate on quantum bits (qubits) that can exist in superposition states. The complexity analysis of quantum algorithms requires new frameworks:

- **Quantum query complexity**: Number of queries to a quantum oracle
- **Quantum circuit complexity**: Number of quantum gates required
- **Quantum space complexity**: Number of qubits needed

The relationship between classical and quantum complexity remains one of the most fascinating areas of theoretical computer science.

Definition 21.5.1 (Quantum State). An n-qubit quantum state is a unit vector in $\mathbb{C}^{2^n}$:

$$|\psi\rangle = \sum_{x\in\{0,1\}^n} \alpha_x |x\rangle$$

where $\sum_x |\alpha_x|^2 = 1$.

21.5.2 Quantum Speedups and Limitations

Quantum algorithms can provide various types of speedups:

Exponential speedups Shor's factoring algorithm runs in $\mathcal{O}(n^3)$ time versus the best known classical algorithm's sub-exponential complexity. This dramatic improvement threatens current cryptographic systems.

Theorem 21.5.1 (Shor's Algorithm). *There exists a quantum algorithm that factors an n-bit integer with bounded error probability in time $\mathcal{O}(n^3)$ using $\mathcal{O}(n)$ qubits.*

Polynomial speedups Grover's search algorithm provides a quadratic speedup for unstructured search, finding an item in an unsorted database of n items in $\mathcal{O}\left(\sqrt{n}\right)$ queries versus $\mathcal{O}(n)$ classically.

Theorem 21.5.2 (Grover's Lower Bound). *Any quantum algorithm for unstructured search requires $\Omega\left(\sqrt{n}\right)$ queries, making Grover's algorithm optimal.*

No speedup For some problems, quantum algorithms cannot outperform classical ones. Total functions cannot have super-polynomial quantum speedups in the black-box model.

21.5.3 Quantum Complexity Classes

The quantum complexity class hierarchy introduces:

- **BQP** (Bounded-error Quantum Polynomial time): The quantum analog of BPP
- **QMA** (Quantum Merlin-Arthur): The quantum analog of NP
- **QCMA**: Where the proof is classical but verification is quantum

The relationship **BPP** $\subseteq$ **BQP** $\subseteq$ **PSPACE** is known, but whether these containments are strict remains open. The conjecture that BQP properly contains BPP would have profound implications for computing.

21.5.4 Quantum Algorithm Analysis Techniques

Analyzing quantum algorithms requires specialized techniques:

Quantum amplitude amplification Generalizes Grover's algorithm to amplify the probability of desired outcomes.

Quantum walks The quantum analog of random walks, often providing polynomial speedups for search problems.

Quantum Fourier transform The cornerstone of many quantum algorithms, implementable in $\mathcal{O}(n^2)$ gates for n qubits.

The complexity analysis must account for decoherence, error rates, and the overhead of quantum error correction, which can significantly impact practical performance.

21.6 Complexity in Machine Learning

21.6.1 Learning-Theoretic Complexity

Machine learning introduces unique complexity considerations beyond traditional algorithmic analysis:

- **Sample complexity**: Number of training examples needed
- **Computational complexity**: Time to train and evaluate models
- **Model complexity**: Parameters or capacity of the hypothesis class
- **Generalization complexity**: The gap between training and test performance

The fundamental trade-off between model complexity and generalization is captured by various complexity measures including VC-dimension, Rademacher complexity, and covering numbers.

Definition 21.6.1 (VC-Dimension)**.** The VC-dimension of a hypothesis class $\mathcal{H}$ is the maximum size of a set that can be shattered by $\mathcal{H}$, where a set S is shattered if for every labeling of S, there exists $h \in \mathcal{H}$ consistent with that labeling.

21.6.2 PAC Learning Framework

The Probably Approximately Correct (PAC) learning framework provides rigorous complexity bounds. A concept class $\mathcal{C}$ is PAC-learnable if there exists an algorithm that, given

$$m = \mathcal{O}\left(\frac{1}{\epsilon}\left(\log\frac{1}{\delta} + \mathrm{VC}(\mathcal{C})\right)\right)$$

samples, produces a hypothesis with error at most ϵ with probability at least $1 - \delta$.

The computational complexity of PAC learning varies dramatically:

- Some concept classes are efficiently PAC-learnable (e.g., conjunctions)
- Others are information-theoretically learnable but computationally hard (e.g., DNF formulas)
- Cryptographic assumptions imply the existence of concept classes that are not efficiently learnable

Theorem 21.6.1 (Hardness of Learning DNF). *Unless* **NP** = **RP**, *there is no polynomial-time algorithm for PAC learning DNF formulas.*

21.6.3 Deep Learning Complexity Paradoxes

Deep neural networks present fascinating complexity puzzles:

Optimization complexity Training neural networks is NP-hard in general, yet gradient descent often finds good solutions in practice.

Overparameterization Networks with far more parameters than training samples should overfit catastrophically according to classical theory, yet they often generalize well.

Implicit regularization The choice of optimization algorithm implicitly affects the complexity of the learned function, with gradient descent exhibiting an implicit bias toward simpler solutions.

21.6.4 Complexity of Neural Network Inference

The inference complexity of neural networks involves:

- **Time complexity**: $\mathcal{O}(W)$ where W is the number of weights

- **Space complexity**: Can be reduced through quantization and pruning
- **Energy complexity**: Increasingly critical for edge deployment

Techniques like knowledge distillation, network pruning, and quantization trade accuracy for reduced complexity. The optimal trade-off depends on the application requirements and deployment constraints.

21.6.5 Learning Algorithm Complexity

Modern learning algorithms exhibit diverse complexity characteristics:

Gradient-based methods Stochastic gradient descent achieves ϵ-optimal solution in $\mathcal{O}(1/\epsilon^2)$ iterations for convex problems, $\mathcal{O}(1/\epsilon^4)$ for non-convex.

Theorem 21.6.2 (SGD Convergence for Convex Functions). *For L-smooth convex functions, SGD with appropriate step size achieves $\mathbb{E}[f(x_T) - f^*] \leq \epsilon$ after*

$$T = \mathcal{O}\left(\frac{L\|x_0 - x^*\|^2}{\epsilon}\right)$$

iterations.

Kernel methods Support vector machines require $\mathcal{O}(n^2)$ to $\mathcal{O}(n^3)$ time for n samples, limiting scalability.

Tree-based methods Random forests and gradient boosting achieve $\mathcal{O}(n \log n)$ training time per tree with careful implementation.

Online learning Algorithms must balance regret (cumulative loss compared to best fixed strategy) against computational efficiency.

21.6.6 Hardness Results and Lower Bounds

Recent theoretical results establish fundamental limits:

- Learning intersection of halfspaces is hard under cryptographic assumptions
- Agnostic learning of halfspaces is hard even with membership queries
- Statistical-computational gaps exist where information-theoretic learning is possible but computationally intractable

These results guide the development of practical algorithms and help explain empirical phenomena in machine learning.

21.7 Conclusion

Modern complexity challenges reflect the evolving landscape of computing. From streaming algorithms processing infinite data to quantum algorithms exploiting superposition, from cache-oblivious designs to energy-aware computing, and from online decision-making to deep learning's complexity paradoxes—each domain extends our understanding of computational complexity.

These challenges share common themes:

1. **Resource diversity**: Beyond time and space, we now optimize for energy, communication, cache misses, and quantum resources

2. **Approximate solutions**: Trading accuracy for efficiency is often necessary and sufficient

3. **Model refinement**: Classical worst-case analysis frequently requires refinement for modern applications

4. **Interdisciplinary connections**: Modern complexity increasingly intersects with physics, statistics, and information theory

As computing continues to evolve, new complexity challenges will emerge. The theoretical frameworks developed to address current challenges provide the foundation for tackling future computational problems. Understanding these modern complexity paradigms is essential for both theoretical computer scientists and practitioners designing systems for the contemporary computing landscape.

The next chapter will examine how these theoretical insights translate into practical algorithm design through detailed case studies, demonstrating how complexity analysis guides the development of efficient solutions to real-world problems.

Part VIII

Case Studies and Applications

Chapter 22

Algorithm Design Through Complexity Analysis

Introduction

Algorithm design is fundamentally an exercise in managing complexity. Rather than viewing complexity analysis as merely a tool for evaluating existing algorithms, this chapter explores how complexity considerations can actively guide the design process. Through detailed case studies spanning diverse computational domains, we demonstrate how theoretical insights into complexity lead to practical algorithmic innovations.

22.1 Complexity-Driven Algorithm Design

22.1.1 The Design Paradigm

Complexity-driven design begins with understanding the fundamental limits of a problem. Before writing any code, we ask critical questions:

Lower Bound Analysis: What is the theoretical minimum complexity for solving this problem? For sorting, we know $\Omega(n \log n)$ comparisons are necessary. For graph connectivity, $\Omega(V + E)$ time is required to examine all components. These bounds provide targets for our design efforts.

Problem Structure Exploitation: Complex problems often contain hidden structure that enables more efficient solutions. The key is identifying which aspects of the input can be leveraged:

- **Sparsity**: When data has many zero or default values, specialized representations can dramatically reduce complexity

- **Locality**: When related data cluster together, cache-aware algorithms can minimize memory access costs
- **Decomposability**: When problems can be broken into independent subproblems, divide-and-conquer or dynamic programming approaches become viable

22.1.2 The Complexity Hierarchy Approach

When designing algorithms, we traverse a hierarchy of complexity goals:

1. **Polynomial vs. Exponential**: First, we seek any polynomial-time solution, even if it's $\mathcal{O}\left(n^{10}\right)$
2. **Practical Polynomial**: Next, we refine to practical polynomial bounds like $\mathcal{O}\left(n^3\right)$ or $\mathcal{O}\left(n^2\right)$
3. **Near-Linear**: For large-scale applications, we target $\mathcal{O}(n \log n)$ or $\mathcal{O}\left(n \log^2 n\right)$
4. **Linear or Sublinear**: For massive datasets, even $\mathcal{O}(n)$ may be too slow, requiring streaming or sampling approaches

22.1.3 Trade-off Navigation

Algorithm design involves navigating multiple trade-offs:

Time vs. Space: The classic trade-off manifests in techniques like memoization (trading space for time) or recomputation (trading time for space). Modern systems with abundant RAM often favor space-intensive solutions.

Preprocessing vs. Query Time: Many problems benefit from expensive preprocessing that enables fast queries. Search engines spend $\mathcal{O}(n \log n)$ time building indices to support $\mathcal{O}(\log n)$ searches.

Exactness vs. Approximation: When exact solutions are intractable, approximation algorithms with provable bounds offer practical alternatives. A 2-approximation running in $\mathcal{O}(n)$ time often beats an exact $\mathcal{O}\left(n^3\right)$ algorithm.

22.1.4 Methodology for Complexity-Driven Design

Our systematic approach involves:

1. **Complexity Characterization**: Determine the problem's complexity class (P, NP-complete, etc.)

2. **Lower Bound Establishment**: Identify theoretical limits through reduction or adversary arguments
3. **Algorithm Space Exploration**: Survey existing approaches and their complexity profiles
4. **Bottleneck Identification**: Profile where current solutions spend most time/space
5. **Targeted Innovation**: Design new techniques specifically addressing identified bottlenecks
6. **Empirical Validation**: Verify that theoretical improvements translate to practice

22.2 Case Study: Fast Matrix Multiplication

22.2.1 The Problem and Its Importance

Matrix multiplication is fundamental to scientific computing, machine learning, computer graphics, and countless other applications. The naive algorithm for multiplying two $n \times n$ matrices requires $\mathcal{O}(n^3)$ operations:

Algorithm 40 Naive Matrix Multiplication

```
for i = 1 to n do
    for j = 1 to n do
        C[i, j] ← 0
        for k = 1 to n do
            C[i, j] ← C[i, j] + A[i, k] · B[k, j]
        end for
    end for
end for
```

With modern applications routinely handling matrices with millions of elements, even small improvements in the exponent yield massive practical benefits.

22.2.2 Strassen's Breakthrough

In 1969, Volker Strassen shattered the assumption that $\mathcal{O}(n^3)$ was optimal by presenting an $\mathcal{O}(n^{2.807})$ algorithm. His key insight: clever algebraic manipulation could reduce the number of recursive multiplications.

The Strassen Formulation: For 2×2 block matrices, instead of 8 multiplications, we compute:

$$M_1 = (A_{11} + A_{22})(B_{11} + B_{22}) \tag{22.1}$$
$$M_2 = (A_{21} + A_{22})B_{11} \tag{22.2}$$
$$M_3 = A_{11}(B_{12} - B_{22}) \tag{22.3}$$
$$M_4 = A_{22}(B_{21} - B_{11}) \tag{22.4}$$
$$M_5 = (A_{11} + A_{12})B_{22} \tag{22.5}$$
$$M_6 = (A_{21} - A_{11})(B_{11} + B_{12}) \tag{22.6}$$
$$M_7 = (A_{12} - A_{22})(B_{21} + B_{22}) \tag{22.7}$$

These 7 products (instead of 8) combine to form the result, yielding:

$$T(n) = 7T(n/2) + \mathcal{O}\left(n^2\right)$$

which solves to $\mathcal{O}\left(n^{\log_2 7}\right) \approx \mathcal{O}\left(n^{2.807}\right)$.

22.2.3 The Quest for the Optimal Exponent

Strassen's algorithm sparked decades of research into the optimal exponent ω for matrix multiplication:

Theoretical Advances:

- 1978: Pan achieved $\mathcal{O}\left(n^{2.796}\right)$
- 1979: Bini et al. reached $\mathcal{O}\left(n^{2.780}\right)$
- 1981: Schönhage obtained $\mathcal{O}\left(n^{2.522}\right)$
- 1987: Strassen improved to $\mathcal{O}\left(n^{2.479}\right)$
- 1990: Coppersmith-Winograd achieved $\mathcal{O}\left(n^{2.376}\right)$
- 2012: Vassilevska Williams refined to $\mathcal{O}\left(n^{2.3729}\right)$
- 2020: Alman and Vassilevska Williams reached $\mathcal{O}\left(n^{2.3728639}\right)$

Theorem 22.2.1 (Matrix Multiplication Exponent Bounds)**.** *The optimal exponent ω for matrix multiplication satisfies:*

$$2 \leq \omega \leq 2.3728639$$

The Complexity Theory Perspective: Many believe $\omega = 2$, but proving this remains one of the major open problems in theoretical computer science.

22.2.4 Practical Considerations

Despite theoretical advances, practical implementations face challenges:

Crossover Points: Strassen's algorithm has larger constant factors than the naive approach. Typical implementations switch to conventional multiplication for matrices smaller than 64×64 or 128×128.

Numerical Stability: Strassen's algorithm can amplify floating-point errors. For applications requiring high precision, stability concerns may outweigh performance benefits.

Cache Performance: Modern fast matrix multiplication must consider memory hierarchy:

- **Blocking**: Partition matrices into cache-sized blocks
- **Loop Tiling**: Reorder operations to maximize cache reuse
- **Prefetching**: Anticipate future memory needs

Parallel Implementation: Matrix multiplication parallelizes naturally, but fast algorithms complicate parallel decomposition. Hybrid approaches combine Strassen's method with parallel blocked algorithms.

22.2.5 Specialized Variants

Complexity analysis has driven development of specialized matrix multiplication algorithms:

Sparse Matrices: When matrices contain mostly zeros, complexity depends on the number of non-zero elements. Compressed representations and specialized algorithms achieve $\mathcal{O}(\text{nnz})$ complexity where $\text{nnz} \ll n^2$.

Rectangular Matrices: For multiplying $n \times k$ by $k \times m$ matrices, complexity is $\mathcal{O}(nmk)$. When dimensions vary significantly, specialized algorithms optimize the dominant factor.

Boolean Matrix Multiplication: Over GF(2), logical operations replace arithmetic, enabling bit-parallel optimizations and connections to graph algorithms.

22.3 Case Study: Integer Factorization

22.3.1 Problem Significance and Complexity

Integer factorization—decomposing a composite number into prime factors—exemplifies how complexity analysis shapes algorithm design in cryptography. The presumed difficulty of factoring large integers underpins RSA encryption, making this problem crucial for information security.

Definition 22.3.1 (Integer Factorization Problem)**.** Given a composite integer n, find prime numbers $p_1, p_2, \ldots, p_k$ and positive integers $e_1, e_2, \ldots, e_k$ such that:

$$n = p_1^{e_1} \cdot p_2^{e_2} \cdot \ldots \cdot p_k^{e_k}$$

Complexity Status: Factorization is in NP $\cap$ co-NP but not known to be in P or NP-complete. This unique position has driven sophisticated algorithmic development.

22.3.2 Evolution of Factoring Algorithms

Trial Division - $\mathcal{O}(\sqrt{n})$

The naive approach tests divisibility by all numbers up to $\sqrt{n}$. For a 100-digit number, this requires $\sim 10^{50}$ operations—impossible even with universe-scale computing resources.

Pollard's Rho Algorithm - $\mathcal{O}\left(n^{1/4}\right)$

Using a pseudo-random walk to find cycles, this probabilistic algorithm excels at finding small factors:

Algorithm 41 Pollard's Rho Algorithm

$x \leftarrow 2, y \leftarrow 2, d \leftarrow 1$
while $d = 1$ **do**
    $x \leftarrow f(x) \bmod n$ ▷ f is typically $x^2 + c$
    $y \leftarrow f(f(y)) \bmod n$
    $d \leftarrow \gcd(|x - y|, n)$
end whilereturn d

The birthday paradox ensures we find factors in expected $\mathcal{O}\left(\sqrt{p}\right)$ time where p is the smallest prime factor.

Quadratic Sieve - $\mathcal{O}\left(\exp(\sqrt{\ln n \ln \ln n})\right)$

This subexponential algorithm revolutionized factoring by finding congruences $x^2 \equiv y^2 \pmod{n}$:

1. Sieve for smooth numbers (those with only small prime factors)
2. Use linear algebra to combine smooth numbers
3. Extract factors from resulting congruences

The complexity analysis revealed that optimal performance requires carefully balancing the smoothness bound based on n's size.

Number Field Sieve - $\mathcal{O}\left(\exp((64/9)^{1/3}(\ln n)^{1/3}(\ln\ln n)^{2/3})\right)$

Currently the fastest known classical algorithm for large integers, NFS works in algebraic number fields:

1. Polynomial selection (finding good polynomials is crucial)
2. Sieving (finding smooth algebraic integers)
3. Linear algebra (solving huge sparse systems)
4. Square root computation (in number fields)

22.3.3 Complexity-Driven Optimizations

Smoothness Testing: The efficiency of modern factoring algorithms depends on identifying smooth numbers. Complexity analysis led to:

- Early abort strategies when partial factorization reveals non-smoothness
- Batch smoothness testing using product trees
- Cache-optimized sieving arrays

Linear Algebra Phase: Solving systems with millions of variables requires specialized techniques:

- Block Lanczos algorithm for GF(2) systems
- Structured Gaussian elimination exploiting sparsity
- Parallel and distributed implementations

Parameter Selection: Complexity analysis provides formulas for optimal parameters:

- Smoothness bounds: $B \approx \exp(\frac{1}{2}\sqrt{\ln n \ln\ln n})$
- Sieve region size: Balancing sieving time vs. relation yield
- Large prime bounds: Allowing partial relations improves efficiency

22.3.4 Quantum Complexity: Shor's Algorithm

Theorem 22.3.1 (Shor, 1994). *Integer factorization can be solved in quantum polynomial time $\mathcal{O}\left((\log n)^3\right)$ on a quantum computer.*

Shor's algorithm demonstrates that factorization is in BQP (bounded-error quantum polynomial time):

1. **Period Finding**: Use quantum Fourier transform to find the period of $f(x) = a^x \bmod n$
2. **Classical Reduction**: Convert period to factors using continued fractions

This exponential speedup over classical algorithms has profound implications for cryptography, driving development of post-quantum cryptographic systems.

22.3.5 Practical Impact and Current Records

Complexity improvements have dramatic practical consequences:

- 1991: RSA-100 (330 bits) factored using Quadratic Sieve
- 1999: RSA-155 (512 bits) factored using Number Field Sieve
- 2009: RSA-768 (768 bits) factored, requiring 2000 CPU-years
- 2019: RSA-240 (795 bits) factored

Each advancement required not just theoretical improvements but careful engineering guided by complexity analysis.

22.4 Case Study: Computational Geometry Problems

22.4.1 The Geometric Complexity Landscape

Computational geometry problems exhibit rich complexity behaviors due to their spatial nature. Unlike discrete problems, geometric algorithms must handle continuous spaces, degeneracies, and robustness issues while maintaining efficiency.

22.4.2 Convex Hull: From $\mathcal{O}(n^4)$ to $\mathcal{O}(n \log n)$

The convex hull problem—finding the smallest convex polygon containing a set of points—illustrates how algorithmic innovation can dramatically improve complexity.

Definition 22.4.1 (Convex Hull)**.** Given a set S of n points in $\mathbb{R}^d$, the convex hull $\mathrm{CH}(S)$ is the smallest convex set containing S.

Naive Approach - $\mathcal{O}(n^4)$

Test all possible triangles; a point is on the hull if it's part of a triangle with all other points on one side.

Gift Wrapping (Jarvis March) - $\mathcal{O}(nh)$

Walk along the hull, finding the next vertex by checking all points. Complexity depends on output size h.

Graham Scan - $\mathcal{O}(n \log n)$

1. Sort points by polar angle: $\mathcal{O}(n \log n)$
2. Process points in order, maintaining convex hull: $\mathcal{O}(n)$

The key insight: sorting provides structure that enables linear-time hull construction.

Divide and Conquer - $\mathcal{O}(n \log n)$

1. Recursively compute hulls of left/right halves
2. Merge hulls using tangent lines

This approach naturally parallelizes and achieves optimal worst-case complexity.

Chan's Algorithm - $\mathcal{O}(n \log h)$

Combining gift wrapping with a clever grouping strategy achieves output-sensitive optimal complexity:

1. Guess hull size m
2. Partition into n/m groups

3. Compute hull of each group
4. Gift wrap using group hulls

Theorem 22.4.1 (Lower Bound for Convex Hull). *In the algebraic decision tree model, computing the convex hull of n points requires $\Omega(n \log n)$ comparisons in the worst case.*

22.4.3 Closest Pair: Beating $\mathcal{O}(n^2)$

Finding the closest pair of points among n points seems to require checking all $\binom{n}{2}$ pairs, but geometric structure enables faster solutions.

Divide and Conquer Approach - $\mathcal{O}(n \log n)$

1. Divide points by vertical line
2. Recursively find closest pairs in each half
3. Check pairs crossing the dividing line

The crucial observation: only points within distance δ of the dividing line need checking, and geometric constraints limit these to $\mathcal{O}(n)$ comparisons.

Randomized Incremental - Expected $\mathcal{O}(n)$

Using randomization and careful data structure maintenance, we can achieve expected linear time by processing points in random order and maintaining a grid of cells.

22.4.4 Voronoi Diagrams: A Geometric Swiss Army Knife

Voronoi diagrams partition space based on nearest neighbors, solving numerous problems efficiently.

Definition 22.4.2 (Voronoi Diagram). For a set of points $P = \{p_1, \ldots, p_n\}$ in $\mathbb{R}^d$, the Voronoi cell of p_i is:

$$V(p_i) = \{x \in \mathbb{R}^d : ||x - p_i|| \leq ||x - p_j|| \text{ for all } j \neq i\}$$

Fortune's Sweep Line Algorithm - $\mathcal{O}(n \log n)$: Using a beach line data structure and event queue, we construct the diagram by sweeping a line across the plane. The algorithm's elegance comes from recognizing that the beach line consists of parabolic arcs.

Applications via Voronoi Diagrams:

- Nearest neighbor queries: $\mathcal{O}(\log n)$ after $\mathcal{O}(n \log n)$ preprocessing
- Largest empty circle: $\mathcal{O}(n \log n)$ by checking Voronoi vertices
- Minimum spanning tree: Extract from Delaunay triangulation in $\mathcal{O}(n \log n)$

22.4.5 Range Searching: The Curse of Dimensionality

Range searching—finding all points within a query region—demonstrates how dimensionality affects complexity.

1D Range Searching:

- Balanced BST: $\mathcal{O}(\log n + k)$ query after $\mathcal{O}(n \log n)$ preprocessing

2D Range Trees:

- Query: $\mathcal{O}\left(\log^2 n + k\right)$
- Space: $\mathcal{O}(n \log n)$
- Construction: $\mathcal{O}(n \log n)$

***d*-Dimensional Range Trees**:

- Query: $\mathcal{O}\left(\log^d n + k\right)$
- Space: $\mathcal{O}\left(n \log^{d-1} n\right)$

The exponential growth with dimension motivates approximate methods for high dimensions.

22.4.6 Robustness and Degeneracy

Geometric algorithms must handle numerical precision and degenerate cases:

Exact Arithmetic: Using rational arithmetic or adaptive precision to guarantee correctness

Symbolic Perturbation: Conceptually perturbing input to remove degeneracies without changing output

Topology-Oriented Approach: Maintaining combinatorial structure separately from numeric coordinates

22.5 Case Study: Bioinformatics Algorithms

22.5.1 The Complexity Challenge in Biological Data

Bioinformatics presents unique complexity challenges due to massive data scales (billions of DNA base pairs), approximate matching requirements, and evolutionary relationships. Algorithm design must balance theoretical efficiency with biological relevance.

22.5.2 Sequence Alignment: From $\mathcal{O}(n^3)$ to $\mathcal{O}(n^2)$

Sequence alignment—finding optimal correspondence between biological sequences—is fundamental to understanding evolution and function.

Global Alignment (Needleman-Wunsch) - $\mathcal{O}(nm)$

Dynamic programming fills an $n \times m$ matrix where n, m are sequence lengths:

$$\text{DP}[i,j] = \max \begin{cases} \text{DP}[i-1,j-1] + \text{score}(A[i], B[j]) & \text{(match/mismatch)} \\ \text{DP}[i-1,j] + \text{gap\_penalty} & \text{(deletion)} \\ \text{DP}[i,j-1] + \text{gap\_penalty} & \text{(insertion)} \end{cases}$$

Space Optimization (Hirschberg) - $\mathcal{O}(n)$ space, $\mathcal{O}(nm)$ time

Using divide-and-conquer with careful bookkeeping, we can reconstruct the optimal alignment using only linear space—crucial for aligning long genomic sequences.

Local Alignment (Smith-Waterman) - $\mathcal{O}(nm)$

Modification allowing alignment to start/end anywhere revolutionized database searching by finding conserved regions.

Heuristic Speedups (BLAST) - $\mathcal{O}(n+m)$ expected

1. Find exact word matches (seeds)
2. Extend seeds without gaps
3. Perform gapped alignment only for promising regions

This heuristic approach sacrifices optimality guarantees for dramatic speedup, making genome-scale searches feasible.

22.5.3 Multiple Sequence Alignment: Confronting NP-Completeness

Theorem 22.5.1. *The multiple sequence alignment problem with sum-of-pairs scoring is NP-complete for $k \geq 3$ sequences.*

Dynamic Programming - $\mathcal{O}(n^k)$

The optimal solution requires a k-dimensional DP table—exponential in the number of sequences.

Progressive Alignment (ClustalW) - $\mathcal{O}\left(k^2n^2\right)$

1. Compute pairwise distances: $\mathcal{O}\left(k^2n^2\right)$
2. Build guide tree: $\mathcal{O}\left(k^3\right)$
3. Align following tree: $\mathcal{O}\left(kn^2\right)$

This greedy approach trades optimality for practical efficiency.

Iterative Refinement (MUSCLE) - $\mathcal{O}\left(k^2n + kn\log n\right)$

1. Fast initial alignment using k-mer distances
2. Iteratively improve by realigning subgroups
3. Complexity reduces through careful profiling

22.5.4 Genome Assembly: From Fragments to Chromosomes

Reconstructing genomes from billions of short DNA reads exemplifies big data challenges in bioinformatics.

Overlap-Layout-Consensus - $\mathcal{O}\left(n^2\log n\right)$

1. Find all pairwise overlaps: $\mathcal{O}\left(n^2\right)$ with suffix arrays
2. Layout overlaps into contigs: $\mathcal{O}\left(n\log n\right)$
3. Consensus from multiple coverage: $\mathcal{O}\left(n\right)$

de Bruijn Graph Approach - $\mathcal{O}\left(n\right)$

Revolutionary insight: represent k-mers as graph edges rather than reads as nodes:

1. Build k-mer graph: $\mathcal{O}\left(n\right)$
2. Find Eulerian path: $\mathcal{O}\left(E\right)$
3. Resolve bubbles and tips: $\mathcal{O}\left(n\right)$

This linear-time approach enabled assembly of human genomes on commodity hardware.

22.5.5 Phylogenetic Tree Construction

Inferring evolutionary relationships demonstrates the interplay between biological models and computational complexity.

Distance-Based Methods:

- UPGMA: $\mathcal{O}(n^2)$ using clustering
- Neighbor-Joining: $\mathcal{O}(n^3)$ naive, $\mathcal{O}(n^2 \log n)$ with heaps

Maximum Parsimony: NP-complete, requiring branch-and-bound or heuristic search

Maximum Likelihood: Even harder than parsimony, but statistical properties justify computational cost

Bayesian Inference (MCMC): Trading deterministic for probabilistic guarantees enables exploring huge tree spaces

22.5.6 Pattern Discovery in Biological Sequences

Finding regulatory motifs and functional patterns requires specialized algorithms.

Suffix Trees - $\mathcal{O}(n)$ construction, $\mathcal{O}(m)$ search

Linear-time construction (Ukkonen's algorithm) enables:

- Exact pattern matching
- Longest common substrings
- Tandem repeat detection

Burrows-Wheeler Transform - $\mathcal{O}(n)$ space, $\mathcal{O}(m)$ search

Compressed full-text index supporting:

- Pattern search in compressed space
- Bidirectional search for approximate matching
- Memory-efficient genome-scale indices

Hidden Markov Models - $\mathcal{O}(nk^2)$ training, $\mathcal{O}(nk)$ decoding

Probabilistic models capturing sequence families:

- Gene prediction
- Protein domain identification
- Sequence classification

22.6 Lessons Learned and Design Principles

22.6.1 Universal Principles from Case Studies

Our case studies reveal recurring themes in complexity-driven algorithm design:

Proposition 22.6.1 (Principle 1: Lower Bounds Guide Innovation). *Understanding theoretical limits focuses effort on achievable improvements. Matrix multiplication research targets the gap between $\Omega(n^2)$ lower bound and $\mathcal{O}(n^{2.373})$ upper bound.*

Proposition 22.6.2 (Principle 2: Problem Structure Determines Approach).

- *Dense problems (matrix multiplication) benefit from algebraic techniques*
- *Sparse problems (graphs, geometry) exploit structural properties*
- *Approximate problems (bioinformatics) trade exactness for efficiency*

Proposition 22.6.3 (Principle 3: Multiple Complexity Measures Matter). *Real algorithms must balance:*

- *Time complexity (primary focus)*
- *Space complexity (memory limitations)*
- *I/O complexity (disk/network access)*
- *Cache complexity (memory hierarchy)*
- *Parallel complexity (Amdahl's law limitations)*

22.6.2 The Theory-Practice Gap

Hidden Constants: Asymptotically superior algorithms may have impractical constants. Fibonacci heaps achieve theoretically optimal complexities but rarely outperform simpler structures in practice.

Average vs. Worst Case: Quicksort's $\mathcal{O}(n^2)$ worst case rarely occurs; its $\mathcal{O}(n \log n)$ average case with small constants makes it practical. Smoothed analysis helps explain why worst cases are often pessimistic.

Input Characteristics: Real-world inputs often have structure:

- Social networks exhibit small-world properties
- Biological sequences show evolutionary conservation
- Geometric data clusters in low-dimensional manifolds

22.6.3 Design Methodology Synthesis

Algorithm 42 Complexity-Driven Design Methodology

```
Step 1: Complexity Characterization
    Determine problem complexity class
    Identify related solved problems
    Establish lower bounds
Step 2: Algorithm Landscape Survey
    Map existing approaches and their trade-offs
    Identify bottlenecks in current solutions
    Recognize unexploited problem structure
Step 3: Innovation Through Combination
    Merge techniques from different domains
    Apply new data structures to old problems
    Exploit modern hardware capabilities
Step 4: Theoretical Analysis
    Prove correctness
    Derive complexity bounds
    Identify worst-case inputs
Step 5: Practical Optimization
    Profile actual performance
    Tune parameters based on input characteristics
    Implement cache-aware and parallel versions
Step 6: Empirical Validation
    Benchmark against existing solutions
    Test on real-world datasets
    Measure all relevant complexity metrics
```

22.6.4 Emerging Directions

Machine Learning Integration: Using learned predictors to guide algorithmic choices, achieving instance-optimal complexity.

Quantum-Classical Hybrids: Combining quantum subroutines with classical algorithms for problems partially amenable to quantum speedup.

Adaptive Algorithms: Dynamically adjusting strategy based on observed input characteristics.

Energy-Aware Complexity: Optimizing for power consumption alongside traditional metrics.

22.6.5 The Ongoing Evolution

Complexity-driven algorithm design remains vibrant because:

1. **New Problems Emerge**: Big data, machine learning, and quantum computing present novel challenges
2. **Hardware Evolution**: GPUs, TPUs, and neuromorphic chips require algorithm redesign
3. **Theoretical Advances**: New mathematical tools enable tighter analysis
4. **Interdisciplinary Insights**: Biology, physics, and economics inspire algorithmic techniques

22.6.6 Conclusion

The case studies in this chapter demonstrate that complexity analysis is not merely an evaluation tool but a creative force in algorithm design. By understanding fundamental limits, exploiting problem structure, and carefully navigating trade-offs, we can develop algorithms that are both theoretically elegant and practically efficient.

The journey from naive to sophisticated algorithms—whether in matrix multiplication, factorization, computational geometry, or bioinformatics—shows that breakthrough improvements often come from:

- Questioning assumptions (Is $\mathcal{O}\left(n^3\right)$ really necessary for matrix multiplication?)
- Finding hidden structure (Can we exploit geometric properties for faster algorithms?)
- Accepting trade-offs (Can approximation provide massive speedups?)
- Combining techniques (Can we merge different algorithmic paradigms?)

As we face increasingly complex computational challenges, the principles and methodologies developed through decades of complexity-driven design will continue to guide us toward efficient solutions. The interplay between theoretical analysis and practical implementation remains the cornerstone of algorithmic innovation, reminding us that the best algorithms emerge when we deeply understand both the mathematics of complexity and the realities of computation.

Exercises

Theoretical Exercises

1. **Matrix Multiplication Lower Bound**: Prove that any algorithm for multiplying two $n \times n$ matrices must examine all $2n^2$ input entries, establishing the $\Omega\left(n^2\right)$ lower bound.

2. **Factorization Complexity**: Show that if integer factorization is in P, then RSA encryption can be broken in polynomial time.

3. **Geometric Duality**: Prove that the convex hull problem in 2D is dual to finding the intersection of half-planes, and analyze the complexity implications.

4. **Alignment Space**: Calculate the size of the search space for optimally aligning k sequences of length n, and explain why multiple sequence alignment is NP-complete.

Implementation Exercises

5. **Strassen Implementation**: Implement Strassen's algorithm with automatic crossover to naive multiplication for small matrices. Experimentally determine the optimal crossover point for your system.

6. **Pollard Rho Variants**: Implement and compare different cycle-finding functions $f(x)$ for Pollard's Rho algorithm. Which performs best for different types of composites?

7. **Geometric Robustness**: Implement a convex hull algorithm that correctly handles colinear points and numerical precision issues. Test with pathological inputs.

8. **BLAST Heuristic**: Implement a simplified version of BLAST for DNA sequences. Compare its speed and accuracy against optimal Smith-Waterman alignment.

Advanced Problems

9. **Cache-Oblivious Algorithms**: Design a cache-oblivious algorithm for matrix transposition that achieves optimal cache complexity without knowing cache parameters.

10. **Approximation Quality**: For the traveling salesman problem, implement and compare the approximation ratios achieved by different polynomial-time heuristics on various graph classes.

Research Questions

11. Investigate the relationship between matrix multiplication complexity and other fundamental problems (matrix inversion, determinant computation).

12. Explore how quantum algorithms might improve the complexity of problems discussed in this chapter beyond integer factorization.

Further Reading

Foundational Papers

- Strassen, V. (1969). "Gaussian elimination is not optimal"
- Shor, P.W. (1997). "Polynomial-time algorithms for prime factorization and discrete logarithms on a quantum computer"
- Fortune, S. (1987). "A sweepline algorithm for Voronoi diagrams"
- Altschul, S.F. et al. (1990). "Basic local alignment search tool"

Advanced Texts

- Brent & Zimmermann. *Modern Computer Arithmetic*
- de Berg et al. *Computational Geometry: Algorithms and Applications*
- Gusfield. *Algorithms on Strings, Trees, and Sequences*

Online Resources

- MIT OpenCourseWare: Advanced Algorithms
- Complexity Zoo: Updated complexity class relationships
- NIST Dictionary of Algorithms and Data Structures

Chapter 23

Complexity in Industry Applications

Introduction

While theoretical complexity analysis provides fundamental insights into algorithm behavior, industry applications present unique challenges that bridge theory and practice. This chapter explores how complexity analysis drives decision-making in production systems, where factors like data distribution, hardware constraints, and business requirements shape algorithmic choices. We examine real-world scenarios where theoretical optimality often yields to practical considerations, and where understanding complexity helps engineers make informed trade-offs.

23.1 Database Query Optimization

23.1.1 The Query Optimization Problem

Database query optimization represents one of the most complex algorithmic challenges in production systems. Modern query optimizers must choose execution plans from an exponentially large search space while meeting strict latency requirements.

Complexity of Query Planning

- Join ordering for n tables: $\mathcal{O}(n!)$ possible orderings
- With bushy plans: $\mathcal{O}\left(\frac{(2n-2)!}{(n-1)!}\right)$ possibilities
- Dynamic programming approach: $\mathcal{O}(3^n)$ time, $\mathcal{O}(2^n)$ space

23.1.2 Cost-Based Optimization

Query optimizers estimate execution costs using statistics about data distribution, making complexity analysis crucial for predicting performance.

Key Components:

- **Cardinality Estimation:** Predicting result set sizes using histograms, sampling, and statistical models
- **Cost Models:** CPU cost $\mathcal{O}(n \log n)$ for sorting, $\mathcal{O}(n \cdot m)$ for nested loops, $\mathcal{O}(n + m)$ for hash joins
- **Index Selection:** Balancing query performance $\mathcal{O}(\log n)$ vs. update overhead $\mathcal{O}(\log n)$ per modification

23.1.3 Join Algorithm Selection

Different join algorithms exhibit varying complexity characteristics:

Nested Loop Join

- Time: $\mathcal{O}(n \cdot m)$
- Space: $\mathcal{O}(1)$
- Optimal for small outer relations with indexed inner relations

Sort-Merge Join

- Time: $\mathcal{O}(n \log n + m \log m + n + m)$
- Space: $\mathcal{O}(n + m)$ for external sort
- Efficient for pre-sorted data or when output ordering is required

Hash Join

- Time: $\mathcal{O}(n + m)$ average case, $\mathcal{O}(n \cdot m)$ worst case
- Space: $\mathcal{O}(\min(n, m))$
- Preferred for equi-joins with adequate memory

23.1.4 Adaptive Query Processing

Modern systems employ adaptive techniques that modify execution strategies based on runtime feedback:

- **Re-optimization:** Detecting cardinality estimation errors and adjusting plans mid-execution
- **Eddies:** Dynamic tuple routing with $\mathcal{O}(1)$ overhead per tuple
- **Progressive Optimization:** Learning from previous executions to improve future plans

23.1.5 Distributed Query Complexity

In distributed databases, network communication adds another dimension to complexity:

- **Data Shuffling:** $\mathcal{O}(n)$ network transfer for redistribution
- **Broadcast Joins:** $\mathcal{O}(n \cdot p)$ total network cost for p nodes
- **Semi-join Reduction:** Preprocessing to minimize network transfer

23.2 Compiler Optimization Complexity

23.2.1 The Compilation Pipeline

Compiler optimization involves numerous NP-hard problems, requiring sophisticated heuristics to achieve reasonable compilation times.

Phase Complexity

- Lexical Analysis: $\mathcal{O}(n)$ for n source characters
- Parsing: $\mathcal{O}(n^3)$ for general CFGs, $\mathcal{O}(n)$ for LL(1)/LR(1)
- Semantic Analysis: $\mathcal{O}(n)$ with efficient symbol tables
- Optimization: Variable, often exponential for optimal solutions
- Code Generation: NP-complete for optimal register allocation

23.2.2 Data Flow Analysis

Compiler optimizations rely on data flow analysis with varying complexity:

Reaching Definitions

- Bit-vector approach: $\mathcal{O}\left(n^2 \cdot b\right)$ where b is number of basic blocks
- SSA construction: $\mathcal{O}\left(n \cdot \alpha(n)\right)$ with dominance frontiers

Live Variable Analysis

- Iterative solution: $\mathcal{O}\left(n^2\right)$ worst case
- Graph coloring for registers: NP-complete, requiring heuristics

23.2.3 Loop Optimizations

Loop transformations significantly impact performance but involve complex analysis:

Loop Invariant Code Motion

- Detection: $\mathcal{O}\left(n\right)$ per loop iteration
- Safety analysis requires alias analysis: undecidable in general

Loop Vectorization

- Dependence analysis: $\mathcal{O}\left(n^2\right)$ for n array references
- Vectorization decision: Must balance SIMD width, memory alignment, and trip count

Loop Tiling

- Optimal tile size selection: NP-hard
- Cache miss estimation: $\mathcal{O}\left(n^d\right)$ for d-dimensional arrays

23.2.4 Interprocedural Optimization

Whole-program optimization faces scalability challenges:

- **Call Graph Construction:** $\mathcal{O}\left(n \cdot e\right)$ for n functions, e call sites
- **Inlining Decisions:** Knapsack-like problem with code size constraints
- **Escape Analysis:** $\mathcal{O}\left(n^3\right)$ for pointer analysis in worst case

23.2.5 Just-In-Time Compilation

JIT compilers balance compilation overhead against execution speedup:

- **Profiling Overhead:** 5-10% runtime cost for instrumentation
- **Compilation Triggers:** Hot spot detection using $\mathcal{O}(1)$ counters
- **Tiered Compilation:** Progressive optimization levels based on execution frequency

23.3 Network Routing Algorithms

23.3.1 Internet Routing Protocols

Internet-scale routing requires algorithms that scale to millions of nodes while maintaining rapid convergence.

BGP (Border Gateway Protocol)

- Convergence: $\mathcal{O}(n!)$ worst case for n AS nodes
- Memory: $\mathcal{O}(n \cdot p)$ for n prefixes, p paths
- Update processing: $\mathcal{O}(p \cdot a)$ for p peers, a attributes

OSPF (Open Shortest Path First)

- Dijkstra's algorithm: $\mathcal{O}\left(n^2 \log n\right)$ with n routers
- Link state database: $\mathcal{O}\left(n^2\right)$ space
- Convergence time: $\mathcal{O}(\text{diameter})$ message complexity

23.3.2 Software-Defined Networking

SDN introduces new complexity challenges in centralized control:

Flow Table Management

- Table size: Limited to ~4K-64K entries in hardware
- Lookup: $\mathcal{O}(1)$ with TCAM, $\mathcal{O}(\log n)$ with software tables
- Update consistency: Two-phase commit with $\mathcal{O}(n)$ switches

Path Computation

- K-shortest paths: $\mathcal{O}(k \cdot n \cdot (m + n \log n))$
- Traffic engineering: Multi-commodity flow (polynomial but expensive)
- Failure recovery: Precomputed backup paths double space requirements

23.3.3 Content Delivery Networks

CDN routing optimizes for latency and load balancing:

Request Routing

- DNS-based: $\mathcal{O}(1)$ lookup, coarse-grained control
- Anycast: $\mathcal{O}(1)$ routing table lookup per packet
- HTTP redirect: $\mathcal{O}(1)$ additional round trip

Cache Placement

- Facility location problem: NP-hard
- Approximation algorithms: 1.463-approximation in $\mathcal{O}(n^3)$
- Online caching: Competitive ratio of $\mathcal{O}(\log n)$ for LRU

23.3.4 Mobile Network Optimization

5G and beyond require handling massive device counts with strict latency requirements:

- **Handover Decisions:** $\mathcal{O}(k)$ for k neighboring cells
- **Resource Allocation:** Integer programming, NP-hard
- **Network Slicing:** Virtual network embedding, NP-complete

23.3.5 Routing in Datacenter Networks

Modern datacenters employ specialized topologies and routing:

Fat-Tree Networks

- Path diversity: $k^3/4$ servers with $k^2/2$ paths between any pair
- Routing table size: $\mathcal{O}(k)$ entries per switch
- ECMP load balancing: $\mathcal{O}(1)$ per packet

Clos Networks

- Non-blocking with $2n-1$ middle switches for n inputs
- Route computation: $\mathcal{O}(n)$ for Benes network configuration

23.4 Cryptographic Algorithm Analysis

23.4.1 Symmetric Cryptography Complexity

Modern block ciphers balance security against performance:

AES (Advanced Encryption Standard)

- Encryption/Decryption: $\mathcal{O}(n)$ for n blocks
- Key schedule: $\mathcal{O}(1)$ for fixed key sizes
- Hardware acceleration: $\sim$1 cycle per byte with AES-NI

Stream Ciphers

- ChaCha20: $\mathcal{O}(n)$ with better cache behavior than AES
- Initialization: $\mathcal{O}(1)$ for key and nonce setup

23.4.2 Public Key Cryptography

Asymmetric algorithms involve number-theoretic operations with higher complexity:

RSA

- Key generation: $\mathcal{O}(k^3)$ for k-bit primes using Miller-Rabin
- Encryption/Decryption: $\mathcal{O}(k^3)$ using fast modular exponentiation
- Signature generation: $\mathcal{O}(k^3)$ with Chinese Remainder Theorem optimization

Elliptic Curve Cryptography

- Point multiplication: $\mathcal{O}(k^3)$ for k-bit keys
- Key size advantage: 256-bit ECC $\approx$ 3072-bit RSA security
- Signature verification: $2\times$ point multiplication cost

23.4.3 Hash Functions and MACs

Cryptographic hashes provide fixed-time operations:

SHA-256

- Compression function: 64 rounds, $\mathcal{O}(1)$ per 512-bit block
- Total complexity: $\mathcal{O}(n)$ for n-byte message
- Merkle tree verification: $\mathcal{O}(\log n)$ for n leaves

HMAC

- Two hash computations: $\mathcal{O}(n)$ for message length n
- Key preprocessing: $\mathcal{O}(1)$ for fixed block size

23.4.4 Post-Quantum Cryptography

Quantum-resistant algorithms introduce new complexity trade-offs:

Lattice-Based (CRYSTALS-Kyber)

- Key generation: $\mathcal{O}(n^2)$ for dimension n
- Encapsulation: $\mathcal{O}(n^2)$ matrix-vector multiplication
- Larger keys: $\sim$1KB public keys vs. 256 bytes for ECC

Hash-Based Signatures (SPHINCS+)

- Signature size: $\mathcal{O}(k \log n)$ for tree height k
- Verification: $\mathcal{O}(k)$ hash computations
- Stateless but larger signatures ($\sim$50KB)

23.4.5 Cryptographic Protocol Complexity

Protocol design involves multiple complexity considerations:

TLS Handshake

- Full handshake: 2 RTT, $\mathcal{O}(1)$ asymmetric operations
- Session resumption: 1 RTT, symmetric crypto only
- 0-RTT mode: Security vs. latency trade-off

Zero-Knowledge Proofs

- zkSNARKs: $\mathcal{O}(n \log n)$ prover, $\mathcal{O}(1)$ verifier
- Setup phase: $\mathcal{O}(n)$ trusted setup required
- Bulletproofs: $\mathcal{O}(n)$ verification, no trusted setup

23.5 Game Theory and Algorithmic Mechanism Design

23.5.1 Auction Mechanisms

Online advertising and e-commerce rely on efficient auction algorithms:

Second-Price Auctions

- Winner determination: $\mathcal{O}(n)$ for n bidders
- Payment calculation: $\mathcal{O}(1)$
- Truthfulness: Dominant strategy incentive compatible

Generalized Second Price (GSP)

- Ad slot allocation: $\mathcal{O}(n \log n)$ sorting
- Not truthful but used by major search engines
- Equilibrium computation: PPAD-complete

Combinatorial Auctions

- Winner determination: NP-hard
- Approximation: $\mathcal{O}(\sqrt{m})$ for m items
- VCG payments: Requires solving $n+1$ optimization problems

23.5.2 Matching Markets

Two-sided markets require stable and efficient matching:

Gale-Shapley Algorithm

- Stable marriage: $\mathcal{O}(n^2)$ for n participants
- Hospital-resident matching: $\mathcal{O}(n \cdot m)$ for n residents, m positions
- Strategy-proof for proposing side only

Online Matching

- Bipartite matching: $(1 - 1/e)$-competitive
- AdWords problem: $(1 - 1/e)$-competitive with large budgets
- Ride-sharing: $\mathcal{O}(n^2)$ for n requests with time windows

23.5.3 Recommendation Systems

Personalization algorithms balance accuracy with computational efficiency:

Collaborative Filtering

- Matrix factorization: $\mathcal{O}(k \cdot (m+n) \cdot i)$ for k factors, i iterations
- Neighborhood methods: $\mathcal{O}(n^2 \cdot m)$ preprocessing
- Online updates: $\mathcal{O}(k)$ per rating

Content-Based Filtering

- Feature extraction: $\mathcal{O}(d \cdot n)$ for d features, n items
- Similarity computation: $\mathcal{O}(n^2 \cdot d)$ for all pairs
- LSH for approximate nearest neighbors: $\mathcal{O}(n^{1/c})$ for c-approximation

23.5.4 Social Choice and Voting

Computational social choice addresses algorithmic voting challenges:

Winner Determination

- Condorcet winner: $\mathcal{O}(n^2 \cdot m)$ for n candidates, m voters
- Kemeny ranking: NP-hard, $\mathcal{O}(n! \cdot m)$ brute force
- Schulze method: $\mathcal{O}(n^3)$ using Floyd-Warshall

Strategic Voting

- Manipulation detection: NP-complete for many rules
- Bribery: Often NP-hard even for simple rules

23.5.5 Network Effects and Viral Marketing

Social network algorithms model information spread:

Influence Maximization

- Problem: NP-hard under independent cascade model
- Greedy approximation: $(1 - 1/e - \varepsilon)$ with $\mathcal{O}(k \cdot n \cdot m \cdot R)$ for R simulations
- Sketch-based methods: $\mathcal{O}(k \cdot (m + n) \cdot \log n/\varepsilon^2)$

Community Detection

- Modularity optimization: NP-hard
- Louvain algorithm: $\mathcal{O}(n \log n)$ typical case
- Spectral methods: $\mathcal{O}(n^3)$ for eigendecomposition

23.6 Real-World Performance Considerations

23.6.1 When Big-O Isn't Enough

Production systems often violate theoretical assumptions:

Hidden Constants Matter

- Quicksort ($\mathcal{O}(n \log n)$) often beats Heapsort despite worse worst-case
- Linear search beats binary search for small arrays (∼100 elements)
- Simple $\mathcal{O}(n^2)$ algorithms can outperform complex $\mathcal{O}(n \log n)$ for small n

Cache Effects

- Sequential access: $\sim 100\times$ faster than random access
- Cache-oblivious algorithms: Optimal across memory hierarchies
- Column vs. row storage: Order of magnitude difference for analytics

23.6.2 Latency vs. Throughput Trade-offs

Different optimization goals lead to different algorithmic choices:

Batch Processing

- Optimize for throughput: Amortize fixed costs
- Example: Batched graph processing in Pregel model

Interactive Systems

- Optimize for latency: Minimize 99th percentile
- Example: Incremental indexing vs. batch rebuilds

Streaming Systems

- Balance latency and throughput: Micro-batching
- Example: Spark Streaming's configurable batch intervals

23.6.3 Scalability Patterns

Distributed systems introduce unique complexity considerations:

Horizontal Scaling

- Sharding: $\mathcal{O}(1)$ lookup with consistent hashing
- Replication: $\mathcal{O}(r)$ storage for r replicas
- Coordination: Consensus protocols $\mathcal{O}(n^2)$ messages

Vertical Scaling

- NUMA effects: $2 - 10\times$ performance variation
- Vector instructions: $4 - 16\times$ speedup for amenable algorithms
- GPU acceleration: $100\times$ for embarrassingly parallel problems

23.6.4 Reliability and Fault Tolerance

System reliability often requires algorithmic redundancy:

Error Detection and Correction

- Checksums: $\mathcal{O}(n)$ computation, $\mathcal{O}(1)$ space overhead
- Reed-Solomon codes: $\mathcal{O}(n^2)$ encoding, $\mathcal{O}(n^2 \log n)$ decoding
- Merkle trees: $\mathcal{O}(\log n)$ proof size for corruption detection

Consensus Protocols

- Paxos/Raft: $\mathcal{O}(n)$ messages per decision
- Byzantine fault tolerance: $\mathcal{O}(n^2)$ message complexity
- CAP theorem: Fundamental trade-off between consistency and availability

23.6.5 Monitoring and Observability

Production systems require efficient monitoring algorithms:

Metrics Collection

- Time series compression: $10 - 100\times$ reduction with bounded error
- Sampling strategies: Reservoir sampling $\mathcal{O}(k)$ space for k samples
- Distributed tracing: $\mathcal{O}(n)$ overhead with sampling

Anomaly Detection

- Statistical methods: $\mathcal{O}(1)$ for running statistics
- Machine learning: $\mathcal{O}(n \cdot d)$ for n points, d dimensions
- Sketch algorithms: Count-min sketch $\mathcal{O}(1)$ update, $\mathcal{O}(1)$ query

23.6.6 Cost Optimization

Cloud computing introduces economic considerations:

Resource Allocation

- Bin packing: NP-hard, first-fit gives 2-approximation
- Spot instance bidding: Online algorithms with competitive ratios
- Auto-scaling: Predictive vs. reactive with different complexity

Storage Tiering

- Hot/cold separation: $\mathcal{O}(n \log n)$ for access frequency sorting
- Compression vs. query performance: Space-time trade-off
- Erasure coding: (n, k) codes with n/k storage overhead

Summary

Industrial applications of algorithmic complexity demonstrate that theoretical analysis, while foundational, must be balanced with practical considerations. Success in production systems requires understanding not just asymptotic behavior, but also constants, hardware characteristics, failure modes, and economic constraints. The examples in this chapter illustrate how complexity analysis guides architectural decisions, helps predict system behavior under scale, and identifies optimization opportunities.

Key takeaways include:

1. **Theory informs practice:** Complexity analysis provides crucial insights even when practical factors dominate
2. **Trade-offs are ubiquitous:** No single metric captures all relevant aspects of system performance

3. **Context matters:** The best algorithm depends on data characteristics, hardware, and business requirements
4. **Approximation is often necessary:** Many real-world problems require heuristics or approximation algorithms
5. **Measurement validates theory:** Production metrics help calibrate theoretical models

As systems grow in scale and complexity, the ability to analyze and reason about algorithmic complexity becomes increasingly critical for building efficient, scalable, and reliable software systems.

Appendix A

Mathematical Reference

A.1 Common Summation Formulas

A.1.1 Arithmetic Series

- **Basic arithmetic sum:**

$$\sum_{i=1}^{n} i = \frac{n(n+1)}{2}$$

- **Sum of squares:**

$$\sum_{i=1}^{n} i^2 = \frac{n(n+1)(2n+1)}{6}$$

- **Sum of cubes:**

$$\sum_{i=1}^{n} i^3 = \left[\frac{n(n+1)}{2}\right]^2$$

- **General arithmetic progression:**

$$\sum_{i=0}^{n-1} (a+id) = \frac{n[2a+(n-1)d]}{2}$$

A.1.2 Geometric Series

- **Basic geometric sum:**

$$\sum_{i=0}^{n-1} r^i = \frac{1-r^n}{1-r}, \quad r \neq 1$$

- **Infinite geometric series:**

$$\sum_{i=0}^{\infty} r^i = \frac{1}{1-r}, \quad |r| < 1$$

- **Modified geometric:**

$$\sum_{i=1}^{n} i \cdot r^i = r\left[\frac{1-(n+1)r^n + nr^{n+1}}{(1-r)^2}\right]$$

A.1.3 Harmonic Series

- **Harmonic number:**

$$H_n = \sum_{i=1}^{n} \frac{1}{i} \approx \ln(n) + \gamma + \frac{1}{2n}$$

where $\gamma \approx 0.5772$ (Euler-Mascheroni constant)

- **Generalized harmonic:**

$$H_n^{(k)} = \sum_{i=1}^{n} \frac{1}{i^k}$$

Converges for $k > 1$ to $\zeta(k)$ as $n \to \infty$

A.1.4 Binomial Coefficients

- **Binomial theorem:**

$$(x+y)^n = \sum_{k=0}^{n} \binom{n}{k} x^k y^{n-k}$$

- **Vandermonde's identity:**

$$\binom{m+n}{r} = \sum_{k=0}^{r} \binom{m}{k}\binom{n}{r-k}$$

- **Hockey stick identity:**

$$\sum_{i=r}^{n} \binom{i}{r} = \binom{n+1}{r+1}$$

A.2 Useful Inequalities

A.2.1 Basic Inequalities

Theorem A.2.1 (AM-GM Inequality). *For non-negative real numbers $a_1, a_2, \ldots, a_n$:*

$$\frac{a_1 + a_2 + \cdots + a_n}{n} \geq \sqrt[n]{a_1 \cdot a_2 \cdots a_n}$$

Theorem A.2.2 (Cauchy-Schwarz Inequality).

$$\left(\sum_{i=1}^{n} a_i b_i\right)^2 \leq \left(\sum_{i=1}^{n} a_i^2\right)\left(\sum_{i=1}^{n} b_i^2\right)$$

Theorem A.2.3 (Triangle Inequality).

$$|a + b| \leq |a| + |b|$$

Theorem A.2.4 (Bernoulli's Inequality). *For $x \geq -1$ and $n \in \mathbb{N}$:*

$$(1 + x)^n \geq 1 + nx$$

A.2.2 Logarithmic Inequalities

- **Log sum:** $\log(a + b) \leq \log(2 \cdot \max(a, b))$
- **Jensen's inequality for log:**

$$\log\left(\sum_i p_i x_i\right) \geq \sum_i p_i \log(x_i), \quad \sum_i p_i = 1$$

- **Useful bounds:**

$$\frac{x}{1 + x} \leq \ln(1 + x) \leq x, \quad x > -1$$

A.2.3 Exponential Bounds

- **Simple bounds:** $1 + x \leq e^x$ for all x
- **Tighter bound:** $e^x \leq 1 + x + x^2 e^{|x|}$ for all x
- **Lower bound:** $e^x \geq \left(1 + \frac{x}{n}\right)^n$ for $x \geq 0, n > 0$

A.3 Stirling's Approximation

A.3.1 Main Formula

$$n! \approx \sqrt{2\pi n}\left(\frac{n}{e}\right)^n$$

A.3.2 Refined Versions

- **With error term:**

$$n! = \sqrt{2\pi n}\left(\frac{n}{e}\right)^n e^{\lambda_n}$$

where $\frac{1}{12n+1} < \lambda_n < \frac{1}{12n}$

- **Logarithmic form:**

$$\ln(n!) = n\ln(n) - n + \frac{1}{2}\ln(2\pi n) + \mathcal{O}(1/n)$$

- **Bounds:**

$$\sqrt{2\pi n}\left(\frac{n}{e}\right)^n e^{\frac{1}{12n+1}} < n! < \sqrt{2\pi n}\left(\frac{n}{e}\right)^n e^{\frac{1}{12n}}$$

A.4 Basic Probability Distributions

A.4.1 Discrete Distributions

Distribution	PMF	Mean	Variance
Binomial	$P(X=k) = \binom{n}{k}p^k(1-p)^{n-k}$	np	$np(1-p)$
Geometric	$P(X=k) = (1-p)^{k-1}p$	$1/p$	$(1-p)/p^2$
Poisson	$P(X=k) = \frac{\lambda^k e^{-\lambda}}{k!}$	λ	λ

A.4.2 Continuous Distributions

Distribution	PDF	Mean	Variance
Uniform $[a,b]$	$f(x) = \frac{1}{b-a}$	$\frac{a+b}{2}$	$\frac{(b-a)^2}{12}$
Exponential	$f(x) = \lambda e^{-\lambda x}$	$1/\lambda$	$1/\lambda^2$
Normal	$f(x) = \frac{1}{\sqrt{2\pi\sigma^2}}e^{-\frac{(x-\mu)^2}{2\sigma^2}}$	μ	σ^2

A.4.3 Concentration Inequalities

Theorem A.4.1 (Markov's Inequality). *For non-negative random variable X:*

$$P(X \geq a) \leq \frac{\mathbb{E}[X]}{a}$$

Theorem A.4.2 (Chebyshev's Inequality).

$$P(|X - \mu| \geq k\sigma) \leq \frac{1}{k^2}$$

Theorem A.4.3 (Chernoff Bound). *For* $0 < \delta < 1$*:*

$$P(X \geq (1 + \delta)\mu) \leq e^{-\frac{\delta^2 \mu}{3}}$$

Theorem A.4.4 (Hoeffding's Inequality).

$$P(|S - \mathbb{E}[S]| \geq t) \leq 2 \exp\left(-\frac{2t^2}{\sum_i (b_i - a_i)^2}\right)$$

Appendix B

Complexity Class Hierarchy

B.1 Fundamental Time Complexity Classes

B.1.1 Deterministic Classes

The fundamental hierarchy of deterministic complexity classes:

$$\mathsf{L} \subseteq \mathsf{NL} \subseteq \mathsf{P} \subseteq \mathsf{NP} \subseteq \mathsf{PSPACE} \subseteq \mathsf{EXPTIME} \subseteq \mathsf{NEXPTIME} \subseteq \mathsf{EXPSPACE}$$

- L (LOGSPACE): Problems solvable with $\mathcal{O}(\log n)$ space
- P (PTIME): Problems solvable in polynomial time
- $\mathsf{EXPTIME}$: Problems solvable in $2^{\text{poly}(n)}$ time
- $\mathsf{2\text{-}EXPTIME}$: Problems solvable in $2^{2^{\text{poly}(n)}}$ time

B.1.2 Nondeterministic Classes

- NL: Nondeterministic logarithmic space
- NP: Nondeterministic polynomial time
- $\mathsf{NEXPTIME}$: Nondeterministic exponential time
- coNP: Complement of NP (problems where "no" instances have short proofs)

B.2 Space Complexity Classes

B.2.1 Hierarchy

$$\mathsf{L} \subseteq \mathsf{NL} = \mathsf{coNL} \subseteq \mathsf{PSPACE} = \mathsf{NPSPACE} \subseteq \mathsf{EXPSPACE} = \mathsf{NEXPSPACE}$$

B.2.2 Key Results

Theorem B.2.1 (Savitch's Theorem). $\mathsf{NSPACE}(f(n)) \subseteq \mathsf{SPACE}(f(n)^2)$

Theorem B.2.2 (Immerman-Szelepcsényi). $\mathsf{NL} = \mathsf{coNL}$

Theorem B.2.3. $\mathsf{PSPACE} = \mathsf{IP}$ *(Interactive proofs with polynomial space)*

B.3 The Polynomial Hierarchy

B.3.1 Definition

The polynomial hierarchy is defined inductively:

$$\Sigma_0^P = \Pi_0^P = \mathsf{P} \tag{B.1}$$
$$\Sigma_{k+1}^P = \mathsf{NP}^{\Sigma_k^P} \text{ (NP with } \Sigma_k^P \text{ oracle)} \tag{B.2}$$
$$\Pi_{k+1}^P = \mathsf{co}\Sigma_{k+1}^P \tag{B.3}$$
$$\mathsf{PH} = \bigcup_k \Sigma_k^P \text{ (entire polynomial hierarchy)} \tag{B.4}$$

B.3.2 Key Classes

- $\Sigma_1^P = \mathsf{NP}$: Existential quantifier
- $\Pi_1^P = \mathsf{coNP}$: Universal quantifier
- Σ_2^P: $\exists\forall$ quantifier alternation
- $\Delta_2^P = \mathsf{P}^{\mathsf{NP}}$: Polynomial time with NP oracle

B.4 Probabilistic Complexity Classes

B.4.1 Bounded Error Classes

- BPP: Bounded-error probabilistic polynomial time (error $\leq 1/3$)
- RP: Randomized polynomial time (one-sided error)
- $\mathsf{ZPP} = \mathsf{RP} \cap \mathsf{coRP}$: Zero-error probabilistic polynomial time
- PP: Probabilistic polynomial time (error $< 1/2$)

B.4.2 Relationships

$$\mathsf{P} \subseteq \mathsf{ZPP} \subseteq \mathsf{RP} \subseteq \mathsf{BPP} \subseteq \mathsf{PP} \subseteq \mathsf{PSPACE}$$

B.5 Circuit Complexity Classes

B.5.1 Basic Classes

- NC^0: Constant depth, polynomial size circuits
- AC^0: Constant depth, unbounded fan-in
- TC^0: Constant depth with threshold gates
- NC^1: $\mathcal{O}(\log n)$ depth, polynomial size
- $\mathsf{P/poly}$: Polynomial size circuits (non-uniform)

B.5.2 Hierarchy

$$\mathsf{NC}^0 \subsetneq \mathsf{AC}^0 \subsetneq \mathsf{TC}^0 \subseteq \mathsf{NC}^1 \subseteq \mathsf{L} \subseteq \mathsf{NL} \subseteq \mathsf{NC} \subseteq \mathsf{P}$$

B.6 Open Problems in Complexity Theory

B.6.1 Major Open Problems

1. **P vs NP:** Is $\mathsf{P} = \mathsf{NP}$?
2. **NP vs coNP:** Is $\mathsf{NP} = \mathsf{coNP}$?
3. **P vs PSPACE:** Is $\mathsf{P} = \mathsf{PSPACE}$?
4. **BPP vs P:** Is $\mathsf{BPP} = \mathsf{P}$? (derandomization)
5. **NP vs BQP:** Can quantum computers solve NP-complete problems efficiently?
6. **PH collapse:** Does the polynomial hierarchy collapse?

B.6.2 Known Separations

Theorem B.6.1 (Time Hierarchy)**.** $\mathsf{TIME}(f(n)) \subsetneq \mathsf{TIME}(f(n) \cdot \log^2(f(n)))$

Theorem B.6.2 (Space Hierarchy)**.** $\mathsf{SPACE}(f(n)) \subsetneq \mathsf{SPACE}(f(n) \cdot \log(f(n)))$

Appendix C

Algorithm Analysis Cookbook

C.1 Step-by-Step Analysis Procedures

C.1.1 Time Complexity Analysis Protocol

1. **Identify Basic Operations**
   - Determine the fundamental operation (comparison, arithmetic, memory access)
   - Count operations, not lines of code
   - Consider both explicit and implicit operations
2. **Establish Input Size**
   - Define n (array length, number of nodes, string length)
   - For multiple parameters, identify relationships
   - Consider worst-case input configurations
3. **Analyze Control Flow**
   - Sequential code: $T(n) = T_1(n) + T_2(n) + \cdots + T_k(n)$
   - Conditionals: $T(n) = \max(T_{\text{if}}(n), T_{\text{else}}(n))$
   - Simple loops: $T(n) = \text{iterations} \times \text{body\_time}$
   - Nested loops: $T(n) = \sum_i \sum_j \text{body\_time}(i, j)$
4. **Handle Recursive Calls**
   - Write recurrence relation

- Identify base cases
- Apply solving technique
- Verify solution

5. **Simplify and Express in Big-O**
   - Drop lower-order terms
   - Ignore constant factors
   - Express using standard complexity classes

C.1.2 Space Complexity Analysis Protocol

1. **Identify Space Components**
   - Input space (usually not counted)
   - Auxiliary space (temporary variables, data structures)
   - Call stack space (for recursive algorithms)
2. **Analyze Each Component**
   - Fixed space: $\mathcal{O}(1)$ for constant number of variables
   - Dynamic allocations: Size of allocated structures
   - Recursive space: Maximum depth $\times$ space per call
3. **Combine Components**
   - For sequential: Take maximum
   - For recursive: Add stack space to auxiliary space

C.2 Common Recurrence Patterns

C.2.1 Linear Recurrences

Recurrence	Solution	Example
$T(n) = T(n-1) + \mathcal{O}(1)$	$\mathcal{O}(n)$	Linear search
$T(n) = T(n-1) + \mathcal{O}(n)$	$\mathcal{O}(n^2)$	Selection sort
$T(n) = 2T(n-1) + \mathcal{O}(1)$	$\mathcal{O}(2^n)$	Tower of Hanoi
$T(n) = T(n-1) + T(n-2) + \mathcal{O}(1)$	$\mathcal{O}(\varphi^n)$	Naive Fibonacci

Recurrence	Solution	Example
$T(n) = T(n/2) + \mathcal{O}(1)$	$\mathcal{O}(\log n)$	Binary search
$T(n) = T(n/2) + \mathcal{O}(n)$	$\mathcal{O}(n)$	Finding median
$T(n) = 2T(n/2) + \mathcal{O}(1)$	$\mathcal{O}(n)$	Tree traversal
$T(n) = 2T(n/2) + \mathcal{O}(n)$	$\mathcal{O}(n \log n)$	Merge sort
$T(n) = 2T(n/2) + \mathcal{O}(n^2)$	$\mathcal{O}(n^2)$	Slow matrix multiply
$T(n) = 3T(n/2) + \mathcal{O}(n)$	$\mathcal{O}(n^{\log_2 3})$	Karatsuba
$T(n) = 7T(n/2) + \mathcal{O}(n^2)$	$\mathcal{O}(n^{\log_2 7})$	Strassen

C.2.2 Divide and Conquer Recurrences

C.2.3 Master Theorem Application

For recurrences of the form $T(n) = aT(n/b) + f(n)$:

Theorem C.2.1 (Master Theorem). *Let $a \geq 1$ and $b > 1$ be constants, and let $f(n)$ be a function. Then:*

1. *If $f(n) = \mathcal{O}(n^{\log_b a - \epsilon})$ for some constant $\epsilon > 0$, then $T(n) = \Theta(n^{\log_b a})$*
2. *If $f(n) = \Theta(n^{\log_b a})$, then $T(n) = \Theta(n^{\log_b a} \log n)$*
3. *If $f(n) = \Omega(n^{\log_b a + \epsilon})$ for some constant $\epsilon > 0$, and if $af(n/b) \leq cf(n)$ for some constant $c < 1$ and sufficiently large n, then $T(n) = \Theta(f(n))$*

C.3 Common Operations Complexity

Operation	Array	Linked List	Hash Table	BST	Heap
Access	$\mathcal{O}(1)$	$\mathcal{O}(n)$	N/A	$\mathcal{O}(\log n)^*$	N/A
Search	$\mathcal{O}(n)$	$\mathcal{O}(n)$	$\mathcal{O}(1)^*$	$\mathcal{O}(\log n)^*$	$\mathcal{O}(n)$
Insert	$\mathcal{O}(n)$	$\mathcal{O}(1)$	$\mathcal{O}(1)^*$	$\mathcal{O}(\log n)^*$	$\mathcal{O}(\log n)$
Delete	$\mathcal{O}(n)$	$\mathcal{O}(1)^{**}$	$\mathcal{O}(1)^*$	$\mathcal{O}(\log n)^*$	$\mathcal{O}(\log n)$

Table C.1: *Average case, **With reference to node

C.4 Sorting Algorithm Complexities

Algorithm	Best	Average	Worst	Space	Stable
Bubble Sort	$\mathcal{O}(n)$	$\mathcal{O}(n^2)$	$\mathcal{O}(n^2)$	$\mathcal{O}(1)$	Yes
Insertion Sort	$\mathcal{O}(n)$	$\mathcal{O}(n^2)$	$\mathcal{O}(n^2)$	$\mathcal{O}(1)$	Yes
Selection Sort	$\mathcal{O}(n^2)$	$\mathcal{O}(n^2)$	$\mathcal{O}(n^2)$	$\mathcal{O}(1)$	No
Merge Sort	$\mathcal{O}(n \log n)$	$\mathcal{O}(n \log n)$	$\mathcal{O}(n \log n)$	$\mathcal{O}(n)$	Yes
Quick Sort	$\mathcal{O}(n \log n)$	$\mathcal{O}(n \log n)$	$\mathcal{O}(n^2)$	$\mathcal{O}(\log n)$	No*
Heap Sort	$\mathcal{O}(n \log n)$	$\mathcal{O}(n \log n)$	$\mathcal{O}(n \log n)$	$\mathcal{O}(1)$	No
Counting Sort	$\mathcal{O}(n+k)$	$\mathcal{O}(n+k)$	$\mathcal{O}(n+k)$	$\mathcal{O}(k)$	Yes
Radix Sort	$\mathcal{O}(nk)$	$\mathcal{O}(nk)$	$\mathcal{O}(nk)$	$\mathcal{O}(n+k)$	Yes

Table C.2: *Can be made stable with modifications

Appendix D

Further Reading and Resources

D.1 Classic Papers and Textbooks

D.1.1 Foundational Papers

1. **"On the Computational Complexity of Algorithms"** – Hartmanis & Stearns (1965)
    - Introduced time complexity classes
    - Established complexity theory foundations
2. **"The Complexity of Theorem-Proving Procedures"** – Cook (1971)
    - Introduced NP-completeness
    - Formulated the P vs NP problem
3. **"Reducibility Among Combinatorial Problems"** – Karp (1972)
    - 21 NP-complete problems
    - Established reduction techniques
4. **"Alternation"** – Chandra, Kozen & Stockmeyer (1981)
    - Polynomial hierarchy definition
    - Alternating Turing machines
5. **"How to Construct Random Functions"** – Goldreich, Goldwasser & Micali (1986)
    - Pseudorandom functions
    - Cryptographic complexity

D.1.2 Essential Textbooks

Introductory Level

- **"Introduction to Algorithms"** – Cormen, Leiserson, Rivest & Stein
  - Comprehensive algorithm coverage
  - Excellent for self-study
- **"Algorithm Design"** – Kleinberg & Tardos
  - Problem-solving approach
  - Real-world applications

Advanced Level

- **"Computational Complexity: A Modern Approach"** – Arora & Barak
  - Complete complexity theory coverage
  - Recent developments included
- **"The Art of Computer Programming"** – Knuth
  - Mathematical rigor
  - Detailed analysis techniques
- **"Randomized Algorithms"** – Motwani & Raghavan
  - Probabilistic methods
  - Advanced techniques

Specialized Topics

- **"Approximation Algorithms"** – Vazirani
- **"Parameterized Complexity"** – Downey & Fellows
- **"Communication Complexity"** – Kushilevitz & Nisan
- **"Quantum Computing: An Applied Approach"** – Hidary

D.2 Research Directions and Open Problems

D.2.1 Active Research Areas

1. **Fine-Grained Complexity**
    - Beyond polynomial/exponential dichotomy
    - Conditional lower bounds
    - SETH and related conjectures
    - Exact complexity of fundamental problems
2. **Quantum Complexity**
    - Quantum supremacy verification
    - BQP vs PH separation
    - Quantum error correction complexity
    - Post-quantum cryptography
3. **Average-Case Complexity**
    - Cryptographic assumptions
    - Random SAT threshold
    - Smoothed analysis extensions
    - Planted problems
4. **Communication and Query Complexity**
    - Log-rank conjecture
    - Direct sum theorems
    - Quantum communication advantages
    - Distributed complexity
5. **Proof Complexity**
    - Lower bounds for proof systems
    - Automatability of proof search
    - Connection to circuit complexity
    - Algebraic proof systems

D.2.2 Major Open Problems

The Big Five

1. **P vs NP** – $1,000,000 Clay Prize
2. **NP vs coNP** – Complexity of verification vs refutation
3. **P vs BPP** – Derandomization hypothesis
4. **P vs PSPACE** – Power of space vs time
5. **NP vs BQP** – Quantum vs classical verification

Other Significant Problems

- **Unique Games Conjecture** – Approximation hardness
- **Log-rank Conjecture** – Communication complexity
- **NC vs P** – Parallel vs sequential computation
- **L vs NL** – Deterministic vs nondeterministic space
- **BPP vs NEXP** – Randomness vs nondeterminism

Barriers to Progress

- Relativization barrier (Baker-Gill-Solovay)
- Natural proofs barrier (Razborov-Rudich)
- Algebrization barrier (Aaronson-Wigderson)

D.3 Professional Development

D.3.1 Conferences

Tier 1

- **STOC** – Symposium on Theory of Computing
- **FOCS** – Foundations of Computer Science
- **CCC** – Computational Complexity Conference
- **ICALP** – International Colloquium on Automata, Languages and Programming

Specialized

- **SODA** – Symposium on Discrete Algorithms
- **APPROX/RANDOM** – Approximation and Randomized algorithms
- **QIP** – Quantum Information Processing
- **ITCS** – Innovations in Theoretical Computer Science

D.3.2 Career Paths

Academia

- Research in theoretical computer science
- Teaching algorithms and complexity
- Interdisciplinary applications

Industry

- Algorithm engineering at tech companies
- Optimization in operations research
- Quantitative analysis in finance
- Cryptography and security
- Machine learning theory

D.4 Tools and Software

D.4.1 Analysis Tools

- **Mathematica/Maple** – Symbolic computation for recurrences
- **CPLEX/Gurobi** – Linear programming solvers
- **NetworkX** – Graph algorithm analysis
- **SageMath** – Open-source mathematics software

D.4.2 Visualization Tools

- **Graphviz** – Complexity class diagrams
- **D3.js** – Interactive algorithm visualizations
- **Manim** – Mathematical animations
- **TikZ** – Publication-quality diagrams

D.4.3 Profiling and Benchmarking

- **perf** – Linux performance analysis
- **Valgrind** – Memory and cache analysis
- **Intel VTune** – Detailed performance profiling
- **Google Benchmark** – Microbenchmarking library

Bibliography

Classic Textbooks and Monographs

Aho, A. V., Hopcroft, J. E., & Ullman, J. D. (1974). *The Design and Analysis of Computer Algorithms.* Reading, MA: Addison-Wesley.

Arora, S., & Barak, B. (2009). *Computational Complexity: A Modern Approach.* Cambridge: Cambridge University Press.

Cormen, T. H., Leiserson, C. E., Rivest, R. L., & Stein, C. (2022). *Introduction to Algorithms* (4th ed.). Cambridge, MA: MIT Press.

Garey, M. R., & Johnson, D. S. (1979). *Computers and Intractability: A Guide to the Theory of NP-Completeness.* New York: W. H. Freeman.

Goldreich, O. (2008). *Computational Complexity: A Conceptual Perspective.* Cambridge: Cambridge University Press.

Kleinberg, J., & Tardos, É. (2006). *Algorithm Design.* Boston: Addison-Wesley.

Knuth, D. E. (1997–2011). *The Art of Computer Programming* (Vols. 1–4A). Upper Saddle River, NJ: Addison-Wesley.

Papadimitriou, C. H. (1994). *Computational Complexity.* Reading, MA: Addison-Wesley.

Sedgewick, R., & Wayne, K. (2011). *Algorithms* (4th ed.). Boston: Addison-Wesley.

Sipser, M. (2013). *Introduction to the Theory of Computation* (3rd ed.). Boston: Cengage Learning.

Seminal Papers

Ajtai, M. (1983). "Σ_1^1-formulae on finite structures." *Annals of Pure and Applied Logic*, 24(1), 1–48.

Blum, M. (1967). "A machine-independent theory of the complexity of recursive functions." *Journal of the ACM*, 14(2), 322–336.

Cook, S. A. (1971). "The complexity of theorem-proving procedures." *Proceedings of the 3rd Annual ACM Symposium on Theory of Computing*, 151–158.

Dijkstra, E. W. (1959). "A note on two problems in connexion with graphs." *Numerische Mathematik*, 1, 269–271.

Edmonds, J. (1965). "Paths, trees, and flowers." *Canadian Journal of Mathematics*, 17, 449–467.

Hartmanis, J., & Stearns, R. E. (1965). "On the computational complexity of algorithms." *Transactions of the American Mathematical Society*, 117, 285–306.

Karp, R. M. (1972). "Reducibility among combinatorial problems." In R. E. Miller & J. W. Thatcher (Eds.), *Complexity of Computer Computations* (pp. 85–103). New York: Plenum Press.

Levin, L. A. (1973). "Universal sequential search problems." *Problems of Information Transmission*, 9(3), 265–266.

Savitch, W. J. (1970). "Relationships between nondeterministic and deterministic tape complexities." *Journal of Computer and System Sciences*, 4(2), 177–192.

Turing, A. M. (1936). "On computable numbers, with an application to the Entscheidungsproblem." *Proceedings of the London Mathematical Society*, 42(2), 230–265.

Specialized Topics

Amortized Analysis

Tarjan, R. E. (1985). "Amortized computational complexity." *SIAM Journal on Algebraic and Discrete Methods*, 6(2), 306–318.

Sleator, D. D., & Tarjan, R. E. (1985). "Self-adjusting binary search trees." *Journal of the ACM*, 32(3), 652–686.

Approximation Algorithms

Hochbaum, D. S. (Ed.). (1997). *Approximation Algorithms for NP-Hard Problems.* Boston: PWS Publishing.

Vazirani, V. V. (2001). *Approximation Algorithms.* Berlin: Springer-Verlag.

Williamson, D. P., & Shmoys, D. B. (2011). *The Design of Approximation Algorithms.* Cambridge: Cambridge University Press.

Probabilistic Analysis

Motwani, R., & Raghavan, P. (1995). *Randomized Algorithms.* Cambridge: Cambridge University Press.

Mitzenmacher, M., & Upfal, E. (2017). *Probability and Computing: Randomization and Probabilistic Techniques in Algorithms and Data Analysis* (2nd ed.). Cambridge: Cambridge University Press.

Parallel and Distributed Algorithms

JáJá, J. (1992). *An Introduction to Parallel Algorithms.* Reading, MA: Addison-Wesley.

Lynch, N. A. (1996). *Distributed Algorithms.* San Francisco: Morgan Kaufmann.

Leighton, F. T. (1992). *Introduction to Parallel Algorithms and Architectures.* San Francisco: Morgan Kaufmann.

Quantum Computing

Nielsen, M. A., & Chuang, I. L. (2010). *Quantum Computation and Quantum Information* (10th Anniversary ed.). Cambridge: Cambridge University Press.

Shor, P. W. (1997). "Polynomial-time algorithms for prime factorization and discrete logarithms on a quantum computer." *SIAM Journal on Computing*, 26(5), 1484–1509.

Modern Research and Applications

Dasgupta, S., Papadimitriou, C. H., & Vazirani, U. (2008). *Algorithms.* New York: McGraw-Hill.

Roughgarden, T. (2016). *Twenty Lectures on Algorithmic Game Theory.* Cambridge: Cambridge University Press.

Spielman, D. A., & Teng, S.-H. (2004). "Smoothed analysis of algorithms: Why the simplex algorithm usually takes polynomial time." *Journal of the ACM*, 51(3), 385–463.

Vitter, J. S. (2008). "Algorithms and data structures for external memory." *Foundations and Trends in Theoretical Computer Science*, 2(4), 305–474.

Online Resources and Surveys

Aaronson, S. (2013). "P =? NP." In *Open Problems in Mathematics* (pp. 1–122). Springer.

Arora, S., & Safra, S. (1998). "Probabilistic checking of proofs: A new characterization of NP." *Journal of the ACM*, 45(1), 70–122.

Immerman, N. (1988). "Nondeterministic space is closed under complementation." *SIAM Journal on Computing*, 17(5), 935–938.

Impagliazzo, R. (1995). "A personal view of average-case complexity." *Proceedings of the 10th Annual Conference on Structure in Complexity Theory*, 134–147.

Wigderson, A. (2019). *Mathematics and Computation: A Theory Revolutionizing Technology and Science.* Princeton: Princeton University Press.

Index

References are given as Chapter.Section.Subsection (e.g., ğ3.2.1 refers to Chapter 3, Section 2, Subsection 1).

Reference Legend:

- §X = Chapter X
- §X.Y = Section Y of Chapter X
- §X.Y.Z = Subsection Z of Section X.Y
- §A, B, C, D = Appendices

www.ingramcontent.com/pod-product-compliance
Lightning Source LLC
Chambersburg PA
CBHW060757240926
51847CB00019B/132

9782488616041